Group therapy is a learning lab—a nonthreatening, safe place where people are free to be themselves and work on their individual concerns, goals, and behaviors.

The Adult Children of Alcoholics (ACOAs) in this book began meeting for group therapy after they learned about the impact of alcoholism in their lives. Even though you may not have grown up in an alcoholic home and your experiences are not identical, you will likely share many common feelings. Dysfunctional family patterns and unresolved issues that children continue as adults are not reserved for families of alcoholics only.

Similar coping styles develop in families where one parent or other family member controls an inappropriate amount of the family's focus. Perhaps you grew up with an emotionally detached father, an overcontrolling mother, or an easily angered parent. Mental or physical illness may have interrupted healthy family relationships. Acknowledging and understanding the resulting feelings and then sharing them with others is a way to get well, whether you, too, are an ACOA, or one who identifies with their experiences.

SZIFRA BIRKE
Director of Alternatives Counseling
West Lafayette, Indiana

TOGETHER WE HEAL

Szifra Birke *and* Kathy Mayer

Formerly entitled
Private Practice

BALLANTINE BOOKS • NEW YORK

Library of Congress Catalog Card Number: 90-91849

ISBN 0-345-36281-0

Manufactured in the United States of America

First Ballantine Books Edition: December 1990

CONTENTS

Thank You   vii
Introduction   1
Introducing Our Therapy Group   33
ACOA MEETINGS
Getting Acquainted   Meeting 1   46
Becoming Aware of
    Alcoholism's Impact   Meeting 2   65
Wishing We Had Known
    About Alcoholism Earlier   Meeting 3   85
Sharing Our Childhood
    Experiences   Meeting 4   105
Realizing We Were So Often
    Alone   Meeting 5   129
Taking on ACOA Roles   Meeting 6   148
Recognizing Our Feelings   Meeting 7   166
Rewriting Our Family Rules   Meeting 8   192
Feeling Powerless   Meeting 9   211
Looking at Our Own
    Addictive Behaviors   Meeting 10   229
Having Fun   Meeting 11   244
Sharing Feedback with Each
    Other   Meeting 12   261
Dealing with Our Families
    Now   Meeting 13   278
Living Today   Meeting 14   295

Where We've Been; Where
    We Want to Go   Meeting 15   311
Using Our Tools for Recovery   Final Meeting   327
What's Your Next Step?   351
A Note to Therapists   367

THANK YOU

FROM CONTRIBUTIONS WE received from ACOAs, we created fictional ACOAs who participate in the meetings in this book. These ACOAs are composites of those who contributed material and ACOAs we know personally and professionally.

Thank you, each of you, for sharing your experiences and feelings with us. Much of your dialogue is exactly as you gave it to us. Your words are more powerful, more deeply felt, and more expressive than any we could create.

The names, biographical information, and family backgrounds in this book are fiction. The sadness, hurt, embarrassment, shame, despair, hope, positiveness, anger, frustration, joy—every feeling each of you has felt and shared—are yours. Thank you for sharing them with us and with all who will read this book.

With special thanks, using the names you requested, to:
Cliff, Penny, Alyson, Mary, Jim, Ann, Karen, Julie, Kathy, Julie, Lori, Ann, Concetta, John, Harold, Randall, "H," Mitzi, Debby, Lynette, Tom, Dennis, Marilyn, Amy, Leslie, Pat, Roxie, Connie, Shortie, Lee, Fran, Mary, Michael, Anne, Jan, Jessica, Sue, Albert, Jennie, Sarah, C.G., Kathy, Joe, Ric, Joe, Phyllis, Pat, Shirley, Carrie, Hank, Lisa, Pat, Ray, Jim, Della, Cindi, Marilyn, Phyllis, Kate, Jane, David, Ray, Kelly, Randy, Marsha, Vera, Bill, Betty, Kelly, Carol, Jim, Wayne, Vicki, Steve, Harriet, Croales, Lee, Wendy, Frank, Jim, Ed, Joyce, Jeff, Kath, Sarah, Susan, Christine, Jean, Laurel, Penny, Christine, Kathy, Susie, Bill, John, Kilroy, Gina, Sarah, Christine,

Marta, Yvonne, Jim, Linda, Cindy, Alice, Kevin, Sherry, Kay, Ellen, Nancy, David, Norm, Claudia, Casey, Dee, "T.," Shirly, Stephen, Charles, Jessie, Ozzie, Bud, Cheryl, Julia, Susan, Gail, William, Karen, Tim, Tom, India, Demory, Dennis, Becky, Jane, Jayne, Earl, Cherri, David, Cheri, Audrey, Eddie, and Paul.

To all ACOAs who have shared their lives with us, thank you. This book is for all of you.

—Szifra and Kathy

To my grandparents, although I never got the chance to know you.

To my mother for your generosity and for having held on to your love of life and your optimism. You showed by your example that grave losses do not have to destroy our ability to nurture and be joyous. I thank you, too, for being a wonderful grandmother.

To my father, too, a thank-you for never giving up. I thank you for modeling perseverance and guts. I remember your humor and wit and cherish your wonderful metaphors.

To my sister Roslyn and brothers Lenny and Rich and their families for their encouragement and backing. A special mention to you, Roslyn.

To my friends for your support, warmth, and special conversations. A special thank-you to old and dear friends Kara Cheek, Hope Gulker, Lesley Guyton, Lannie Le Gear, and Dorothy O'Byrne.

To Mel Morgenbesser, Nancy Frenzel, and Bernie Gulker for your friendship and for input that made the book more readable. Thanks to John Femino for valuable feedback in the earliest stages, and to Lyn Doyle for your expertise as editor of our first edition. And to Betsy Nahas and Millie McCormack for the last-minute editing.

To Jack Fahey, our first publisher. You inspired us with notes of encouragement and enthusiasm for a book about an ACOA group.

To Claudia Black, who generously read and commented on the book as it progressed. Thank you for the gift of your time and expertise.

To Cheryl Woodruff, our editor at Ballantine, for communicating so clearly what you wanted and what you liked. Telling me right away that you really liked this book felt terrific. A special thanks for the title.

To Kathy, without whom there would be no book. Thanks for being a mascot (recovering, of course!). Your humorous running commentary and positive attitude helped make all the hard work fun.

To all the ACOAs who have shared their lives and experiences with me. An extra thanks to the three ACOAs whose poems are used in *Together We Heal*.

To my husband, Joluut. My heartfelt thanks for your unending support, encouragement, patience, and love. Thanks to JoSelle, too. I'm grateful to have you in my life.

To my children, Tov and Kol, for being fun and funny, inspiring, and supportive. You are great guys to be around and have enriched my life. Mostly, though, I want to thank you just for being.

—Szifra

To Szifra, for years of help and encouragement, for believing in me, and for teaching me to believe in me.

To the ACOAs who shared with me in our group.

To my sisters and brothers, for reading the ACOA material I gave you and for growing, yourselves, as we learned about alcoholism.

To Mom and Dad, although you never discovered the joy of recovery, you gave everything you could to your children.

Thank you

—Kathy

INTRODUCTION

EARLY IN MY work with young and Adult Children of Alcoholics (ACOAs), I realized there was a need for a book such as *Together We Heal*. Many of my clients felt alone, believing they were the only ones who'd ever had certain thoughts and feelings. They also carried needless guilt. I knew that a group experience could offer them the opportunity to feel more connected, empowered, and encouraged. As part of a group they would feel less alone, less isolated, and less guilty.

Even though ACOAs grow up in different families, miles and years apart, they share many common experiences and feelings. Because reading can be a significant part of treatment for alcohol-affected families, I decided to write a book capturing the common experiences and feelings of a number of my clients. Through reading, they can learn about alcoholism, codependency, and their impact on children. They learn, too, about the resulting survival strategies that children adapt—and, equally important, they come to recognize that others have similar backgrounds, experiences, and feelings.

In 1980, when I first began thinking about the importance of group treatment for Adult Children, few such groups were available, primarily because of time, child care, money, or transportation problems. A gap existed that needed desperately to be filled. If ACOAs could not get to a group, I reflected, maybe a group could get to them.

About the same time, Kathy joined my ACOA therapy group. Kathy had long wanted to be a writer; she had a degree in journalism but had never taken what she termed "the risk of writing." Eventually, she began to resolve her ACOA issues; she also began writing and submitting free-lance copy to magazines. Her first publications were victories for both of us.

Working together to write this book seemed the natural next step. Having Kathy as my writing partner has been wonderful. As an ACOA and a writer, her insights and perceptions have been invaluable.

ALCOHOLISM TREATMENT AND THE ACOA MOVEMENT

In 1970 Congress passed the "Comprehensive Alcohol Abuse and Alcoholism Prevention, Treatment, and Reha-bilitation Act" and the National Institute on Alcohol Abuse and Alcoholism (NIAAA) was established. These actions by the government indicated that alcoholism and its treat-ment were to be taken seriously. The focus, though, was only on the alcoholic. Very little attention was given to helping the children or spouses of alcoholics. Jael Greenleaf presents the issue so well in her publication *Co-alcoholic, Para-alcoholic: Who's Who and What's the Difference?* She writes, "A program that treats only the person with the disease of alcoholism and not those within the alcoholism syndrome is comparable to a garage that specializes in changing only the right front tire and not the other three."

In the last decade inpatient facilities for the treatment of alcoholism have opened at unprecedented rates. Courts be-gan offering alcoholics rehabilitation in lieu of jail. And alcoholism became a public issue. With this increased awareness, attention focused on the families of alcoholics. Initially, professionals had difficulty understanding that the codependènt (earlier called co-alcoholic) and Children of Alcoholics also needed treatment for their own problems.

Most practitioners simply did not understand the issues involved, let alone know how to help.

Early work by pioneers in the Adult Children of Alcoholics movement helped professionals understand the needs of family members. Claudia Black, Sharon Wegscheider-Cruse, Janet Woititz, and Robert Ackerman, among others, blazed a trail of enlightenment about alcoholism and its effect upon all family members. At the same time, increased attention in the criminal justice system helped bring the issue to public awareness. Treatment facilities tried to adapt their programs to meet the changing needs. In many cases, however, these early attempts at involving the family were halfhearted—still focused primarily at helping the alcoholic stay sober. In fact, many well-intentioned professionals unwittingly reinforced "all the wrong things." Some told children who had been hypermature for years, "Take care of your dad; he'll need your help, and your mom told me you were a great little helper." Others told spouses who needed to focus on themselves, "He'll be in rough shape at times. Try to be supportive. He'll need understanding because it'll be stressful for him."

Recently many programs have begun to include the family in treatment so they can learn to address their own issues. Family members' problems are identified so they can be helped to find new and better options—independent of what the alcoholic does. Spouses and children deserve primary attention. Now they, too, can get treatment. At last we are in a position to stop the generational passage of alcoholism and rewrite the many associated inappropriate and destructive rules for living.

WHAT'S THERAPY ALL ABOUT

The Toolbox
My goal in therapy is to help you obtain or augment the tools you need to live more contented, rewarding lives. Tools are skills, behaviors, and attitudes that are used in

daily living to solve problems. As a recovering ACOA, you will 1) learn that options *are* available; 2) increase your knowledge of alcoholism and codependency; 3) add to your general living skills; and 4) deal with your feelings. Recovery takes time, but many tools are available to facilitate the process: grieving, active listening, assertiveness, living in the moment, self-care, talking about what really matters, trusting, identifying and expressing feelings, setting limits, and asking for help . . . all are invaluable and crucial to your development.

Together we find out what tools you need to help you deal effectively with problems that come up. How complete is your toolbox? Which tools are in good working order? Are some tools rusty because they have not been used since someone in authority inappropriately discouraged their use? Which tools need to be cleaned or sharpened? Through careful discussion, we identify each tool and whether or not it may still be useful. Some have collected much residue in the forms of guilt, shame, fear, or pain over the years. Rusty tools may be cleaned up, modified, or thrown away, depending upon condition and need. Sometimes essential tools are missing altogether; we identify those and work to acquire them. The goal is to add quality, workable tools to the toolbox.

Learning About Options

You also learn about alternatives, options, and choices. These are the keys that unlock the toolbox for Adult Children of Alcoholics. As children, you had no choices about the family you lived in. You were powerless over your parents' relationship, which was often terribly conflictual. You were powerless over your alcoholic parent's drinking. No matter how much you tried to be good, to dilute or hide the alcohol, to get good grades, or even to act out, hoping that might help, you couldn't fix the problem. You were powerless over whether, how much, and when the alcoholic drank, and powerless to affect the resulting behavior. You were also powerless over your nonalcoholic parent's behavior and level of codependency. Even though you may have planned for a month to go to Grandma's for dinner at four P.M. on Christmas Day, if Dad got drunk at three, you stayed home.

You were powerless, too, because you didn't understand that Dad was either thinking about drinking, drinking, or trying desperately not to drink. Mom was thinking about Dad's drinking, maybe drinking with him, using prescription drugs, or trying desperately not to think about his drinking.

A primary purpose of therapy is to help empower clients. You were powerless as children and often still feel powerless as adults. Instead of feeling stuck, you can learn to ask yourself empowering questions at times of conflict or distress. Asking "What options do I have in this situation?" "What choices are available to me?" will give you power you did not have as a child.

Increasing Alcohol and Codependency Knowledge

Knowledge is another important tool. As you learn about alcoholism and codependency, you more fully understand how and why you were affected. You understand how and why early adaptive behaviors continue in adulthood, even when they're no longer needed. With knowledge comes freedom. At last you can make your own choices in life, empowering yourself to find the happiness, meaning, and rewards so elusive until now.

Adding to General Living Skills

Therapists can help ACOAs by teaching needed skills. Tools may be as diverse as parenting, negotiating, asserting rights, self-nurturing, communicating, relaxing, making friends, and trusting, as well as myriad other life skills.

Besides learning about the availability of options, increasing alcohol and codependency knowledge, and adding to general living skills, Adult Children need help with feelings. Often it is in therapy that Adult Children first learn to identify, express, and become comfortable with a wide range of feelings.

HOW I GOT STARTED

There's clear and abundant evidence that people benefit from talking to others about what happens in their lives. Self-help groups are proliferating. People are meeting together in record numbers.

I organized my first therapy group for "grown Children of Alcoholics" in 1979, before the term Adult Children of Alcoholics had been coined. I remember vividly how it all began. Three women with whom I'd worked for a few months were not making much progress. Hoping I'd uncover something, I reread the notes I'd kept from the first meeting. What stood out in my intake summaries was the notation that each woman had reported some version of "husband drinks too much" at the initial consultation. Since I lacked primary training in addictions, I requested feedback from our addictions staff member. He was a strapping six-foot-three-inch recovering alcoholic who spoke his mind unhesitatingly. I asked him if it was relevant that each client had said "My husband drinks too much." He proceeded to blast me out of my chair, and, thus, I began to learn about alcoholism!

I soon realized that two of these three women also had an alcoholic parent. Very little information or training was available, but I learned what I could about the impact of having a parent who was alcoholic. Ultimately I decided that my clients needed experience in a group.

At the time, mental health and addiction professionals did not understand the special needs of Adult Children of Alcoholics. I asked to organize and then facilitate a group for "grown Children of Alcoholics." The mental health center staff didn't see the need for a separate group for people with an alcoholic parent but agreed to let me lead such a group if I included spouses of alcoholics.

That was in 1979. It's amazing how far we've come since then. I am thankful, relieved, and encouraged.

In commenting on this evolution, I'd like to see us go one step further and create a new term that includes the nonalcoholic parent as well. Children do have two parents, not just one. The codependent parent is an essential piece of the alcoholism equation. COACPs (Children of Alcoholics and Codependent Parents) is a cumbersome yet far more accurate label. Some inappropriate behaviors were learned from your codependent parent. Some of the nurturing you didn't get is because your codependent parent was not able to provide what you needed emotionally. Many ACOAs describe a warmer, more loving childhood relationship with their alcoholic parent than with the nonalcoholic codependent. In adulthood, too, many feel closer to and believe they learned more skills from the alcoholic parent. Just like alcoholism, codependency creates its own problems—making good parenting difficult.

Many ACOAs have parents who got sober or were absent from the family as they grew up. These children, too, suffer from many of the same feelings as the ACOAs who lived with an actively alcoholic parent. But because they were not around the alcoholism, many may not feel justified in having "Adult Children" problems. They deserve and may need ACOA recovery, too.

THERAPY GROUPS

I like to describe group therapy as a learning lab—a nonthreatening, safe place where people are free to be themselves and work on their individual concerns, goals, and behaviors. It is a low-risk environment where you can meet others who share similar backgrounds and who likely have experienced feelings similar to yours. It's a place to try new behaviors and to practice new skills without fear of reprisal. Everyone shares the common goals of getting help for themselves and encouraging others as they work to reach their own goals.

Some Adult Children face discouragement from their families when they attempt to make changes in their lives. In alcohol-affected families, change is often shunned or avoided. After several weeks of group therapy, many ACOAs hear comments from their families such as "Did your therapist tell you to let your kid walk all over you? All that kid needs is a good smack."

After such family interactions, many ACOAs get together in group and offer comments such as these:

"When I come here, I feel supported in trying to be a better mother."

"In my family they make fun of me and point out all the things that go wrong."

"I end up discouraged about trying so hard. But when I'm in group, I realize everyone here wants to break the addiction cycle, raise better families, be happier. I always feel more normal and encouraged here."

Group members offer one another encouragement and support for the changes they are making. It's a powerful dynamic that offers a structure for learning about yourself and others in the spirit of common helping.

Group may be the only place in your life where individual needs are the most important. Group may be the only place where you feel a part of rather than apart from the people around you. Many ACOAs have told me it was in group that they felt they belonged for the first time in their lives. "I feel so separate everywhere else. In here I feel like I fit, like I belong," one ACOA told me. In group you learn that others share similar thoughts, feelings, and experiences and you learn that none of us always knows all the rules. A woman I know used to say, "This is a situation in which I want to call the Bureau of Right Answers." In group ACOAs find out, much to their dismay, that there is no one place to learn all the answers.

When I try to reassure my clients that their thoughts and feelings are normal, they are often skeptical. When another group member says, "You thought that? Really? I thought I was the only one," the skepticism dissolves.

In group ACOAs learn to identify, express, and become comfortable with a wider range of feelings; to practice assertiveness and asking for help; to break isolating patterns and rigid family roles. ACOAs learn to trust themselves and others more and to think of alternatives in their lives. They learn to talk about the real issues and to listen, too.

MORE SPECIFICS ON THERAPY GROUPS

There are many kinds of groups facilitated by leaders. Some are psychodynamic—leaving the group's process almost entirely up to the group. As you will see in *Together We Heal*, I am more directive, especially at first. I ask questions, make comments, and invite quiet group members to speak. Many therapists are less active in group even at the beginning.

Because a therapist's personality, style, and orientation will determine much about the group, it is difficult to give you a picture of the average group. There really is no way to generalize. Besides the therapist's individual orientation, the personalities and styles of participants in the group will also determine the structure and rules. How helpful a group will be depends on how it's run, who leads it, how motivated the other people attending are, and whether it feels right to you.

MY GROUP

Most therapy groups meet once a week, generally for an hour and a half. Groups with leaders or co-leaders are usually limited in size. Most therapy groups have between five and eight members, which is the size of the groups I facilitate. *Together We Heal* offers a larger group, but in my practice in general, when there are more than six I work with a cofacilitator.

The groups I lead are closed to create the predictability and consistency absent from the homes most of my clients grew up in. *Closed groups* are generally made up only of those who were present when the group began. The same people are there each week. Groups where others are allowed to join at almost any stage are called *continuous* or *open groups*. My groups borrow slightly from the continuous model in that new members may join at strategic times or when current members leave. I do this carefully and infrequently to decrease disruption in communication, continue group cohesiveness, and assure comfort for current members.

The opening and closing of my group are consistent and predictable. Participants know what topic is planned for the following week. Many times the group changes direction as the discussion evolves. In *Together We Heal* this happens in Meeting 10. The planned topic was "fun," but soon it was clear that substance abuse needed to be addressed instead.

Goal setting is another important part of group. I want to know why my clients are participating in group therapy and what they hope to gain so I know how to best assist them. You will see this happening with Roger and others in *Together We Heal*. Roger wants to be more assertive, so group members and I reinforce him when he clearly asks for what he needs or wants.

Therapy groups often have clear ground rules and expectations for behavior for the benefit of all involved. Individual rights and responsibilities exist, as do group rights. For example, in my group ACOAs are asked to give at least two weeks' notice before they leave the group. This happens in Meeting 15, when Linda announces that she will be leaving. Group members are allowed closure—that is, they are given the time to talk about how it feels and what they think.

As you'll see in *Together We Heal*, therapists and other group members are apt to prod people in the group; soul baring is encouraged. It's not okay for a person to never talk. Someone is there to help "put the person together" if the meeting has been especially difficult. I am there to monitor inappropriate remarks or behavior and to encourage and reinforce healthy behavior.

Rules for outside interactions among members differ depending upon the particular group. Some groups are purely psychoanalytic, while others are support groups with a therapist convening and facilitating.

Strictly psychoanalytic group leaders generally ban all outside interactions. Members can communicate only with each other within the group. Other group leaders say little about interacting outside; they wait to see what develops. Some therapy groups encourage the camaraderie. As you read, you'll see that I am in the middle group—the laissez-faire group—with one condition. Anything that occurs outside between group members is potentially group material, meaning we can discuss it and process it fully. In this way we minimize the chance that people will feel excluded—a common childhood carryover.

SUPPORT GROUPS

Support groups for ACOAs have a leaderless structure and fall into two general categories: Al-Anon–based Adult Children groups, which follow Al-Anon's meeting format, and Adult Children of Alcoholics Support Groups, which are usually affiliated with the National Association of Children of Alcoholics (NACOA) or Adult Children of Alcoholics, Inc.

Al-Anon Adult Child Meetings

In Al-Anon Adult Child meetings, the format follows a prescribed style, and materials are limited to literature provided by Al-Anon. Some Al-Anon meetings allow other material on a side table as long as it is clear that it is not a part of the official meeting. If members want to read a passage or mention a book that helped, they must first get permission from the group, typically by asking, "This is not conference-approved literature, does anyone object if I read it or mention it?'' If no one objects, they may refer to it.

National Association of Children of Alcoholics and Adult Children of Alcoholics, Inc., Adult Child Meetings

Support groups affiliated with NACOA or Adult Children of Alcoholics follow a variety of meeting formats and seem to have proliferated in greater numbers than the Al-Anon–based groups. These groups may or may not use the Twelve Steps and Twelve Traditions of Alcoholics Anonymous/Al-Anon and the Serenity Prayer. Some states have formed coalitions or intergroups where a representative of each of the various groups in the state attends to share information and new meeting format ideas.

Cross-Talk

Generally, both kinds of support groups discourage cross talk. In some groups members arc asked to accept without comment what others say. For the most part they adhere to the following guideline: ''We accept, without comment, what others say because it is true for them. We work toward taking responsibility for our own feelings, thoughts, and actions instead of giving advice to others.'' Other support groups have more flexibility. For example, many, if not most, who enter support groups believe they can cause, cure, and control alcoholism. They are told immediately, by those who have themselves learned, ''You did not and cannot cause it, you cannot cure it, nor can you control it.''

In a support group, participants are not required to attend each week; they are free to come when they want or need to. Support groups can have as few as three people or as many as one hundred. In some cities large support groups may break up into smaller meetings, often by topic or smoking/nonsmoking.

Individuals could attend support groups for months without ever speaking up. Many do. It is entirely up to the ACOAs whether or not to speak or share.

In support groups, ACOAs reveal as much as, go as deep as, and deal with whatever issue feels comfortable. It is up to the individuals to be assertive, to speak up if something that has been said is troubling or hurtful to them.

While styles and goals of groups vary depending on whether they are therapist-led or drop-in support, it's important to keep in mind that no one format is better than the other. Your decision will rest upon your needs, goals, available groups, and your therapist's recommendations.

To give you an idea of the range involved, the following list details a number of differences between the two. Therapy and self-help groups do not duplicate or replace each other, but instead offer differing approaches to recovery that frequently complement each other. Different groups may be accessed by ACOAs at different times.

Therapy Groups	Self-Help Groups
Confidentiality	Anonymity and confidentiality (first names only)
Size limited	Open to any member
Weekly attendance expected	Members may attend as needs dictate
Cost for attendance	Optional donation
Format depends on therapist	Format depends on Twelve Steps and Twelve Traditions of AA/Al-Anon or other group

Therapy Groups	Self-Help Groups
Therapist prods and intermember dialogue encouraged	Members share goals with sponsor when ready
Good-bye policy	Can leave/discontinue attendance without notice
Monitoring changes	Members share experience, strength, and hope
Participation expected	Participation optional
Closed	Open
Therapy is provided	Support is offered, and free material is provided
24-hour emergency coverage by therapist	Telephone list for 24-hour support from sponsor and members.

THE PEOPLE IN *TOGETHER WE HEAL*

In *Together We Heal*, ACOAs begin group therapy after already having learned a great deal about the impact of alcoholism on their lives. Some have participated in support groups. Others have read about alcoholism, codependency, and ACOA-ism. Most have been in individual counseling, where they have discussed and worked through some aspects of trust, fear, and intimacy problems. They have begun to understand how growing up in an alcoholic home is affecting their lives today. Joining this therapy group is one more step in their recovery.

Each has confided in a therapist and maybe in a friend or relative. Now they'll open up to more people. They're nervous, yet ready to take the risks for the gains they want to make. Most people start group with some anticipation and anxiety. That doesn't mean they're not ready; most of us get nervous when we are about to do something that is "one step above our comfort level." It's normal and natural to feel nervous in this situation. If you're feeling this way, please don't let it stop you from taking a step in your own behalf.

The ACOAs in our book are quite open to sharing soon after meeting each other. They are well past the early stages of recovery. I mention this so you will understand their willingness to be more open than you might be right now. If you are thinking of joining a self-help group, you will be free to attend and participate at your level of comfort and progress. If you want to join a therapy group, talk to the group leader about how much you will be asked to participate early on. I tell people who want to join my groups that I will ask them to continue taking small, manageable steps toward their goals, not giant stretches that will be painful.

To cover as many topics as possible, this book presents a shortened version of what most groups would discuss over a longer period of time. Many of the changes that the ACOAs in this book make occur more rapidly than they generally do in real life. For example, in Meeting 6, Kathy announces that she is going to begin free-lance writing. In reality Kathy made this decision after a few months, not after six weeks. We've escalated similar progress and changes to enhance the book's readability. Many of the ACOAs in my groups stay for a year or longer to accomplish the goals they set. Typically, people make changes over a greater length of time than the thirty weeks presented in this book. You cannot rush the process. Be patient with yourself.

Some of the material the members in *Together We Heal*

deal with is very intense. It is developmentally appropriate for their stage of recovery. These are ACOAs who have already done much work in exploring their pasts and their pain. They have learned ways to deal with sad feelings and strong memories. If you are just learning about the impact of alcoholism and codependency in your life, you need a group that is either educational or informational in focus, or one designed for early-stage recovery. The childhood memories and issues dealt with by the *Together We Heal* group members may be too intense (in content and pace) for you.

MY ROLE

As therapist, my role in *Together We Heal* is to highlight the patterns and themes emerging from the dialogue and help the group members tie them together. The ACOAs' dialogues and interactions are the most crucial ingredient in *Together We Heal*.

YOUR ROLE- SURVIVAL STRATEGIES

Family members affected by alcoholism find a number of ways to cope with its presence in their lives. Although individuals react differently, some common characteristics shared by family members have been identified. These characteristics are generally referred to as *family roles* or *survival strategies*. How these continue in adulthood and affect ACOAs' new relationships and adult lives is one of the most significant themes that emerges in the ACOA recovery process.

Children need ways to adapt to the stresses in their families. The higher the stress, the more likely the child will end up with survival strategies that do not promote lasting self-esteem. Survival strategies are ways we adapt, ways we cope, as children.

Claudia Black categorizes these characteristics within the following roles: responsible one, adjuster, placater, and acting-out child. Sharon Wegscheider-Cruse, who developed the inner and outer circle graphics to reflect feelings and behaviors common for these roles, refers to them as family hero, lost child, mascot, and scapegoat.

A summary of the characteristics of each role follows. Not every alcohol-affected family member fits the mold for one specific role; most family members take on pieces of one or more. These are not meant to be rigid definitions, but rather a collection of the kinds of feelings and behaviors different family members experience and exhibit.

The Family Hero

Often the oldest child or, in very traditional families, the first boy, is what Claudia Black calls the *responsible child* and Sharon Wegscheider-Cruse calls the *family hero*. These are children who measure their self-worth almost exclusively by their achievements. As children they frequently volunteer and manifest a strong drive to be on top. They are often the class leaders and may be parental or bossy with peers. They may also be the "teacher's pet."

Beneath this facade of responsibility and success is a person who feels okay only when achieving or accomplishing a goal. Although it doesn't often show, these are children who are overly needy of attention and approval from others because they are not good at reinforcing themselves.

The Scapegoat

Other children adapt by rebelling. The *acting-out child* or *scapegoat* often follows the hero child in the birth order. No matter how smart or capable you are, if you're younger, it's very difficult to look smarter or more capable than an older sibling. The scapegoat unconsciously recognizes that the hero spot is taken. To carve out their own spot, these children take on a rebellious "you can't make me" facade. They tend to talk back, neglect schoolwork, and engage in delinquent behavior. Some act out by being sexually promiscuous; girls may become pregnant very young. They manage to get attention from parents and adults around them, as does the hero. Even though the attention focused on the rebel is generally negative, it takes the spotlight off the alcoholic. The rebel's behavior may disrupt the fighting between the parents by bringing them together temporarily to work out solutions to their child's problems. Beneath the acting out is a child who assumes that no one except others choosing a similar path will accept them, which partly explains their tendency to develop a strong peer group.

The Lost Child

As the rebel is visible, the *adjuster* or *lost child* is invisible, fading into the background and causing little or no trouble to anyone. Teachers and adults sometimes can't even remember this child's name. Lost children tend to have few if any friends and often work and play alone. This is the child from whom the family feels no pressure. Without an astute observer, this child is unlikely to get help.

The Mascot

In most families, a clown or *mascot* child emerges later in the birth order. This child, Claudia Black's *placater*, tends to be funny or distracting to get attention—making faces, acting silly, trying very hard to get others to laugh. "As long as they're laughing, I feel comfortable and liked," may be the inner feelings of the mascot. Sometimes these children seem hyperactive because they pick up the tension of the family and discharge it with frenetic behavior.

The diagrams presented on the pages that follow were adapted from *Family Freedom*, a booklet by Sharon Wegscheider-Cruse. The outer circles of each role contain the feelings usually visible to others; the inner circles are the feelings often kept hidden.

The descriptions and information alongside the circles were accumulated from a variety of sources: years of clinical observations and treatment, workshops I've attended, and books I've read. It's difficult to credit anyone specific.

In addition to the roles outlined, I thought it useful to list the characteristics of the chemically dependent person and the chief enabler, usually the spouse, now referred to as the codependent.

For in-depth information on family roles, we encourage you to read Sharon Wegscheider-Cruse's *Another Chance: Hope and Help for the Alcoholic Family*; Claudia Black's *It Will Never Happen to Me;* and *Let Go and Grow* by Robert Ackerman.

THE CHEMICALLY DEPENDENT PERSON

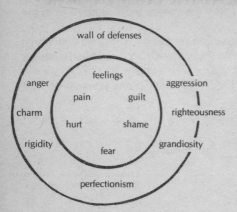

Characteristics:

- Always right
- Resentful
- Charming
- Blaming
- Hostile
- Self-Pity
- Workaholism
- Depression
- Withdrawal
- Arrogance
- All-or-nothing thinking

As the chemically dependent person goes through the progression of the illness, the feelings of guilt, shame, and fear grow. They must be hidden under outside behavior that convinces others that everything is fine.

As the chemical disease progresses, each family member compulsively represses his or her feelings and learns to react with a survival behavior. This behavior serves to build a wall of defenses for protection from pain.

Needs of the Chemically Dependent Person:

Confrontation
Support
Accountability
Love
Acceptance by others
Acceptance of self
Forgiveness

CODEPENDENT/THE CHIEF ENABLER

Characteristics As an Adult:

- Super-responsible
- Martyr (others first)
- Illness common—
  migraine, back pain,
  colitis, high blood
  pressure
- Can't say no
- Difficulty with limit setting
- Frequently exhausted and emotionally drained

The chief enabler is the person who is closest to and most depended on by the chemically dependent. The enabler becomes totally involved in the mood swing of the dependent. To maintain the semblance of normalcy, the enabler needs to become more and more responsible.

Because there is no forum for expression of straightforward anger, the spouse uses silent treatment, sarcasm, blame, and/or a passive-aggressive style.

If the alcoholic is drinking, tries to keep him/her from getting drunk.

If the alcoholic gets drunk, tries very hard to keep him/her from getting hurt.

If the alcoholic gets drunk, tries to keep him/her from driving.

If the alcoholic drives, tries to keep him/her from getting hurt.

Needs of the Chief Enabler:

Support
Self-care
Confrontation
Expression of feelings
Involvement with others
Talking about the real issues
Assertiveness skills
Limit setting

THE RESPONSIBLE ONE/THE FAMILY HERO

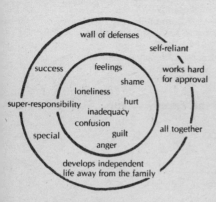

Characteristics During Childhood and Adolescence:

- High achiever/low feeler
- Focus on performance over-developed
- Focus on emotions underdeveloped
- Perfect—does what's "right"
- Brings self-worth to the family system (family can be proud)
- Successful, performs well
- Perfectionistic expectations
- Seeks approval
- All-or-nothing approach to life and to projects
- Perceptive
- Helpful
- Independent

The family hero can see and hear more of what is happening in the family and begins to feel responsible for the family pain. The hero works hard to make things better for the family and works diligently to improve the situation. Hero seems to bear no scars of the difficult home situation.

The Family Hero Didn't Learn:

- How to listen to others
- Flexibility/spontaneity
- To trust others
- How to relax, play
- How to accept common mistakes or failures
- To take satisfaction in his/her achievements

23

As an Adult, the Family Hero:

- Takes on leadership roles
- Ties self-worth to accomplishments
- May live type A life-style and suffer with stress-related disorders
- Imposes unrealistic expectations on self and others
- Always looks to please; seeks approval
- Tend toward workaholism and burnout
- May be too serious and rigid to enjoy self and others
- Is "never wrong"
- May be a dependent person (emotionally, chemically)
- May go to career in helping profession

Needs of the Family Hero:

Allow mistakes
Recognize choices
Take risks
Play
Be vulnerable
Accept self
Express feelings
Move from external worth to internal worth

THE ACTING-OUT CHILD/THE SCAPEGOAT

Characteristics During Childhood and Adolescence:

- Defiance, anger
- Acts out
- "Bad kids"
- Provides change in focus of the family (takes focus off the alcoholic)
- Visible because of behavior
- Reliance on peers
- Gives up easily
- Difficulty with responsibility
- Internalization of family chaos; externalization of inappropriate behavior

The scapegoat does not wish to work so hard to prove her/himself worthy. The scapegoat looks to others for peer support.

As an Adult, the Scapegoat:

- Keeps people away by his/her style
- Might "act out" on the job
- Elicits anger from employers and family
- Works hard to keep others from seeing hurt inside
- Likely uses and abuses chemicals
- May become involved with the law

Needs of the Scapegoat:

Support of feelings
Acceptance
Challenge of inappropriate behavior and patterns
To be listened to
Accept responsibility for own behavior
Appropriate release of anger
Get in touch with range of inner feelings

THE ADJUSTER/THE LOST CHILD

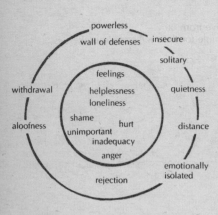

Characteristics During Childhood and Adolescence:

- Follower
- Timid
- Avoids conflict and involvements
- In own room a lot
- Solitary activities (collects things, reads)
- Considers own needs unimportant
- Withdrawn
- "Don't make waves"
- Lets others get away with inappropriate behavior
- "Invisible"
- "I don't care—it doesn't matter," "Whatever you want"
- Behaviors not obviously apparent

The lost child suffers loneliness even though being alone is the situation where there is most comfort for that child. The growing chaos of the family pressures the lost child to look for validation within personal resources, such as fantasies. The lost child provides relief for the family—one less to worry about.

As an Adult, the Lost Child:

- Feels like he/she is boring
- Is afraid to take risks, fear of being hurt
- Suffers from stress-related problems (anxiety attacks, colitis, allergies, asthma)
- Is quiet, aloof, isolated, passive (feels helpless)
- Has trouble making decisions/takes whatever comes
- May be anorexic, bulimic
- Takes path of least resistance

Needs of the Lost Child:

Invitation
Consistency
Encouragement
Rewards for efforts
Consider self needs
Learn to accept/receive from others
Let others be responsible for their lives and mistakes

THE PLACATER/THE MASCOT

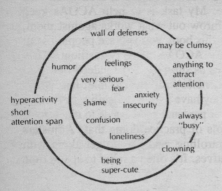

Characteristics During Childhood and Adolescence:

- "Fun"
- Provides humor/fun to deflect and reduce tension and anxiety in the family (may be accurate barometer of stress in family)
- Fear of not belonging
- Fear of breaking down
- Strong sense of abandonment

Mascots are often cute, fun to be around, and able to use charm and humor to survive in a painful family system. No one sees the fear and insecurity deep within.

The mascot is sheltered even more from knowing real feelings in the family: "Don't tell the baby." Filled with his/her own feelings and perceptions—few, if any, of the facts. Less maturity exhibited.

As an Adult, the Mascot:

- May have eating problems
- Experience sense of impending doom
- Appears cheerful, witty
- Is entertaining
- May marry a hero
- Has sense of obligation to others

Needs of the Family Mascot:

Physical touch
Be taken seriously
Information
Be asked for input
Develop alternative behavior
To learn to laugh on inside as well

Adults often feel locked into these roles, even when they are no longer adaptive. My task is to help ACOAs keep what's working well, throw out what works against them, and modify the rest. In this book you will see people in our group doing this. Many ACOAs are very resilient. They often refer to themselves as survivors, and indeed they are. People with "hero tendencies" are responsible, hardworking, and productive. They have a fantastic ability to persist, to succeed. They can put personal needs aside to meet goals because they've had lots of practice doing that. Adjusters can be flexible, noncontrolling, and easy to get along with among friends and relatives. It's often a relief to spend time with someone who has few demands. Mascots continue to entertain, making them fun to be around. They are funny and enjoyable.

Many Adult Children grew up constantly reading the emotional climate in the family. As soon as they opened the front door, their emotional barometer turned on. A sense of trouble, doom, or "it's okay today" met them as they returned from school. Today they have great capacity to "read" other people. They can be unusually sensitive and effective in the helping professions. These can be valuable strengths in making necessary changes that allow ACOAs to really enjoy themselves and their lives. Recovery can be fun and exciting. Making changes we want is empowering.

As you read the descriptions above and in Meeting 6 of *Together We Heal,* many of you will identify with several roles. You may have played different ones at different times in your childhood or adolescence. You may be a blend of two or more. Some of you have one role in public and another in private. The goal is not to label, but to understand as much as you can about yourself in order to make decisions in your best interest today.

IF YOU DO NOT HAVE AN ALCOHOLIC PARENT

Even though you may not have grown up in an alcoholic home, you may find yourself identifying with some of the ACOAs in this group. You may share many common feelings. This is only natural: many of us grew up with codependent parents and suffered losses similar to the ACOAs in this group. Dysfunctional family patterns and unresolved issues are not for Children of Alcoholics only.

Similar coping styles develop in families where a parent or other family member controls an inappropriate amount of the family's focus. Perhaps you grew up with an emotionally detached father, an overcontrolling mother, or an easily angered, "rageaholic" parent. Mental or physical illness may have interrupted healthy family relationships. Acknowledging and understanding the resultant feelings and then sharing them with others is a way to get well, whether you are an ACOA or someone who identifies with their experiences.

Alcoholism is a family illness. A strong rule is to deny that it exists: "Never tell anyone about us. Never talk about the alcoholism." The ACOAs in this book break that family rule. As you read, you may feel you are betraying your parents by identifying yourself as the Child of an Alcoholic. Many ACOAs begin therapy feeling this way. You are breaking the denial that shielded you from seeing your parents and your past clearly. Removing this shield may produce intense feelings. Reading others' experiences may remind you of your own. You may recall incidents you haven't thought about in years. You may wonder if you are making excuses for your problems. These, too, are common feelings. Try to be gentle with yourself and understand that you will have mixed feelings about such sensitive issues.

We hope that *Together We Heal* helps you feel less isolated and allows you to identify with and learn from other ACOAs who share some of your perceptions, experiences, and feelings. We hope this added understanding helps you live a freer and happier life.

There is no right or wrong way to read *Together We Heal*. Trust yourself. You may find it easier to take it slowly, attending a meeting or two each time you read, instead of trying to read too much at once. (ACOAs sometimes want to fix everything yesterday!) Some experiences will strike a chord in you; others won't. Use whatever fits. Take the time to feel and to think through your own experiences as you read.

If you do read the book intellectually from beginning to end in one or two sittings, reread it, this time allowing your feelings to surface. Give yourself permission to feel.

At times as you read, you may feel sad, tearful, or even overwhelmed. Or you may be shocked or feel angry. Other times you'll feel hopeful, relieved, perhaps even elated. It's natural for you to experience intense feelings as you read. It's okay and healing, too. Tell yourself, "It's okay for me to feel whatever I'm feeling. I'll be all right."

Reach in or reach out, as needed, while you read. Think of something you can do for yourself. Go to an ACOA meeting, exercise, start a journal, call someone, read a magazine, take a hot bath, or go for a walk.

The ACOAs who contributed to this book are very courageous. You are, too. Take time to recognize this. It's hard work to look at yourself and your family and to open yourself up. It's healing, too, and can be very exciting. I congratulate you on your efforts and encourage you to continue your recovery journey.

Since you'll encounter my name frequently as you read, I'd like you to know that I was named after my maternal grandmother, who was killed in the Holocaust. My mother and others who knew my grandmother tell me she was a special woman. I was born four years after my parents left Europe following World War II, and I'm proud to have my grandmother's name. It's pronounced "Shifra."

Dear Fellow ACOAs,

My dad always wanted to be a writer, but he never wrote. There were lots of things he never did. And I know now alcoholism had a lot to do with why that was.

I always wanted to be a writer, too. And for a long time, I never wrote, either. Until I learned how Dad's alcoholism impacted upon my life.

I've been more fortunate than Dad. He died from alcoholism without ever knowing the hope and excitement of recovery. He died while he and everyone else in our family pretended everything was fine. I knew it wasn't fine, but I lived as though it were. I didn't know I had any other choice. I ignored my internal pain. I concentrated on working hard, achieving, helping others, and acting happy.

Then one day I read a newspaper article about Szifra Birke, a therapist who counsels Children of Alcoholics. ACOAs, the article read, often have every reason to be happy. Many have good jobs and nice homes. But they're not happy.

I cried reading the article. I called Szifra the next day. Since then I've cried a lot more, hurt a lot more, and thought at times I only wanted out. But I've also smiled and laughed a lot more, reached out to others, and healed a lot.

One of the most rewarding changes I made while learning about families and alcoholism was my decision to write. Before, the risk of someone else's reading what I wrote, the risk that it wouldn't be good enough, kept me from ever trying.

There are other rewards, too. I'm closer to my family. I have friends. I have hopes. And I have times when I'm incredibly happy and content.

I'm Kathy in the meetings in this book. I chose to use my real name and talk about my own life. It's my way of reaching out and saying, "I understand your feelings, I understand your hurt. But you don't have to hurt alone anymore. Together, we can help each other. We can recover from our families' alcoholism."

—Kathy

INTRODUCING
OUR THERAPY GROUP

AS YOU READ *Together We Heal* you'll meet and get to know ten ACOAs. Anne, Michael, Linda, Roger, Sarah, Susan, Trina, and Kathy arrive for the first meeting.

Bob and Mark join the group in Meeting 7.

Information sheets summarizing the backgrounds of each ACOA follow. We've included a blank sheet for you, too, to complete as a member of our therapy group. One blank on the information sheet asks for "Role Assumed." We use the roles developed by ACOA experts Claudia Black and Sharon Wegscheider-Cruse. If you're not familiar with these roles, you may want to review the introduction or wait until after reading Meeting 6 to fill in your role.

The last page of each meeting lists the ACOAs attending, with space for you to note your observations, the progress you feel group members are making, and your own reactions to the meeting.

The group you're attending is a composite of many kinds of groups, adopting pieces of format and style from each. The ACOAs in this group have all counseled individually with Szifra and have begun to learn about alcoholism's effects on them. The purpose of the group is to provide a supportive environment where ACOAs can learn from each other and move forward in their recovery. They'll share childhood experiences, discuss issues affecting their lives today, and encourage each other as they take new risks and make changes in their lives.

As you read this book and share with us, we hope you, too, will learn from the ACOAs and move forward in your own recovery.

ACOA Group Information Sheet

Name: Anne
Age: 39   Female

FAMILY OF ORIGIN INFORMATION:
  Birth Order: Second
  Role Assumed: Lost child
  Brothers/Sisters: 2S/1B
    Any Chemically Dependent? Brother
  Alcoholic Parent: Father
    Still Living? No
    Still Drinking? At death, 7 years ago

CURRENT LIFE SITUATION:
  Marital Status: Married
  Children: 2 sons, 2 daughters, adolescent to teens
  Occupation: Child care/day care
  History of Chemical Use: Minimal, none now
  Knowledge of Alcoholism/Counseling Background:
    Szifra
  Original Reason for Counseling: Problems with parenting and self-esteem
  Counseling Experience Before Group: Individual counseling with Szifra, 8 months
  Referred By: Friend

ACOA Group Information Sheet

Name: Bob
Age: 50   Male

FAMILY OF ORIGIN INFORMATION:
   Birth Order: Oldest
   Role Assumed: Scapegoat
   Brothers/Sisters: 1S
     Any Chemically Dependent? Bob, recovering 6
      years
   Alcoholic Parent: Mother
     Still Living? No
     Still Drinking? Sober 5 years before death

CURRENT LIFE SITUATION:
   Marital Status: Second
   Children: 2, first marriage; son, 28; daughter, 26
   Occupation: Alcoholism counselor
   History of Chemical Use: Recovering, 6 years
   Knowledge of Alcoholism/Counseling Background:
     AA, Certified Alcoholism Counselor
   Original Reason for Counseling: Professional interest,
     realization that ACOA issues were impacting on his
     life
   Counseling Experience Before Group: Inpatient treat-
     ment for alcoholism 6 years ago; family counseling
     2 years ago
   Referred By: Self; knew of Szifra's group through his
     own counseling practice

ACOA Group Information Sheet

Name: Kathy
Age: 33   Female

FAMILY OF ORIGIN INFORMATION:
   Birth Order: Third
   Role Assumed: Mascot/responsible
   Brothers/Sisters: 2B/3S
      Any Chemically Dependent? 1B
   Alcoholic Parent: Father
      Still Living? No
      Still Drinking? At death, 4 months ago

CURRENT LIFE SITUATION:
   Marital Status: Divorced
   Children: None
   Occupation: Secretary
   History of Chemical Use: Alcohol use, socially
   Knowledge of Alcoholism/Counseling Background:
      Szifra.
   Original Reason for Counseling: Unhappiness
   Counseling Experience Before Group: Only minimal;
      postdivorce
   Referred By: Saw newspaper article on Szifra's coun-
      seling ACOAs

ACOA Group Information Sheet

Name: Linda
Age: 36   Female

FAMILY OF ORIGIN INFORMATION:
  Birth Order: Oldest
  Role Assumed: Responsible
  Brothers/Sisters: 2S/1B
    Any Chemically Dependent? Users; some abuse
  Alcoholic Parent: Both
    Still Living? Both
    Still Drinking? Both

CURRENT LIFE SITUATION:
  Marital Status: Second
  Children: 2 daughters, 12 and 14
  Occupation: Nurse
  History of Chemical Use: Alcohol use, nondrinker now
  Knowledge of Alcoholism/Counseling Background: 1 year, Al-Anon; individual counseling with Szifra
  Original Reason for Counseling: Low self-esteem; desire to feel better
  Counseling Experience Before Group: 1 year individual counseling, local agency; 1 year couples counseling; 2 months individual counseling with Szifra
  Referred By: Al-Anon member

ACOA Group Information Sheet

Name: Mark
Age: 30   Male

FAMILY OF ORIGIN INFORMATION:
  Birth Order: Fourth
  Role Assumed: Scapegoat
  Brothers/Sisters: 1B/4S
    Any Chemically Dependent? Mark, recovering 8 years
  Alcoholic Parent: Father
    Still Living? No
    Still Drinking? At death, 6 years ago

CURRENT LIFE SITUATION:
  Marital Status: Divorced
  Children: None
  Occupation: Welder
  History of Chemical Use: Heroin-addicted, recovering 8 years; previously abused other chemicals
  Knowledge of Alcoholism/Counseling Background: Treatment in two resident addiction programs; individual counseling with Szifra
  Original Reason for Counseling: Awareness of ACOA issues
  Counseling Experience Before Group: Inpatient treatment and after-care counseling for chemical dependency
  Referred By: Sister

ACOA Group Information Sheet

Name: Michael
Age: 38   Male

FAMILY OF ORIGIN INFORMATION:
   Birth Order: Second
   Role Assumed: Responsible
   Brothers/Sisters: 2B/1S
      Any Chemically Dependent? 1S
   Alcoholic Parent: Father
      Still Living? Yes
      Still Drinking? Yes
      Mother, prescription drug dependent; still living;
         still using

CURRENT LIFE SITUATION:
   Marital Status: Married
   Children: None
   Occupation: Advertising/public relations
   History of Chemical Use: Minimal
   Knowledge of Alcoholism/Counseling Background:
      Szifra; also participates in another ACOA group
   Original Reason for Counseling: Falling apart
   Counseling Experience Before Group: Three sessions
      years ago related to father's alcoholism; individual
      therapy with Szifra for 5 months
   Referred By: Szifra; knew of group through relative

ACOA Group Information Sheet

Name: Roger
Age: 20 Male

FAMILY OF ORIGIN INFORMATION:
  Birth Order: Middle
  Role Assumed: Lost child/scapegoat
  Brother/Sisters: 1B/1S
    Any Chemically Dependent? Roger
  Alcoholic Parent: Mother
    Still Living? Yes
    Still Drinking? No, recovering 4 years

CURRENT LIFE SITUATION:
  Marital Status: Engaged
  Children: None
  Occupation: Student
  History of Chemical Use: Recovering 14 months
  Knowledge of Alcoholism/Counseling Background:
    Inpatient treatment, AA, Szifra
  Original Reason for Counseling: Learn to deal with
    feelings and learn to express himself better
  Counseling Experience Before Group: 30-day inpa-
    tient program; individual after-care counseling with
    addictions counselor for 8 months; individual coun-
    seling with Szifra for 6 months
  Referred By: University safe house for chemical-free
    students

ACOA Group Information Sheet

Name: Sarah
Age: 36   Female

FAMILY OF ORIGIN INFORMATION:
   Birth Order: Oldest
   Role Assumed: Responsible
   Brother/Sisters: 2B
      Any Chemically Dependent? 1B
   Alcoholic Parent: Father
      Still Living? No
      Still Drinking? At death, 5 years ago

CURRENT LIFE SITUATION:
   Marital Status: Divorced, 3 years
   Children: Two sons; 13, 15
   Occupation: High school teacher
   History of Chemical Use: Minimal
   Knowledge of Alcoholism/Counseling Background: Al-Anon, some counseling with Szifra
   Original Reason for Counseling: Divorce aftermath; sleep disturbance
   Counseling Experience Before Group: Surviving divorce group, 8 weeks; individual counseling, 3 months
   Referred By: Physician and a friend in Al-Anon

ACOA Group Information Sheet

Name: Susan
Age: 32   Female

FAMILY OF ORIGIN INFORMATION:
  Birth Order: Oldest
  Role Assumed: Lost child/responsible
  Brother/Sisters: 1B/1S
    Any Chemically Dependent? No
  Alcoholic Parent: Father
    Still Living? No
    Still Drinking? At death, 2 years ago

CURRENT LIFE SITUATION:
  Marital Status: Married
  Children: None
  Occupation: Accountant, manufacturing plant
  History of Chemical Use: Minimal, social drinker
  Knowledge of Alcoholism/Counseling Background: Szifra
  Original Reason for Counseling: Anxiety, stress
  Counseling Experience Before Group: Individual counseling with Szifra, 10 months
  Referred By: Physician

ACOA Group Information Sheet

Name: Trina
Age: 45   Female

FAMILY OF ORIGIN INFORMATION:
   Birth Order: Third
   Role Assumed: Scapegoat
   Brothers/Sisters: 3B/2S
      Any Chemically Dependent? 2B/1S
   Alcoholic Parent: Father
      Still Living? Yes
      Still Drinking? No, quit drinking a few years ago on doctor's orders

CURRENT LIFE SITUATION:
   Marital Status: Divorced
   Children: 2 grown daughters, 3 grandchildren
   Occupation: Receiving department, manufacturing facility
   History of Chemical Use: Recovering 2 years
   Knowledge of Alcoholism/Counseling Background: AA, Szifra
   Original Reason for Counseling: Problems with family of origin and guilt over sexual abuse
   Counseling Experience Before Group: 30-day inpatient treatment of alcoholism, 1 year of individual after-care counseling; 6 months of couples counseling
   Referred By: Counselor and AA member

ACOA Group Information Sheet

Name:
Age:

FAMILY OF ORIGIN INFORMATION:
   Birth Order:
   Role Assumed:
   Brother/Sisters:
      Any Chemically Dependent?
   Alcoholic Parent:
      Still Living?
      Still Drinking?

CURRENT LIFE SITUATION:
   Marital Status:
   Children:
   Occupation:
   History of Chemical Use:
   Knowledge of Alcoholism/Counseling Background:
   Original Reason for Counseling:
   Counseling Experience Before Group:
   Referred By:

Getting Acquainted

IT'S BEEN RAINING off and on all day. How appropriate, Kathy thought, as she drove. This is the kind of weather I'd pick if I were making a movie of this.

Thank goodness it's not a movie, though, or I'd never go, Kathy continued in her reverie, driving much slower than her normal speed. Imagine being filmed as I say my father was an alcoholic. I'm barely comfortable saying it to myself.

"Okay," Kathy murmured aloud, like a parent gently reprimanding, "there's no camera. Don't be so dramatic. What will I say? Why did I decide to be in this group? Keep it objective and I'll do okay."

As she pulled into the parking lot, Kathy saw someone else getting out of a car, probably going the same place. She stalled, thinking, I'm not ready to talk to anyone yet. After a minute, she went in.

Walking into the waiting room of Szifra's office, Kathy nodded and smiled at those already there, then quickly walked over to the bulletin board, busying herself reading notices and newsletters.

Kathy has arrived at her first meeting of a group of Adult Children of Alcoholics organized by Szifra Birke, a therapist in private practice.

Kathy is thirty-three years old, divorced, and the third of six children in her family. Her father died from alcoholism.

46

Although her family never discussed it, they had all been aware of her father's drinking and her mother's efforts to control it. A newspaper article about ACOAs and the formation of the group led Kathy to call.

Tonight's meeting was the first for all eight ACOAs attending. They had committed to participating in the group every Tuesday night for at least six weeks, the minimum commitment Szifra asked when they began "group." They were welcome, though, to attend longer, she had explained. Szifra planned to continue the group indefinitely, adding new members when others left.

Just as Kathy finished reading the notices on the bulletin board, Szifra walked into the waiting room from her office.

An outsider would have been hard-pressed to identify Szifra from the others assembled in the room. She was dressed casually in brown leather sandals and cotton slacks, and her long brown hair was slightly windblown. Szifra's warmth and ease in welcoming her clients conveyed more comfort than the others seemed to be feeling. She invited everyone to help themselves to coffee, then come into her office and find a comfortable chair.

Even though everyone had met Szifra before, most had not met each other, so the group moved quietly and somewhat awkwardly into Szifra's large office. An assortment of chairs formed a loose circle at one end. The lighted floor lamps and woven wall hangings added warmth. Szifra's cluttered desk filled the far end of the room. Bookcases lined two walls.

Szifra's brown eyes conveyed acceptance as she welcomed each ACOA individually.

She joked with Sarah, the first to walk in, which helped Sarah relax. Sarah had been in a divorce support group, so she had some idea what tonight would be like. And she'd been to Al-Anon meetings. Her lingering problems with sleeplessness and a vague, hard-to-define discontent had motivated her to take Szifra's suggestion and join the group.

Sarah had been referred to Szifra by her physician. As a

teacher, Sarah thought her fast-paced schedule might be getting too strenuous for her now that she was well into her thirties. She was learning instead that she had some unresolved issues about how her father's alcoholism had affected her family.

Sarah appeared expectant as she sat down and folded her hands in her lap. Her smile lit up bright green eyes and showed off two dimples on each cheek. With her light brown hair pulled back in a ponytail, she seemed both modern and old-fashioned.

Sarah was glad to see Linda come in. They had been in an Al-Anon group together. Linda's walk was more hesitant than usual. As a hospital nurse, Linda had developed a brisk, efficient walk. But she wasn't feeling that confidence and efficiency tonight. Even though she'd long been aware of alcoholism's impact on her life, thinking about it tonight felt scary.

Linda is thirty-six and married for the second time; she had met her husband in a couples' substance abuse support group. Tonight, as she faced the new group, she reminded herself of his support and encouragement.

Sitting down, Linda straightened her print wraparound skirt, fidgeted with the collar on her blouse, then ran her hands through her short, curly red hair. Finally she felt in place and able to glance around the room. It will seem very different to be in this room with so many people, she thought. After many sessions alone with Szifra, sharing the room with others felt strange.

Susan and Roger arrived next, looking as if they wanted to acknowledge each other. They had never met, though, and neither felt ready to offer an introduction.

As Susan sat down, she unconsciously scooted her chair back slightly from the circle. Susan grew up in a small, quiet family. She and her sister had learned early the ladylike behavior expected by their mother, and talking about your family troubles was certainly not ladylike. She'd broken the family code by joining a group that would discuss these experiences. And even though she felt like running,

Susan knew this was an important step in conquering her social fears. As her fear of crowds and the accompanying physical symptoms escalated, Susan's doctor had referred her to Szifra. The very anxiety she felt tonight was her reason for being here.

Susan is married. Her father died from alcoholism two years ago. Framed by straight blond hair, Susan's round face appeared warm and gentle. Her long, slender fingers gripped the arms of her chair tightly, revealing her discomfort.

Roger picked up on Susan's anxiety but didn't say anything. Speaking was difficult for him, anyway. Tonight was even more so since he was meeting new people. Roger surveyed the remaining chairs, trying to decide where he could best stretch out his long legs. He took the chair next to Linda. Her careful dress contrasted sharply with Roger's casual appearance. His brown hair was tousled. He wore faded jeans and a sports jersey. He's an attractive man who doesn't realize it, Linda thought as he sat down.

Roger is the youngest member of the group—twenty years old, and a college student. He's been recovering from his own alcoholism for more than a year and is ready now to deal with related issues, such as how his mother's alcoholism may have impacted on his life. She began her recovery several years ago. Like Susan, Roger wants to conquer social fears and develop more comfort interacting with people.

Roger smiled as Michael walked in, coffee cup in hand.

"Hello," Michael said to the group. His blue eyes briefly made contact with the others as he settled his tall, muscular frame onto the chair next to Szifra. His smile helped cover up the apprehension he was feeling. He was dressed casually but wished he had the protection of his work clothes, tie, and wingtips. As a public relations and advertising account executive, it wasn't often he could dress casually. He wondered if people thought he felt relaxed and open. He knew he didn't.

Michael attends some drop-in ACOA meetings of a self-help group. He decided to join Szifra's group, hoping it would have more focus and direction. His mother and father are both chemically dependent. Michael doesn't remember a peaceful family time in all his thirty-eight years. Now he avoids family gatherings.

Anne shyly followed Michael into the room. For Anne three was a group, so this was intimidating. If it was a group of children, though, she'd feel fine. She was always comfortable with children, which was probably why she chose child care for a career. Anne offered a surprisingly strong "Hello." Anticipating Anne's discomfort, Szifra gestured for her to sit on her right. As Anne sat down, Szifra gently touched her arm, offering Anne a little extra support.

At thirty-nine, Anne was determined to improve her self-esteem, and she hoped coming to tonight's meeting would take her a step further. Anne's father died from his alcoholism seven years ago. It was only recently that she realized her childhood had anything to do with her adult insecurities.

Anne was attractive in an unusual way, with large brown eyes and sharp features. She was perhaps too thin, however; her tailored clothes fit loosely. She fidgeted on her chair, pulling her skirt well over her knees. Then she checked the button at the neck of her blouse, not sure what to do with her hands. My mouth feels so dry, Anne thought. I wish I had a diet pop.

Trina filled her coffee cup, asking Kathy what had brought her to the group. Everyone heard Trina's question, her deep voice booming. Her language was clear and direct, her hair cut simply. She wore jeans and a knit shirt. At forty-five, Trina had seen a lot of life, as she phrased it.

Through her own recovery from alcoholism, she'd become aware of how many in her family were chemically dependent. This group, she felt, offered her a chance to be around sober people and to learn what it was like to interact with people who were not abusing alcohol or drugs. She had a commonsense, practical approach to life's problems these days. And she didn't waste time with small talk. Finding out why Kathy joined the group seemed like the sensible thing to do.

Kathy, though, was taken aback by Trina's direct question. She laughed nervously as she responded, "Well, I'd tried everything else." Kathy and Trina walked in together. Kathy took the nearest chair, trying to regain the relative calm she'd talked herself into as she drove to the meeting. It's not a movie, she reminded herself again. She felt self-conscious and eager for the focus to move away from her.

Sarah noticed Kathy was dressed conservatively, especially considering her casual hairstyle. She wondered if Kathy dressed so neutrally because she was overweight or because of her job. She looked as if she had just come from an office.

Trina took the last chair, crossing her legs and leaning back with obvious ease. A veteran of many AA meetings and group therapy during treatment, Trina felt comfortable, even in a new group. She was pleased with her comfort, remembering how anxious she used to feel in situations with new people.

Szifra smiled at the circle of ACOAs, and their first meeting began.

"Welcome, everyone," Szifra said. "I want to congratulate each of you for coming here tonight. It's not easy to step into unknown territory. For Adult Children of Alcoholics, that's too often been scary and hurtful. You trusted yourselves enough to share your feelings, thoughts, and perceptions with me individually."

She paused a minute to give everyone time to relax a little. "I'm excited you're ready to trust some more by participating in this group. You may be feeling uncomfortable. It's okay. In fact, I'd be surprised if you weren't. As time goes on, you'll feel increasingly more comfortable."

After covering the ground rules for group, Szifra spent some time reviewing the purpose and focus of their meetings. She explained the planned format, stressing she would be flexible, depending on individual and group needs. As she spoke, Kathy found herself relaxing a little. Szifra's warmth helped her. And learning there would be some structure to the group was reassuring to Kathy, who tended to schedule her life, not feeling comfortable if she didn't know how her time would be spent.

Szifra paused in her conversation a minute, looking at each group member. Her eye contact was reassuring and encouraging. They all appreciated that extra encouragement.

"I asked each of you to be prepared to share some brief information about yourself and your family," Szifra continued, "to tell us why you decided to participate in this group, and what you hope to gain. Would someone start?"

After only a slight pause, Sarah said, "I'll start. My name is Sarah. I have two teenage sons. My father was an alcoholic, but I didn't realize that as a child. My father died almost five years ago. No one ever talked about his drinking problem, though. My ex-husband was also an alcoholic. I've been divorced three years. I'm just starting to feel like I'm getting settled again, inside. I originally came to see Szifra because I just didn't feel right, especially since my divorce. I had friends and a rewarding job; I teach high school. But I still felt scared and empty." Sarah sat quietly a moment before saying, "I felt like a bad, worthless person."

Sarah's voice raised in pitch, revealing her growing discomfort as she spoke of personal issues. As she talked, she leaned forward on her chair.

"Szifra asked me in our second session if one of my parents was an alcoholic. I was shocked. I couldn't figure out how she could have known that. Since then, I've learned why she asked me. So many connections are obvious now. I've been working on 'Adult Child' issues."

Leaning back, Sarah finished up, "I'm here to get feedback about myself, to tell you about experiences I had as a child and as an adult related to alcoholism. I also want to hear other people's experiences. And I want to practice being assertive in group so I can be more assertive in the world. I'm usually either passive or aggressive, and I'd like to change that." Sarah nodded, indicating that was all. She felt relieved she had been able to say most of what she had planned.

"Thanks, Sarah," Szifra said. Looking around the circle, she asked who would like to go next.

"I will," Trina said with a sincere eagerness. "I'm Trina. I'm forty-five years old and a recovering alcoholic. I come from a big family, five brothers and sisters. Half are alcoholic or drug addicts. The other half are all crazy. I'm the only sober one. That's made it hard for me. I'm like the outcast, the black sheep." She spoke easily, conversationally.

"My mom and dad are still alive, but my dad's health is real bad. He's an alcoholic. He quit drinking a few years ago, when the doctor told him he'd die if he didn't. I'm trying hard to make it, to learn to be happy. I've been sober two years and found out from Szifra about Adult Children of Alcoholics."

Trina continued, looking around at everyone as she spoke. "In the past several months seeing Szifra, I've read articles and books. I've started to learn about the family issues of alcoholism. Now I'd like to learn more, from other people's experiences. For a long time I thought I was the only one who had lived in hell. I'm realizing I don't have to feel alone any longer. So that's why I'm here. I want to do anything I can to feel better."

There was a short lull before Szifra acknowledged Trina's input. Knowing Anne would need her encouragement, Szifra turned to her, asking her to speak next.

"I'm Anne," she began. "I'm married and have four children. I'm here because Szifra said I should come," she said, only half joking. Susan and Roger exchanged smiles; it was true for them, too.

Knowing she was expected to say more, Anne tried to pretend she was speaking to her day care class so she'd feel more comfortable. She continued slowly, "I need to speak out and get more comfortable with myself and people. My father was an alcoholic. He died seven years ago from al-

coholism. We never talked about it in my family, either."
Anne's eyes filled with tears, but she held them back.

"Thanks, Anne," Szifra said, acknowledging what she
knew had been difficult.

Recognizing Anne's risk as well as her success, Roger
decided to go next.

"I'm Roger," he began, looking only at Szifra. "I'm a
student and a recovering alcoholic. My mother is an alcoholic, too. She's been recovering several years. I'm engaged to someone I've known a long time. I need to learn
to speak out more, too. I have a hard time talking to people.
I do go to AA, but I'm pretty quiet. I also need to learn
about feelings. I don't understand them very well. My sobriety seems okay now; it's been fourteen months, so Szifra
suggested I move on to this group. I never thought my
alcoholism or shyness was related to my mother's drinking,
but now I realize it is. I have gotten a little better. I want to
keep going."

Roger sat up, tucking his long legs under his chair. He
was glad he had spoken out, but also glad it was over. It
didn't feel quite as scary as he'd thought it would.

"Good, Roger." Szifra smiled. "Who's next?"

"I guess I'll get it over with." Kathy laughed, and the
others smiled with her. It was typical of her to keep things
light, especially when the subject matter was heavy. "I'm
Kathy," she began. "I'm divorced and I don't have any
children. My father was an alcoholic. He died four months
ago. I'm here because I've realized a lot of my unhappiness
comes from growing up in an alcoholic home."

She spoke quickly, sounding efficient. But as she continued with more personal issues, she bit her top lip and slowed
her speech. "I know I have reasons to be happy, but I'm
not." It seemed as though she were starting to cry, but it
was hard to tell because of her extreme control and because
her glasses blurred her eyes. Kathy paused, then continued
rapidly, "I'm not very comfortable discussing personal
things, and I keep people at a distance. But if there's a
chance this will help, I'll try it."

"Thank you, Kathy," Szifra said, pausing while Kathy sat back on her chair. "Michael?"

"Okay, I'll jump in." Michael smiled nervously. "I'm Michael. I'm married. No kids. My father is actively drinking; my mother abuses prescription drugs."

Michael spoke softly for a man his size. "I started seeing Szifra originally because I was so stressed out I didn't think I could go on. Opening up was not something I felt comfortable doing, so I resisted seeking help before. When I'd hit bottom, though, I felt so scared, calling for an appointment to see a 'shrink' seemed better than enduring what I was. I've seen Szifra individually for five months now."

Michael shifted on his chair and glanced around the room before he continued, "I believe I'm ready to try trusting more people. After I learned I could trust Szifra, it seemed logical I could learn to trust one more person, and perhaps even more. I have problems with stress and with thinking everyone's better than I am.

"I work in advertising and public relations. I often feel like I'm a fraud about to be discovered. I know my work well and come up with creative ideas. But because I don't feel confident and assured with my clients, I often think if my clients really knew me, they'd be disappointed. I also have problems with closeness and intimacy I'd like to resolve."

"Thanks, Michael," Szifra said, surprised he'd shared so much. Then she turned to Susan, asking her if she'd go next.

"I'm Susan," she began. She spoke so quietly, Trina and Kathy leaned forward to hear her better. "I'm married. I work as an accountant. I'm absolutely terrified to be here, but I know I need to be. I've been seeing Szifra individually for eight months."

Susan's eyes filled with tears, and her voice trembled as she continued, "I want to feel more comfortable in groups, less self-conscious. Especially when I cry, like now."

Susan remembered past times when she'd cried, and a lump in her throat choked off her words. She'd since learned that sharing her self-consciousness helped her continue. She felt worse for the moment but knew she'd feel better later. She felt brave for continuing despite her tears, and she reminded herself of something Szifra often said: "It takes courage to cry."

Acknowledging Susan's tears, Szifra reassured her, "It's okay to cry here. This is a safe place where it's okay to express sadness, fear, joy, apprehension, happiness, and any other feelings."

She turned to the group, reminding them, "You were not able to express these feelings in many of your families and have them accepted. You may wonder what everyone is thinking of you when you express your feelings in here. Try to check that out with us. We all share these feelings. Each of us gets sad, confused, defensive, and so forth. I hope you can be yourselves here. We will not treat your feelings as your families did."

Taking a tissue from the box Linda had passed over, Susan said, "I'm okay now," and continued. "My father was alcoholic. He's no longer living. Mother never drank. My mother was very protective of my sister, brother, and me." Susan hesitated a minute, then concluded, "That's really all for now."

"Susan, thank you," Szifra said warmly.

After a minute, Linda began. "I'm Linda. I'm married for the second time. My first marriage was a disaster. I married just to get away from home, although I didn't realize it then. This marriage is good. I have two daughters, twelve and fourteen.

"Both my parents are alcoholic. They're alive and still drinking. I want a better relationship with them, but I think it's a fantasy. I'm here to get a better perspective on them. I'm too hooked in to them and get dragged down emotionally. I need to work on not being too involved with my sisters' and brother's craziness. They use drugs and are involved with irresponsible people. I always think it's my job to help them. I know logically I can't fix everything, but when I'm in the situation, I forget that. I'm dealing with that by trying to follow Al-Anon's slogan "One Day at a Time." Linda appeared relatively relaxed, comfortable with being in the group. Her discomfort showed only when she spoke about her parents.

Linda organized her thoughts the way she organized her nursing charts. She moved from a description of her family to her reasons for joining the group. "I feel bad about myself too much. I want to feel better. I'm too hard on myself. Like what you said, Sarah, sometimes I feel like a bad, worthless person. My parents said so many damaging things to me as a child, I guess now they seem true, even though I know that's ridiculous. I'm trying to change that, and I have changed a lot already. The fact that I can be here and be this comfortable is a big deal. A year ago, I wouldn't have come. So, I'm glad I'm here!"

"I'm glad you're here, too, Linda," Szifra said. To the group, she said enthusiastically, "You all did great! Make sure to give yourselves credit for being open. You've taken another step. In individual sessions many of you predicted that at worst you'd say nothing, and at best, just a couple of sentences. Without exception, you opened up very well. The reward is you get to open up more!

"Really," she continued, "what I want you to do is tell us how you feel now, compared with how you felt when you first came in. Michael, are you willing to start?"

"All right," Michael said. "I feel relieved. Hearing others say things I could relate to makes me feel much better. Trina, when you said half your family is alcoholic and the other half is crazy, I felt so much better. Mine is like that, too."

Trina laughed and nodded her head several times.

"I feel relieved, too," Kathy said, looking at Michael. "I'm glad that 'first time' is over with. I was nervous while speaking, though. I liked hearing who you all are and why you're here. It made me feel less different, hearing things I could have said."

"Boy, I felt like I could have talked forever," Trina jumped in, "but I shut up to give everyone a chance. I feel good in here. Mike—is it okay if I call you Mike? Michael sounds too formal for me!"

Michael nodded amiably as Trina continued, "Anyway, Mike, maybe we can talk about our really messed-up families more sometime."

"I feel better than at first, too," Roger spoke up. "I'm not sure why exactly, but I'll take it." He realized admitting his shyness earlier had been easier than he'd thought it would be.

Sarah spoke next. "I really like this. Laying our cards on the table. It feels like freedom to me. I think I'm going to be able to get into this."

"Me too," Linda agreed. "I know what you mean, Trina, about going on and on. I could, too. I've got so much stuff inside me, it's unbelievable. Even after all those Al-Anon meetings, I still have unresolved things. I'm hopeful about this group." She smiled at Szifra as she finished.

Szifra nodded, acknowledging Linda, then turned to Susan. "How are you feeling, Susan?"

"I'm pretty uncomfortable still," Susan responded, "but better than at first. I feel shaky and hate crying in front of everyone. But I'm okay."

"It is hard to let ourselves cry in front of others," Szifra confirmed. "We feel self-conscious and out of control, vulnerable. Others' acceptance of you with and without your tears will help you become more comfortable. Many of us will cry in the coming weeks. It's okay."

"I'm sure I'll cry often," Linda said. "I did a lot of crying in Al-Anon.".

"How are you feeling, Anne?" Szifra asked, drawing her into the conversation.

"This is very hard for me," Anne responded. "To be honest, it's a miracle I'm here. Talking is difficult. I am a little more comfortable than at the beginning because you all seem so friendly. It's still difficult, though," she said, looking down at her lap.

Szifra acknowledged Anne's feelings. "It's significant you were willing to tackle something difficult. You're not used to talking about yourself. Tonight you did. I hope you give yourself a pat on the back for opening up. You said much more than you thought you would, and you seem far more comfortable than you predicted.''

Anne blushed as she responded, ''I really am more comfortable than I expected.''

''I'm glad you talked, Anne. I liked what you had to say,'' Roger said, surprising himself that he was saying something like this so early in group.

Anne smiled shyly. Hearing compliments wasn't easy for her.

Szifra paused a minute before going on, giving everyone a chance to think about what had been shared in their first meeting.

''Thanks for opening up,'' she said to the group, ''for letting us know how you're feeling. I commend you. Take time now and after you leave to think of positives to say to yourselves about your participation tonight.'' She laughed a little at herself as she continued, ''I'll bore you to tears about focusing on the positive—unless you get so good at it that I don't have to remind you.

''It may help if you think of yourselves as newspaper reporters who can only write positive stories. You might say, 'I talked more than I thought I could.' Or 'I felt more comfortable than usual.' Then add a compliment, like 'Good for me,' or 'That's great.' ''

Szifra spent several minutes urging them to congratulate themselves for their decisions to participate in group and their openness at the first meeting. She gave them suggestions for recognizing achievements they might otherwise have overlooked. Szifra knew how difficult it was for ACOAs to focus on their emotional successes, and she frequently reminded them about the importance of recognizing these accomplishments.

''One reminder before we stop for tonight,'' Szifra continued. ''I spoke about confidentiality with each of you individually and again when we covered the ground rules for group. I just want to remind you before we leave tonight: It's essential to all of us that we keep whatever happens in this room to ourselves. I want this group to be a secure, safe place so each of you can feel free to share your feelings and experiences. Any questions?''

Trina said she didn't have a question but wanted to confirm what Szifra said about confidentiality. ''I won't be able to open up if people don't keep everything to themselves.'' Several group members nodded their agreement.

''Thank you,'' Szifra said. ''That's it for tonight. I'll see everyone next week.''

My Observations and Reactions to Meeting 1

Anne, 39, child care worker, lost child role in family, father died from alcoholism seven years ago.
Observations:

Kathy, 33, secretary, mascot/responsible role in family, father died from alcoholism this year.
Observations:

Linda, 36, nurse, responsible role in family, both parents are alcoholic, living.
Observations:

Michael, 38, PR/advertising, responsible role in family, father is alcoholic, mother prescription drug–addicted, both living.
Observations:

Roger, 20, student, lost child/scapegoat in family, recovering, mother also recovering.
Observations:

Sarah, 36, high school teacher, responsible role in family, father died from alcoholism five years ago.
Observations:

Susan, 32, accountant, lost child/responsible role in family, father died from alcoholism two years ago.
Observations:

Trina, 45, shipping clerk, scapegoat role in family, recovering, father quit drinking a few years ago.
Observations:

Szifra, therapist
Observations:

Observations about me during my first meeting:

My feelings during this meeting:

Issues I'd like to explore further:

My reactions to this meeting:

What I learned about myself during this meeting:

Becoming Aware of Alcoholism's Impact

I WONDER IF this will ever get any easier, Susan thought as she walked into Szifra's waiting room. She was one of the first to arrive, as she had planned. It was easier for her not to walk into a room full of people.

Susan could often predict when she'd be uncomfortable in social situations. She did her best to prepare for the times she was unable to avoid socializing entirely. Her extreme discomfort with people, even the other accountants on staff, was what had brought her to therapy in the first place. She was determined not to let her anxiety control her life, even though the easier choice was to hide out at home. She noticed her heart was racing as she walked into Szifra's office.

Linda smiled at her warmly. "Hello, how are you?"

Susan thought, She seems like a nurse, warm and friendly. "I'm doing pretty well," she responded softly. "How about you?" They chatted briefly about being there for their second meeting.

Linda had dressed very carefully again tonight; everything coordinated, even her makeup. Susan wore dress slacks, a long-sleeved silk blouse with a bow at the neck, and a sweater vest. She always looks so neat, Linda thought, not realizing she gave the same impression.

The music on the radio filled the lull in conversation that followed until Sarah and Michael arrived. After surviving the first meeting in casual clothes. Michael had decided to opt for physical comfort again, hoping he wouldn't need the protection of his "PR clothes" identity. Sarah appeared friendly and ready to jump in again. Susan wondered how she could still have energy left after teaching all day.

Anne arrived next, relieved that she was early enough to collect her thoughts after a tense drive in from the country. Then Kathy breezed in with a burst of greetings and smiles, but, characteristically, she withdrew once the initial polite conversation was over.

Nods and hellos were offered whenever someone came through the door. Although everyone seemed a little more relaxed this time, the long silences between their brief exchanges revealed the discomfort they felt.

"I sure wish I could play the guitar like that," Michael said, commenting on the music.

"Do you play?" Sarah asked.

"Only a little," Michael responded.

"I play the guitar, too," Sarah said, "but not that well, either. I should get one of my students to teach me, I guess."

Trina arrived with a bag of cookies. "I thought we could all use a little reward tonight," she said. She'd worn her favorite jeans again and her comfortable loafers. Working in shipping enabled her to dress casually, which had attracted her to the job in the first place.

Just before seven, Szifra stepped out of her office to say she needed to make a phone call, but the group would be starting on time. Knowing there would soon be an end to the waiting room waiting helped Anne relax. She shifted slightly on her chair, wishing the evening were already over.

Szifra returned in a minute and welcomed everyone. As the group walked into her office, there was some shuffling around as everyone decided whether to sit where they had last week or try a new place. Some took the same places, including Szifra. "I guess sometimes I like ruts," she said, laughing.

Kathy looked around the room, reading the book titles, the long-established habit of an avid reader.

Trina noticed Kathy was often busy doing something else. Kathy seemed like someone she'd enjoy knowing better, if she could figure out how to reach her. Maybe I'll try to catch her after the meeting, Trina decided to herself. Thinking of Kathy made Trina realize how much she herself had changed from a year ago. The thought of catching someone after a meeting would not have crossed her mind, and even if it had, she would have been too apprehensive to do anything about it.

Once everyone was seated, Szifra again welcomed the group. Her long hair was pulled back in a big silver barrette, and, as usual, she wore her favorite sandals and a jean jumper. I wish I could dress like that, Kathy thought. Szifra has such a consistent style. Her clothes reflect the kind of life-style I wish I had. It makes me miss the idealism of the sixties.

"Hi, everyone," Szifra began. "Glad you are all here. It's great when the whole group is present. Tonight's topic is 'Becoming Aware of Alcoholism's Effects.'

"Before we start, though, I want to let you know I'll leave a few minutes at the beginning of each meeting for brief comments, reactions, or questions from our preceding meeting. This is your chance to get closure from our last meeting before we start a new topic. Does anyone have a leftover from last week?"

"I do," Trina remarked. "I saw my family this week. Because of last week's group, I think I was able to handle them a little better. Hearing others share the same kinds of experiences helped me not feel so out of place when I was with them."

Michael said he identified with Trina's family situation, even though he hadn't seen his family for months. "I also found my first meeting here helped me already. I went to another ACOA meeting, a support group. I think I was able to get more out of it because of coming here."

"Do you know why, Michael?" Szifra asked.

"Well," Michael said, frowning a little as he thought, "I think I understood more the need for some of us ACOAs to talk about our childhoods. Just talk about it. Before, I couldn't understand others' need to talk so much about their pasts. I guess I didn't appreciate the value of sharing your own story and hearing others. After I talked about my own background in here last week, which was the first time I ever had in a group setting. I felt like a tiny bit of weight had been lifted. I think I'm more aware of the value now."

"I agree, Michael," Szifra said. "Sometimes in therapy, ACOAs focus so squarely on today, they forget the value of looking at their past and its impact. Talking about the past can be a way to identify codependency patterns, decrease that negative impact, and recognize some of what was positive."

Roger took advantage of the pause in the conversation that followed. With his legs stretched out in front of him, crossed at the ankles, he looked more relaxed than last week. He, too, wore blue jeans again and worn tennis shoes, the wardrobe of most college students. "I'd like to say something about how I felt after last week's meeting. It was real hard saying I'm an alcoholic in front of everyone here. I thought I was used to that, because of my involvement with AA, but it was hard in here. Maybe because I was admitting my alcoholism to people who are not alcoholics."

"I understand what you mean, Roger," Trina said warmly. "It was hard for me at first, too, when I admitted to others I was an alcoholic. Maybe we still expect a non-alcoholic will judge us. Time and practice has made that a little easier for me."

Roger nodded at Trina. He appreciated her support.

The discussion continued as others commented on how they felt after their first meeting and thoughts they had about group during the week.

"Anyone else?" Szifra asked, after allowing a pause so everyone had the opportunity to speak. No one else seemed to want time, so she proceeded.

"These 'leftovers' were excellent. I encourage you to share at the beginning of each meeting if you have anything remaining from last week.

"Okay. Let's move on to tonight's topic, Becoming

Aware of Alcoholism's Effects. As painful as it is to realize one or both of your parents is alcoholic, it can be a tremendous opportunity, too. Knowing the reason for the turmoil, hurt, and pain can open doors to understanding. You can learn about the addiction and its impact on you and your family. Many of you grew up without ever realizing your parent was an alcoholic. Others of you knew, but never talked about it. Or maybe you knew but didn't think it affected your life.''

The group was attentive as Szifra spent several minutes discussing how alcoholism impacts on families. She concluded, ''You may have experienced emotional or physical neglect or abuse. You may have experienced terror if your parents fought, or sadness when you saw them in pain. Some of you never saw drinking or heard fighting, but you felt inexplicably sad, fearful, or anxious. There might have been tension in the air, unexplained but felt. Some of you may have wondered if your mother's or father's personality change was a result of cocktails before dinner. Perhaps one parent totally dominated your family, and the rest of the family withdrew. The specific family situations can differ; the common threads are the coping skills, the feelings, and the impact today.''

As Szifra looked at each ACOA while she spoke, she knew she was addressing issues very close to them. Kathy's eyes filled with tears, and she bit her upper lip. Roger's hands were joined at the fingertips as he opened and closed his hands. Susan sat perfectly still.

Szifra went on, her manner gentle and caring, ''Perhaps you had no explanation for these experiences until you found out alcohol was the root. It's difficult for an alcoholic to admit alcohol is a problem. It's also extremely hard for Children of Alcoholics to admit their parents are alcoholic and codependent.

''It can be significant in your own recovery to share how you first became aware that you were affected by alcoholism. Pieces of your past tie in to who you are today, how you feel, and what you do.

"So . . . who feels ready to address tonight's issue?" Szifra asked.

After a brief pause, Kathy began, "I usually want to speak first, so sometimes I force myself to give others a chance to be first. But I'd like to start tonight.

"I don't think I'll ever forget the first time I realized that alcoholism had something to do with me today.

"Growing up, I knew things weren't right at home. I remember when I was in the third or fourth grade, our family went to a novena for world peace. That's nine days of prayer, I think it was, for Catholics. I remember sitting in church and saying to myself, 'How can I care about world peace when we don't even have peace at home?' "

Struggling to overcome tears, Kathy opened her eyes wide and blinked rapidly. She swallowed a few times, then continued, "Even though deep inside I knew Dad was an alcoholic, I wouldn't admit it. I believed we could not have an alcoholic in our family. It would just be too horrible. Dad was a good man. He worked every day and provided for us. He was never violent. He used to say, 'All I want is a moment's peace.' I thought if I admitted he was an alcoholic, that would have to mean he wasn't a good man.

"I felt sorry for Dad. He grew up during the Depression and didn't have money for college. He always worked at jobs beneath his intelligence. One of my clearest memories, and saddest for me, is when Dad applied to be director of the student union at a small college where we lived. I remember him sitting at the typewriter in the living room, working on his résumé. I was probably fourteen or fifteen, and that was the first I even knew Dad could type. He was so excited, talking about the possibility of getting that job," Kathy said, starting to cry.

Taking off her glasses and wiping her eyes, she resumed, "I knew Dad would love that job, because he enjoyed people so much. But he didn't get it. I felt so sorry for him. I really wanted him to get that job. It would have been so much better than his freight dock job. Because I felt Dad had so much disappointment and sadness in his life, I rationalized his drinking by saying, 'Who wouldn't drink under those circumstances.'

"Gee, I really got sidetracked," Kathy said, breathing deeply as she tried to control her tears. "I haven't forgotten the original question: 'When did I first become aware I was affected by Dad's alcoholism?' Well, because I could understand why Dad drank, I buried the issue of his drinking and concentrated instead on keeping things running smoothly at home, keeping our lives in order. That was my whole existence. Keeping everything all right. Keeping it fine.

"Then Dad died, from alcoholism. We all knew it, but we didn't talk about it even then. It hurt too much, and I guess we thought it was too late anyway.

"Shortly after Dad died, which was only four months ago, I read a newspaper article about Szifra. She talked about adults who have every reason to be happy, but are unhappy. Adults who grew up in a home with a parent who drank too much. I read that article and had this rush of feelings. I knew she was talking about me. So I cut just her name out of the newspaper and decided to call her the next day."

Laughing a little, she continued, "I only cut out her name. I couldn't put the whole article in my purse because, if I died unexpectedly, someone would look in there and see the article and know." Deflecting her hurt with humor helped relieve Kathy's building emotion. She found it easier to go on then.

"Reading that article was my first inkling that alcoholism might have something to do with my life today. And that's how I got here," Kathy concluded. "I'm sorry I took so long," she added quietly.

"Kathy," Szifra said, "you have come so far. From carrying just my name in your purse to being here tonight. I'm glad the newspaper ran that article, and I'm glad you were ready to deal with your feelings.

"You didn't take too long speaking. So often Adult Children have broken gauges. When they take a little time for themselves, they feel they've taken too much. Giving is so easy, taking so hard. Many of you will feel you are taking too much time. Try to check it out with the group. Remember about broken gauges, too. When in doubt, assume you're fine instead of assuming you've messed up.''

"I guess I do have a hard time taking," Kathy agreed. "I'd much rather give." She said she was finished, ready for someone else to talk so the focus would shift.

Michael began slowly, looking down. Kathy's crying had unnerved him more than he would have guessed. He told the group he remembered recently looking through an advertising annual of award-winning ad campaigns and feeling disgusted because so many liquor ads had won awards. He knew he could never write advertising for booze. He also remembered so many times when both his parents were out of it because of their drinking and prescription drug abuse. Abuse that still went on.

"When my father drank," Michael said, "I hated him. My feelings were cold and distant. I finally began admitting to myself that all the yelling and sick feelings I had inside were somehow connected to the fact that my dad drank so much. I didn't realize this until I was in high school, though."

"In a way, Mike," Trina said, "you're lucky you realized it in high school. I was forty-three years old before I had any idea my family's insanity was linked to alcoholism. I knew something was desperately wrong in my family, but I didn't realize what it was until I battled my own alcoholism." Trina moved a lot when she spoke, not from discomfort, but because it was not her style to sit still. She spoke as much with her hands and her body as she did with her words.

"Trina," Szifra joined in, "are you saying you wish you'd had that information much earlier?"

"You bet. I think I'd be much healthier now, and have saved myself and my kids a lot of grief." After a pause, she continued, "Maybe if I'd understood a lot earlier, I wouldn't have become alcoholic, or if I had, maybe I would have gotten sober a lot sooner. I might have had a better relationship with my kids, been able to be open with them. Instead, I re-created my sick family with them. My kids didn't benefit from my recovery until they were saddled with so much sickness themselves. Szifra and I talked at length about my guilt and sadness about this. It's still pretty hard at times, but mostly I've stopped beating myself up about it. It's amazing, you know, to hear how different it was for all of us, yet we have so many of the same feelings. We all need to realize the connection alcoholism and dysfunction had in our families.''

''Did you want to add anything, Michael?'' Szifra asked, turning back to him.

''Well, just that it seemed like one day I had no answers. Then the next day I just knew. Dad's drinking was screwing up our family. And Mom was getting more messed up all the time, too.''

There was a lull in the conversation as each thought how relevant Michael's comment was to their own lives. Then Sarah, slipping into her classroom style of keeping discussions going, spoke up.

''My realization came at a different age from either Trina's or Michael's,'' Sarah said. ''I was older than Michael, but younger than you were, Trina, when things began to click for me.

''The movie *Dr. Jekyll and Mr. Hyde* helped me understand my dad. Dad was the man I admired the most. Yet I despised him the most, too. I loved the Dr. Jekyll in my dad, but I sure despised the Mr. Hyde. Here was this loving father who called me 'kitten' until I was thirty-one, when he died. He was a very sensitive, caring, and intelligent man.'' Sarah's face reflected a wistfulness as she recalled those times.

''When I was a child,'' she continued, ''I never understood how Dad could suddenly not show up at home for evening meals, or how he could call in sick at work when he didn't seem sick. He would scream at us for no reason. If we told him the next day about his rage, he'd say he didn't remember. I thought either he was lying or I was losing my mind.

"Becoming aware, for me, wasn't like a 'bolt of lightning' had hit. Mom had finally asked for help and was going to Al-Anon. It became her life preserver. When she started practicing Al-Anon's principles of firm sympathy and detachment with love, my father went into a tailspin. When she left for Al-Anon meetings, he accused her, saying she was really out selling herself to other men. He was terribly cruel and angry.

"I was scared stiff. I thought I was losing my father to mental illness and my mom was leaving me behind, too. Finally, one day I had the nerve to ask Mom about her meetings. I almost wished I hadn't. I heard her use the words *alcoholism* and *alcoholic*, and that turned me off. My father wasn't any bum who slept in gutters, licked a bottle dry, and had fits," Sarah said with apparent disgust for those who did. "I thought he had mental problems, not alcohol problems."

"I was a mess. I was confused, frightened, and afraid to hear the truth. I just wanted it all to go away. I finally got so confused and frightened that I went to an Al-Anon meeting with my mother. It was an amazing experience, entering a room full of strangers and then leaving with a feeling that I knew them, a feeling of belonging. All those men and women had a common bond, an illness.

"Gosh, I've talked so long, too. That's how my awareness was, too, a long time coming," Sarah finished.

Linda picked up the dialogue. "Sarah, what you said hit home for me in so many ways. I became an adult thinking I had survived growing up in an alcoholic home. Then the rude awakenings began. I was faced with situations I was unprepared for. I thought all there was to a fulfilling life was marrying and having children. I married a year out of high school so I could get away from my parents. I had a child that first year, and suddenly I was faced with responsibilities I couldn't handle. I couldn't figure out how I could have been so naïve. The marriage was over in three years, but even then I didn't think I had any problems other than a bad marriage."

Surprised at how comfortable she was feeling, Linda continued, "After I was divorced I got into relationships with men who drank a lot. I wasn't able to handle my money. My friendships were shallow and meaningless. Then I got so depressed I couldn't sleep at night.

"Finally I realized I had to do something, so I saw a counselor. That eventually led me to discover what I dreaded the most, how much I was like my parents. Not that I was alcoholic, but that my behavior ran parallel to their alcoholic behavior. Szifra says it was alcoholic-like.

"I'm here now," Linda continued, "because I want to change that. I don't want to be sick. Although I'm better, I want to keep progressing."

"Thanks, Linda," Szifra said. "Your determination is great." Turning to Anne, who'd been quiet all evening, she asked, "What was becoming aware like for you, Anne?"

Anne's face flushed as she replied, "I always knew Dad drank too much. It made me sad. I thought he could stop if he wanted to. After he died, my sister started learning about alcoholism and Children of Alcoholics. She'd mail me articles and brochures, so I read them. I was surprised to find out I'd been so affected, but it's been helpful, too." The shakiness in Anne's voice subsided more quickly this time, Szifra noted to herself. Perhaps she was feeling more comfortable tonight.

Realizing nearly everyone had spoken, Susan decided to go next. With an effort to appear relaxed, she began, "I never saw Dad drink. He never drank at home. I had no idea he was an alcoholic. I knew things were very strange, there was a lot of unspoken friction and odd behavior, but I never knew why until I was in college." Her voice trembled, but she tried to ignore it as she went on, "Mom told me the truth when I was twenty. It really came as a shock. But it was sort of a relief, too, because I finally had a reason for all those troubling times."

"That must have been hard," Michael said. "Living

with it, but not knowing what it was. Even though I was living in the midst of the alcoholism, and I knew it, I didn't think that much about it. I got used to it, I thought. I guess I thought all families were like that. But when I got older and I'd spend the night at somebody's house, I started recognizing there was something different between my family and the other kid's family."

"I had some of that, too," Roger said. "I kept telling myself I had a nice, middle-class home. Things didn't appear that crazy on the surface. It seemed like home was secure. Everything was always so in control. Mom and Dad didn't fight in front of me.

"But it didn't feel good, either." Roger paused a minute, looking up at the ceiling as he searched for the right words. "I wasn't really happy," he continued. "I thought if I'd work harder, I could get things under control. It was a pretend serenity." He nodded as he spoke. "Yeah, a pretend serenity. Only since I've stopped drinking did I realize Mom wouldn't have needed to drink and Dad wouldn't have been so nonemotional if everything was great. It's still hard to admit, though, that things weren't great."

Leaning back, Roger realized he'd spoken more tonight than he probably ever had in a group. He never spoke up in his classes in college. He felt a little embarrassed but reminded himself that speaking up was one of his goals. He smiled as Szifra acknowledged his efforts.

Anne surprised the group and herself when she added, "It's hard for me, too, to admit that things weren't great—and it's even harder to talk about it." Although Anne's words said it was hard, she had mustered a presence that seemed to contradict her words. Her voice was clearly audible, almost loud. Only her hands betrayed her calm demeanor. She alternately clasped them together and gripped the arms of her chair.

"I know I hurt," she continued, "and I knew Dad hurt, too. I wanted him to let me in so maybe he wouldn't hurt so much. I wanted to get to know him. I wanted to like him." Her words became shaky as she neared what was most painful to her. "I wanted him to know me. I wanted to ease his pain and make him feel good so we could be friends," she said as a few tears rolled down her cheeks. "But alcoholism kept it from happening."

Szifra waited to be sure Anne was through, then said, "Roger and Anne have brought up the difficulty of admitting things weren't great. This is a serious issue for many of you. It's like breaking a law in your family and in society: 'Never say anything bad about your parents.' It's sometimes even more difficult if your parent has died.

"Adult Children also have to overcome years of keeping the family secret. It's hard to learn to feel okay with yourself when you say, 'My mother was an inadequate parent,' or, 'My father really hurt me.' Eventually you'll learn to deal with the conflicting feelings you have for your parents. We can love them, yet hate what they've done to us and our families. One day many of you will be able to say, 'My father really hurt me. I love him nonetheless.' Or, 'My mother's drinking prevented her from adequately nurturing me. I missed that nurturing. I also understand she did the best she could, given the alcoholism.' "

Easy for Szifra to say, Sarah thought to herself. Dad's been gone five years and it hasn't gotten any easier for me. Every time I see a student struggling with a family relationship, I remember my own struggles.

"It takes time to get out of the either-or thinking," Szifra continued, "the 'either I love him or I hate him' thinking."

Time, Sarah thought. How much time?

"Some of you may eventually realize you don't love your parents," she heard Szifra saying, "nor do you have to love them. There may have been just too much pain. It takes time to admit that, too, to come to terms with it. Some of you will decide that even though you love your parents, you need to limit your contact with them to keep yourself healthy. It may feel like betrayal." Looking at the reactions of group members, Szifra asked, "Would it be useful to spend a few minutes addressing betrayal in this context?"

"I would like to do that," Sarah agreed, her usual enthusiasm mixed with some sadness. "My father died, and I feel rotten saying this stuff about him. Much of the time I want to retract everything I do say. After I say things, I feel guilty. I worry about God not liking what I'm doing, including being here. Sometimes I even question if Dad really was alcoholic. I think I do this because I feel guilty calling him an alcoholic, wanting to believe it still was a willpower or moral thing. Then I remind myself of Al-Anon's slogan, 'Let Go and Let God.' My mind just spins with all this. I'd like to know when it's going to get easier for me."

"Hopefully, soon," Szifra said kindly. "Yes, it has been years since your father died, but you've largely shut down your feelings about him and his alcoholism, closing yourself off from the pain, and from the healing, too. Hopefully, processing your feelings in here and on your own will lead to more resolution for you, Sarah, and for all of you."

"I used to feel terribly guilty, too," Michael said, looking at Sarah, "thinking I'd betrayed my parents. But I don't anymore. I struggled for a long time, feeling guilty because I hated my dad. Now I really don't hate him anymore, but I never visit my parents, either. I don't even write or call them. We have no contact. I realize they are very sick. Somehow, the better I feel about myself, the less guilty I feel about accepting my parents' bad points. They did the best they could, I guess, but it still was a lousy job."

"Even though I think like you, Mike," Trina joined in, "I still feel a little bad talking about them. A bit like a traitor."

"Sometimes I feel like a traitor, too," Linda admitted. "Then I'll get so mad at my parents. I feel basically okay saying my parents are alcoholic and I'm an Adult Child of Alcoholics. When my self-confidence is low, though, everything gets crazy. It's at these times I feel guilty. Years ago I would never have told people my parents are alcoholics. Now sometimes I like to say it. It helps me get some feeling of acceptance for myself. I think Al-Anon helped me with that some," she concluded.

"Admitting my father's alcoholism to myself and in individual therapy was one thing,'' Kathy said. ''Saying it to a group feels a lot different. My mom always said, 'Your father works hard.' To me, that meant, 'Dad is doing the best he can. Don't say anything otherwise.' Then added to my interpretation was the Catholic-taught guilt about honoring and respecting your parents. Sometimes it still feels wrong to admit my parents were human and had some faults. If I admit they weren't perfect, I take this illogical emotional step that translates it to, 'They were no good.' I'm working for a balance. Understanding alcoholism as a disease has helped, as well as accepting that Mom and Dad had both good and bad points.''

Pausing a minute, Kathy added, ''I'm also trying to realize this is true in friendships and relationships, too.''

Nodding agreement, Linda spoke up. ''That's a good point. That's important for me, too. If someone is close to me, it becomes against the law for me to look at them clearly.''

''I wonder if this is a common issue,'' Szifra speculated. ''Susan, is this an issue for you?''

''Yes, I think it is,'' Susan acknowledged, wishing she had been able to speak up on her own, but glad Szifra had drawn her out. ''I don't like saying anything negative about anyone. It seems petty. Improper.''

Sorting out their comments, Szifra said, ''It seems that allowing others to be imperfect is very difficult. Do you feel imperfections diminish your own self-worth?'' She looked around at everyone, inviting feedback. Shrugs and nods confirmed her summation of the discussion.

''It's an issue I suggest you try to keep in mind as you learn to accept people as they are,'' Szifra continued. ''You'll be much happier when you let yourselves, and others, off the 'need to be perfect' hook.''

Glancing at her watch, Szifra realized they'd gone well over their time. She looked up and smiled at everyone. ''I want to thank you all for your openness tonight. I believe your willingness to share is beneficial to you and the rest of us. A lot of experiences were shared tonight. You've begun to relate to each other. As you get to know each other better, there will be even more interaction.

"Our time is up for tonight. Next week we'll talk about some of the things we know now that we wish we had known earlier. When you can during the week, make mental notes along the lines of 'What I wish I had known.' Feel free to write some down. I think doing this will help you realize how far you have come, how much you have learned."

With obvious relief that the meeting was over, Anne quietly got up to leave. She looked up with surprise when Linda spoke to her, asking her if this week had been any easier for her. Because Linda had said earlier that she, too, used to be very nervous in these situations, Anne found responding easier than she would otherwise. "Somewhat easier." She smiled. "Everyone's so kind, it helps. I'm spending a lot of time worrying, though, about what to say when it's my turn."

"I still do a lot of that myself," Linda said. "It's hard to do this."

"Thanks," Anne said. "Well, see you next week."

"Good-bye!" Trina waved to the group as she headed across the parking lot. "One day at a time," she reminded them, giving the thumbs-up sign.

My Observations and Reactions to Meeting 2

Anne, 39, child care worker, lost child role in family, father died from alcoholism seven years ago.
Observations/progress noted:

Kathy, 33, secretary, mascot/responsible role in family, father died from alcoholism this year.
Observations/progress noted:

Linda, 36, nurse, responsible role in family, both parents are alcoholic, living.
Observations/progress noted:

Michael, 38, PR/advertising, responsible role in family, father is alcoholic, mother prescription drug–addicted, both living.
Observations/progess noted:

Roger, 20, student, lost child/scapegoat in family, recovering, mother also recovering.
Observations/progress noted:

Sarah, 36, high school teacher, responsible role in family, father died from alcoholism five years ago.
Observations/progress noted:

Susan, 32, accountant, lost child/responsible role in family, father died from alcoholism two years ago.
Observations/progress noted:

Trina, 45, shipping clerk, scapegoat role in family, recovering, father quit drinking a few years ago.
Observations/progress noted:

Szifra, therapist
Observations:

Observations about me during this meeting:

My feelings during this meeting:

Issues I'd like to explore further:

My reactions to this meeting:

What I learned about myself during this meeting:

Wishing We Had Known About Alcoholism Earlier

NOT SURE IF needing to go to his ACOA group was a welcome reason to break for the day, Roger closed his books and left the library. All in all, it had been a pretty good afternoon. Lots of studying, but it was coming easier to him now than it had first semester. He missed not having more time to do what he wanted, like lie back and listen to a good album. Still, he was pleased with his determination to get through school.

"I'll have to get a tape deck for my car," Roger said to himself as he headed across campus, dressed in his usual jeans and jersey. "Maybe with some of the money I make this summer."

Driving to Szifra's office, Roger tried to remember if he was supposed to prepare anything for tonight's meeting. He laughingly called it his "homework" for group. "Oh, that's right," he remembered. "I'm supposed to figure out what I know now that I wish I had known a long time ago. Well, that'll be easy for me. To think of, anyway. Maybe not to talk about."

He remembered he was expected to talk at the meeting tonight. With most of the AA meetings he attended, sitting and listening was not unusual, yet he noted with a bit of surprise that he wasn't feeling all that anxious. Maybe it's because the topic doesn't seem as heavy as others we've tackled, he thought. Or maybe, just maybe, it's getting easier for me to speak in a group.

He'd been trying to give himself credit for changes. "Try to notice improvement, then pat yourself on the back," Szifra had suggested. Roger thought about the time he'd said, "That was so stupid. I can't believe I did that." Szifra had suggested he try nurturing sentences instead, like "I wish I'd done that differently. I feel embarrassed now."

Another ACOA, she'd told him, talked about his father putting him down as a child, with the presumed intention of motivating him to do better. "But you can't build up by tearing down," he told her once he'd realized how mistaken his father was. I want to remember that, Roger thought. Maybe I'll start using that when I'm critical of myself.

A few minutes later Roger walked into Szifra's office, feeling more comfortable than he had at the last two meetings. He smiled a greeting at Anne, Susan, and Linda, who were already settled in the waiting room. They were in the midst of a discussion, unlike previous weeks when they and other group members had only exchanged polite greetings. Roger listened as Anne told Susan and Linda about a child in her day care who had learned to tie his shoes that day.

"You must have so much patience with children, Anne," Susan said. "I don't know how you do it."

"I really love it," Anne said shyly.

"What's a typical day like for you, Susan?" Linda asked.

"Nothing like a hospital's pace," she said. "Very dull. Organized and precise. Manufacturing is installing machining centers, and I'm doing the inventory accounting conversions. Numbers all day. No kids or sick people!"

"Can't wait until I can give up books and join the work world full-time," Roger joined in, laughing.

Linda asked Roger how he'd been. "Pretty good," he said.

"I wish I could say the same," Linda responded.

Roger noticed Linda's eyes looked puffy, her makeup not quite concealing the fact that she had either been crying or was tired.

"What's up," he asked, more because he felt he should

than because he wanted to get involved in Linda's private life.

"My parents," Linda said. "I spent more time with Mom and Dad than usual this week. It's got me down. I could hardly wait for tonight."

Roger thought, If I were having a rough time, I wouldn't be excited about coming in. I'd be afraid others would notice. I don't think I could talk about something that was going on right now. Maybe Linda's more used to opening up to people when she's upset. I know Szifra has said that most people grow when they start opening up more. I can do that with Szifra individually, but I don't think I'm ready to do it in group yet.

As Linda talked, Trina and Sarah came in, already engaged in their own conversation about the sports program at the high school where Sarah taught.

"If I hadn't already been so screwed up," Trina said, "I think I would have liked sports in high school. Of course, there wasn't much for girls then, anyway."

Trina and Sarah seem so comfortable, Susan thought as she watched them. So relaxed. Here I sit obsessing about how I'm going to get through tonight's meeting, and they come in like it's the most fun thing in town to do. I'd love to be that relaxed. Shifting on her chair, she smiled at Anne. She didn't know Anne was wishing for the same kind of comfort with people.

Anne sat straight on her chair, her back rigid and her shoulders tense. She looked almost prim. Her tailored clothing made her look more severe than she really was. Tonight she wore a dark blue skirt and plain white blouse. It was only when Anne talked about her work with children that she seemed to soften.

The next few minutes passed quickly, first with Kathy's arrival and then with Michael's.

As Michael grabbed a cup of coffee, Trina joined him at the coffeepot for some of her "new addiction," as she called it, chuckling.

Szifra welcomed the group as they settled in. There's a

little more chatter tonight, she noted to herself. The group members are starting to make connections with each other.

She noticed Susan was dressed in blue jeans tonight. Much more casual than her usual attire. She still looked perfectly neat, though, with a plaid, ruffled blouse tucked in at the waist.

Linda, meticulous in a tailored dress with a short jacket and heels, was not as casual. As she sat down, she stretched her legs out on a padded footstool, new to the office furnishings.

Kathy sat next to her but seemed distant from the group— not physically, but by her style of closing herself off. Her manner didn't encourage others to attempt a personal conversation. Kathy glanced around the room and noticed a new picture on the wall, a delicate pencil drawing of several pastel irises. It was a gift from a former client, one of several that decorated the office: a framed sculpture, photographs, and needlework . . . an eclectic blend of thankyous.

"Hello," Szifra said, smiling a big welcome to everyone. "You seem so much more relaxed and at ease. I'm glad."

She took a seat, ready to begin business. "Does anyone have any reactions to bring up from last week's group?" she asked.

There was a pause as the group members looked at Szifra and each other. Not really wanting to start, but anxious about the silence, Michael began.

"I was depressed for a day or two after last week's meeting," Michael said. "It was hard to concentrate. In an advertising meeting, I went blank. I had a lot of internal churning, mostly about my family, I guess. I usually don't think about them much, but everyone talking about family things last week opened something up, I think."

Michael seemed to speak more softly than at previous meetings. He seemed sad, not as quick to smile.

"I had some of that, too, Mike," Trina said. "Only I think I was more nervous and edgy than depressed. Not so much that night, but all the next day. Recalling the past can really hit me in the gut,'' she said wryly.

Trina spoke with conviction. She had looked at her past in treatment and hadn't liked what she'd seen. It had been hard for her. She knew what it was like to look back and then reel from the terror it caused. Thinking about that to herself for a minute, Trina tuned out the group without realizing it. She leaned back in her chair, gazing into space.

"I guess I'm glad to hear that's true for others, too," Kathy said, picking up the topic. "Not that I want any of us to be depressed. But I've had a hard time with that myself, feeling so desperately sad. I didn't realize you were experiencing it, too," she said, looking to Trina and Michael.

Most of the time Kathy preferred not to look at anyone as she spoke, unless it was to glance at Szifra for reassurance or encouragement. The connection she was beginning to feel with Trina and Michael felt new to her, even nice. She continued to look at them as she spoke. "After group on Tuesday nights I go home and cry and read about alcoholism. And Wednesdays are basically out-of-it days for me. I feel sad all day," she said.

Michael spoke up. "I really disliked that feeling of depression. I started wondering if this was worth it. I came in feeling good, left feeling kind of neutral, then I felt lousy the next day."

Nodding, Sarah said, "I had some of those feelings, too. I talked to Szifra about it. I was scared after the first meeting, thinking I couldn't handle it. I've also been concerned that I'm thinking too much about myself, being selfish, really. My religion teaches me to care for others, so I haven't felt comfortable focusing on myself so much."

"Sarah and I talked about ACOAs and feeling selfish, where the broken gauge might come from," Szifra explained. "As a survival skill, many ACOAs learn to freeze their feelings. When the years of frozen feelings begin to thaw, it's often very uncomfortable, very unfamiliar. And, like Sarah, you feel very selfish any time you focus on yourselves.''

Szifra encouraged them to process those thoughts for a few minutes before moving on. There was a fine line between selfish and self-caring, most thought.

"It helps to realize that Adult Children of Alcoholics aren't necessarily used to feeling sad in response to sad things, or feeling hurt in response to hurtful things," Szifra continued gently. "These meetings have contained some sadness. It is only normal that you would feel sad in response."

"Well, if you're going to put it in terms of what's 'normal,' " Sarah said, laughing a little, but meaning it sincerely, "that's what we've all wanted, to be normal! . . . Kidding aside, I understand what you mean. When sad things happened in my life, I always forced another feeling in there. I would never let myself feel sad or feel any other negative feeling. I thought once I did, there'd be an avalanche and I'd never feel good again. Not that I'm thrilled about feeling sad after these meetings, but talking this over with Szifra helped me accept that I might not always feel wonderful after our meetings."

She adjusted her skirt as she sat back, folding her hands in her lap. After a moment, she continued quietly, "I'm not comfortable with feeling sad yet. But I keep telling myself I'm going to feel some sadness for a while because I'm remembering some very unhappy times. I remind myself I'll feel better, and happy, again. Or maybe even really happy, for the first time. I'm still panicking sometimes, though, despite telling myself all that. I want to run away from these feelings and the events that brought them on. After our second meeting, I was expecting to feel sad, so when I did, it didn't feel as scary. And it didn't seem as though it lasted as long. 'Easy does it,' I'm telling myself."

Realizing many in the group had difficulty letting themselves feel sad, Szifra expanded the discussion. "Many factors determine how affected you might be after each group. For example, How used to sharing your feelings were you before you started attending our meetings? How many secrets have you kept? How trusting are you? Do you feel okay when others see you vulnerable, crying, trembling, not all together? What issues are most sensitive or unresolved for you? Can you reach out to others?

"Regardless of how sad or panicked you have felt after our first two meetings, let me assure you, it gets better." Szifra smiled sincerely. "You will become more comfortable in time. These initial weeks may be a time to schedule more individual therapy, to help process those things surfacing for you early in group. Many ACOAs start group seeing a therapist individually as often as once a week. But that doesn't continue indefinitely. Within a month or two, most ACOAs reduce the frequency of individual sessions because they have become more comfortable in the group meetings."

Szifra checked the time, then continued, "We're going beyond our usual reaction time, but this is an important issue, and I don't want anyone to feel inhibited because of time. Even our rules are made to be broken. We want to be flexible and get rid of black-and-white thinking. Does anyone else want to comment on this?"

"I'd like to," Linda said. "In spite of how upset I was at the beginning of tonight's meeting, I really have felt okay after our meetings. I've felt good, in fact. I was glad about that, but now I wonder if I'm blocking my feelings. Or maybe I'm not feeling a lot afterward because I've talked to others about my feelings before this."

Looking a little surprised, Trina asked, "Who have you talked to?"

"Friends in Al-Anon," Linda responded. "And people I met at some alcohol education classes. I also have two close friends I discuss things with, and my husband."

"Wow," Trina said, impressed with Linda's openness with so many people. "You share a lot. That's amazing."

"And probably does account for your early comfort in here," Szifra added. "You likely aren't feeling a lot of sadness because you have worked through some of what others are looking at, and feeling, for the first time in the presence of people." She paused and glanced around the circle.

"Susan, Roger, or Anne, how about you?" she asked.

Susan began less hesitantly than in previous weeks: "I feel most nervous the day before we meet. I wear myself out with it. I feel nervous afterward, too, but it's more manageable. Maybe I feel less nervous then because I'm relieved it's over."

She sat with her legs crossed, appearing at ease. Her voice gave away only a little nervousness as she continued, "I also know it's worth it for me. I want to get over being uncomfortable in groups. I know I'm learning what my feelings are by coming here. I trust I'm going to be better. Even though I'm terrified, I sense I'm doing what I need to be doing for myself. I really know I am," she finished softly. Her palms were sweaty, but at least she hadn't cried. She felt good about that and about what she'd said. She was glad she'd been able to convey some of the positiveness she was feeling.

Szifra smiled at Susan, then looked to Anne for any comments. Anne said, "I feel scared before I come and relieved I lived through each meeting. I'm usually mad at myself for not saying more, though. Like Susan, I feel I'm doing the right thing, for me and my kids, too. I think I'll get better. I really want to."

Noticing Susan's reactions to Anne's comments, Szifra said, "Susan, you nodded your head when Anne spoke."

Susan responded, "Yes, I'm hard on myself, too, for not speaking up more. I wish I spoke out as much as others."

"You will," Linda reassured her—and Anne, too. "I used to be much more quiet. I had to force myself to speak up. I called it 'practice speaking.' Now I'm comfortable speaking in groups, so I've moved on to other things. I'm using these meetings as my safe place to practice."

"That seems like a good idea," Anne said, trying to speak up without having to be invited to. She wanted to express the gratitude she felt for Linda's kindness.

"While we're on the subject of speaking up," Roger began, "I'm feeling self-conscious because I haven't. I feel nervous when it's my turn to talk. I'm not always sure what to say or how to say it. Maybe if I think of it as practice instead of the real thing, it'll be easier. Thanks for the idea, Linda. I also feel like you do, Susan. I'm helping myself get better by being here.''

Roger thought back to the beginning of the meeting when he'd wondered about Linda's level of comfort opening up. He was right; she was used to being open with people. He wondered if he'd ever get to that point.

The group lapsed into silence, and all eyes gradually turned to Szifra. She asked if they felt ready to move on to tonight's topic. Their nods gave her the signal to proceed.

She began by mentioning the kinds of things ACOAs usually learn about alcoholism and its impact on the family. From there she went on to discuss how useful it would have been to them as children to know some of the things they know now.

"Did you spend time this week thinking about what you wish you had known earlier about alcoholism?" she asked. Several nodded, and Linda and Kathy both took papers from their purses. They had written some notes.

Szifra explained that it would be helpful to explore this subject. "It's important to realize you are not saying, 'I wish I had . . .' as a way of feeling sorry for yourselves," she said. "We identify what we wish we had known earlier in order to fill in the gaps now and help nurture the child within—and also to stop the 'I'm so stupid' or 'It's my fault' spirals. Sometimes you may blame yourselves for things you didn't do or thought you should have done differently. It's important to remember that you acted and behaved the way you did because you did not have the kind of information and tools you now have. You would respond differently today if you faced the same situations with today's skills and understanding.''

Szifra's manner conveyed a real caring for the group members. She spoke with sensitivity, maintaining eye contact. Every now and then she pulled her long hair away from her face, wrapping it in a ponytail and then letting it fall. Her casual hairstyle and appearance were an integral part of her person, making it easier for group members to relate to her.

"Sharing some of what you wish you had known may bring new awareness to others here," she continued. "You have not all learned the same things. As you all know, your learning is an ongoing process." She paused, giving everyone time to consider what she'd said.

After a minute, Linda spoke up. "I'm glad you explained that. In Al-Anon we always referred to the 'pity pot,' and I try to be careful not to spend a lot of time feeling sorry for myself. What you said helps me see the difference between looking back to recognize what information I didn't have and looking back to feel regrets or pity for myself."

"That's a good way to distinguish the difference, Linda," Szifra confirmed. "You seem to have a good sense of tonight's issue. How about starting? What are some of the things you know now that you wish you had known earlier in your life?"

"Okay, I'll begin," Linda agreed. "I did think about it a lot this week, as you can see," she said, waving her notebook paper. "I kept my pad at the nurses' station and made notes during the week. In a nutshell, I wish I had known everything I now know." Other group members smiled and nodded with understanding.

Glancing at her notes, Linda continued, "Specifically, I wish I'd known why my parents didn't come home. I wish I'd known they were alcoholics. I never understood why they stayed out all the time.

"I wish I'd known why I felt so rejected and unlovable," she added hesitantly. "Then, when I got a little older, I wish I'd known that all the time I spent trying to keep my parents from fighting wouldn't make any difference anyway. They're still together. They're still fighting. And they're still drinking. All my work wasn't necessary. Or even useful." Linda's earlier perkiness was muted somehow as she talked about personal issues.

"I used to feel I was the only person who could see that our family had a problem. I thought I was the only one who cared and wanted us to be happy.'' She reached for a tissue to wipe her eyes, saying to Susan, ''See, I told you I'd cry in here.'' She remembered Susan's embarrassment when she had cried at their first meeting.

'' 'Once I'd left home,' '' Linda read from her notebook, '' 'I wish I'd known earlier that my life was screwed up. As I've said, I thought I was a normal person until I got married.' ''

Offering her understanding, Sarah joined in, ''I agree with you, Linda. I can see why you wish you had known those things.'' Sarah shifted on her chair, thinking a minute. She found herself reacting more to Linda's sadness than she'd thought she would. She wished she could take away her pain, the way Linda was able to soothe her hospital patients.

''Well, I guess I'll give my thoughts on the subject,'' Sarah began. ''I wish I'd known that I didn't have to carry the weight of the world all on my shoulders, that I didn't have to solve everything for everyone. That's something I still try to do, so I wish I could get it through my head that I don't have to solve everything.

''I wish I'd known that I could have talked about my feelings without being made to feel guilty about betraying the family trust,'' she added, then sat back and looked around at the other group members.

Michael decided to speak next. The meeting took on a somber mood as everyone grew pensive. ''I wish I'd known that what we suffered as a family was a disease,'' Michael began cautiously. ''It would have made the living nightmare a little easier, I think. I wish I'd known my father was so caught up in his drinking and my mother in attempting to control it, that it was essentially beyond their control.''

''I wish those same things, Michael,'' Kathy said. ''I think if my family had understood alcoholism, things would have been different. I spent a lot of time and energy, too, trying to keep everything fine. But it still wasn't.'' She felt her face get hot as she spoke. Letting herself feel vulnerable was a new experience.

"This is incredible," Trina said, raising her arms to emphasize her words. "We have so many different things we wish we'd known, but they're not all that different, really. I can't believe how much we do all have in common. . . . Well, since I've interrupted," she continued, trying to look guilty, "I'll go ahead with the things I thought were so unique to me. Now I'm finding out they aren't unique to me at all!

"Anyway, the biggie for me," she said, "is that I wish I'd known at a much earlier age about recovery. I sure wish I'd gotten sober sooner. I wish I'd known how much damage alcohol could do to my body. If I'd only known it could be this good. I mean that." She grinned at the group. "I also wish I'd known that my problems were related to someone else's alcoholism. I wish I'd known it was no great honor that my father held his liquor so well." Her voice softened as she concluded, "Maybe I wouldn't have spent so much energy trying to match his skill."

As Trina spoke, Linda thought, isn't it ironic? We can recognize these problems in our parents, but then we end up becoming like them without even realizing it.

Susan, too, had been touched by Trina's sharing. She decided to speak up. "I wish I'd known perfect does not exist."

"It doesn't?" Kathy said, raising her eyebrows with mock surprise. "I'm still trying for that! Even though it seems like I'm trying to be funny, the truth is, too much of the time I get caught up in trying to be perfect. I guess I should say I wish I had known years ago what a useless goal that is."

The group nodded agreement in the pause that followed. Then Roger began to speak, leaning forward on his chair and glancing up from time to time. "I thought about this during the week. My background in AA tells me to be careful about looking back and wishing the past had been different, so I'm cautious about this, but I think I've kept my perspective. The biggest thing I wish I had known when I started drinking was how miserable I'd be and how I'd make such a mess out of my life.

"I also wish I'd known my brother and sister were feeling many of the same things I was. Then it wouldn't have taken until now before I could start developing real relationships with them," he added. "But I'm glad I am doing that now."

Szifra was about to ask Anne for her thoughts when Anne surprisingly began on her own. "I wish I had known even a fraction of the little I know now about alcoholism. I wish I had known about the disease concept of alcoholism, like so many of you have said. Maybe I could have been more understanding of my father." She shook her head sadly. "Maybe I would have been able to do something about our family situation."

"Our talking like this makes me think of even more," Trina said. "I wish I'd known that people do understand those bitter, debilitating feelings, those fears and stresses that cause people like me to escape through chemicals. And I surely wish I'd known that chemicals only compound those feelings and add even more fears and stresses."

"You know," Michael said, "I'm finding that I agree with much of what is being said, too. I'd like to add one other thing. I wish I'd known I wasn't alone. That was a big thing for me. I wish I'd known that other people also felt different, isolated, and alone, and that there was hope for feeling better."

"And that help was available," Roger emphasized. "I think all our lives would have been better if we had faced Mom's alcoholism and dealt with it, rather than trying to ignore it. But I believed, and I guess we all did, that it would be better if we could just keep on going. Keep quiet, do our things."

"We believed that, Roger," Anne agreed. "It was our lot in life to put up with what we'd been dealt. Another 'I wish I'd known' is, I wish I'd known that you cannot stop the alcoholic from drinking. It sure would have made living much easier at my home if I'd known that. I was always trying to figure out ways to keep Dad from drinking. Make a pitcher of orange juice. Have dinner ready early, not wake him up if he fell asleep on the couch."

"Another good one is, I wish I'd known that it happens everywhere, to all kinds of people," Sarah added.

"Why did we always believe no one else had an alcoholic in their family?" Linda asked rhetorically.

"I also wish I'd known my parents' alcoholism was in no way my fault," Linda added.

"We are on a roll," Trina said, laughing. "Here's one more. I wish I'd known that I didn't make myself crazy. That I really wasn't crazy! And that I didn't give myself alcoholism."

The conversation continued without Szifra needing to facilitate. The group shared several more bits of knowledge and understanding they'd learned recently. Some of it seemed so obvious now, Michael said, but wasn't even vaguely familiar when he was younger.

"How about the alternatives issue?" Kathy asked: "That's one of the most important things I'm learning. It helps me a lot. I wish I'd known earlier that I had choices and alternatives. So many times I felt locked into situations. I felt I had no choices. It never even occurred to me that I might have options. It's been wonderful learning to look for alternatives, and even better finding them."

"I wish I'd known I was an okay person," Michael said.

"It's good you know it now," Sarah said.

Michael thought, Well, I'm just learning I might be. He decided he'd say that out loud sometime.

"Really," Linda agreed. "And that my parents' alcoholism had a lot to do with my emotional problems."

"I wish I'd known my father's weekend binge drinking was alcoholic," Sarah said. "And that his double message, 'Do as I say, not as I do,' was part of the disease. It would have been better, too, if I'd understood that my mother was emotionally drunk from the effects of alcohol without even drinking."

"I like that way of conceptualizing codependency, Sarah," Szifra said. "Family members' emotions can be severely damaged from alcoholism.

"So, are there any other comments?" she asked, and a pause followed. Looking around at all the members of the circle, Szifra felt positive about tonight's meeting. Perhaps tonight's topic wasn't as intense as last week, she thought, or maybe people felt more comfortable speaking up. They are also getting to know each other and feeling more free. Anyway, it's good. More trust and intimacy are developing.

Since no one had anything to add, Szifra proceeded. "I loved your willingness to jump in and share so much with each other. You are all clearly becoming more comfortable. Yes, I noticed plenty of shaky voices and a few tears. That's okay. You must feel safer, because you kept right on.

"Hopefully, this discussion will increase your acceptance that you did the best you could in the many difficult situations you found yourselves in as Children of Alcoholics and codependent parents. You were children, with children's skill levels and knowledge. Today you are different. You have more knowledge and more skills. You have more power and more strengths. If you were facing the same situations today, you'd handle them very differently. If you'd known then what you now know, you would have responded differently. Today, you can begin to use your increased power and strength." She spoke encouragingly, conveying her belief that they could and would all become stronger.

"I hope this helped you recognize how much you have already learned both about alcoholism and yourselves. Congratulations. Give yourselves credit for the hard work you've done. I know you won't disagree with me that it was hard work!"

"It feels good to hear we did something right," Kathy joked.

"Hooray for us!" Sarah agreed. "We're pretty neat people."

Szifra encouraged the group to bask in their good feelings a few minutes. The light chatter was fun and useful. Then she continued by addressing the agenda for their next meeting.

"Next week we're going to move on to another topic.

You won't have to do any advance thinking, though. No homework, Roger. At least not for this class! At the beginning of next week's group, we're going to listen to a song written by the daughter of an alcoholic. After we hear it, we'll share the feelings that surface.''

Signaling that the meeting was over, Szifra encouraged everyone to have a good week.

The meeting broke up more noisily than in previous weeks. Group members stood around a few minutes; some engaged in intense conversation, others joked a little.

My Observations and Reactions to Meeting 3

Anne, 39, child care worker, lost child role in family, father died from alcoholism seven years ago.
Observations/progress noted:

Kathy, 33, secretary, mascot/responsible role in family, father died from alcoholism this year.
Observations/progress noted:

Linda, 36, nurse, responsible role in family, both parents are alcoholic, living.
Observations/progress noted:

Michael, 38, PR/advertising, responsible role in family, father is alcoholic, mother prescription drug–addicted, both living.
Observations/progess noted:

Roger, 20, student, lost child/scapegoat in family, recovering, mother also recovering.
Observations/progress noted:

Sarah, 36, high school teacher, responsible role in family, father died from alcoholism five years ago.
Observations/progress noted:

Susan, 32, accountant, lost child/responsible role in family, father died from alcoholism two years ago.
Observations/progress noted:

Trina, 45, shipping clerk, scapegoat role in family, recovering, father quit drinking a few years ago.
Observations/progress noted:

Szifra, therapist
Observations:

Observations about me during this meeting:

My feelings during this meeting:

Issues I'd like to explore further:

My reactions to this meeting:

What I learned about myself during this meeting:

Sharing Our Childhood Experiences

LOOKING FORWARD TO her ACOA meeting that evening, Linda hurried back to the nurses' station to finish her paperwork in time for the shift change. She was beginning to feel that the once-a-week groups helped her keep her life in balance. It's easy to get caught up in the craziness with Mom and Dad's drinking, she thought. Knowing I have people to reach out to who understand what it's like makes it easier.

Linda pulled her charts from the rack and began to put everything in order before leaving the hospital. The satisfaction she got from this was important. It allowed her to feel that she was in control of some part of her life, anyway. Especially compared with the disorder of her childhood and the continued disorder of her relationship with her parents.

Leaving everything as it should be, Linda hurried to the nurses' lounge to change. She dressed carefully and decided to stop for a light supper before group. Smiling to herself, she thought, I'm doing something for me. It feels different, but it feels great, too.

Linda had spent her childhood looking after her brother and sisters, keeping the laundry done even when no money meant hand washing and trying to keep her parents from hurting each other physically when they fought. Now she found it difficult to take time for her own needs. Even though she'd spent several years in counseling and had learned about responsibility to herself, this didn't come automatically.

She stopped for supper at a fast-food restaurant, enjoying the solitude after a busy day. She spent the time thinking about her fourteen-year-old daughter, Lynn. Out of the blue, it seemed, Lynn wanted to live with her father. Linda was crushed, thinking Lynn no longer loved her—although she knew she did.

Perhaps it was adolescence and the attraction of fewer rules at Dad's. Lynn's dad seldom disciplined the girls. But Linda knew it would be different if Lynn were to actually live with her father. She remembered how watched and regulated she'd felt married to him. She didn't want to say no to Lynn, but she didn't want her to go, either.

She tried not to let herself slip into either-or thinking: "Either Lynn wants me, or she wants her father." She reminded herself that Lynn might want both of her parents.

She finished eating, bought a soft drink to take to group, and decided she'd not worry about Lynn's leaving unless her daughter brought it up again. "Let Go and Let God," she murmured, reminding herself of the Al-Anon slogan.

Arriving at Szifra's office, Linda smiled warmly at Susan, Anne, and Roger, who were already there. For a few moments they chatted about work.

Susan asked Anne if there were any new child care stories. Anne and I are so different, she thought. I work with figures all day, debits or credits, black or white. Anne works with kids all day. I'd go nuts. How would I ever know if I was doing the right thing?

Roger asked if anyone wanted coffee as he got himself a cup. Just then Szifra emerged from her office and joined the group for a refill. She usually had coffee, always decaffeinated, and always in a handthrown pottery mug.

Trina commented on the variety of pottery mugs beside the coffeepot as she came in and helped herself to coffee. "I've been meaning to ask you about these," she said. Szifra explained that she was once a potter. That fits, Trina thought, remembering Szifra's office decorations, which included several attractive pots. And there's something about butterflies, too, she recalled. Szifra had told her she'd chosen a butterfly logo for her counseling practice because to her they represented freedom, risk and choice. She'd also explained that children in concentration camps had drawn butterflies a lot as a way of expressing their hope for freedom. Most members of Szifra's family had been killed in the Holocaust. Trina knew, too, that the butterfly was a symbol used by Al-Anon.

The group members moved into Szifra's office, chatting easily with one another. Once everyone was seated, Szifra glanced around the room, smiling. Noticing Anne's chair was pulled back from the circle, Szifra asked her to pull in a little closer.

Sarah commented, "I noticed Anne's chair was back, but I didn't know what to say. I wanted you to move in closer, too, Anne."

"I thought about saying something, too," Kathy added, "but I took the safe way out. No extra risks for me!"

Roger laughed. "I didn't even notice. I'm not sure what that says about me."

"I'd like to point something out to you," Szifra said. "As recently as three weeks ago, you would have kept these thoughts to yourselves, Sarah, Kathy, and Roger. Yet tonight you seemed comfortable letting Anne know what you were thinking. That's progress, guys! Just wanted you to take note."

The group spent a couple of minutes concurring that it would have felt too risky before. "I knew we'd be fast learners!" said Trina.

When it was clear everyone was through, they signaled their readiness to move on. Szifra said, "How about reactions to last week, to our 'I wish I'd known' topic, or anything else we discussed?"

"I felt relieved after last week," Sarah began. "As if a burden had been lifted. I liked being able to say some things about alcoholism I hadn't expressed before. And I didn't feel as guilty. Maybe because so many of you said things that fit for me, too. If you say them, it's okay. It used to be if I said them, or even thought them, I thought I was bad. Even my religion reinforced that. Bad thoughts were the same as bad actions. I've decided that's not true. Maybe now I can let go of some of the bad feelings about myself.''

"Good deal, Sarah. You sound more free," Szifra said. "I'm glad you shared that with us. Anyone else?"

Speaking slowly at first, Anne said to Roger, "It helped me to hear you say you wished you'd known how miserable you'd be because of your drinking. That helped me understand my dad a little better.''

Roger acknowledged Anne's comments, appreciating her openness.

Michael said, "I felt more okay than usual all week. Whenever I'd think, How can I feel that way? I'd remember group and realize we all have these thoughts and feelings. I'm learning it takes time to get it together.''

"I loved saying my parents' alcoholism was in no way my fault," Linda said. "I've never said it out loud in a group before. A few times this week I thought about that and smiled to myself. I used to think it had to be my fault. I must be bad, or they would love me more and treat me better. If I were good, they'd want to spend time with me. That was so awful. Even though I knew it wasn't my fault, I still felt it acutely. My logic and my emotions just wouldn't come together. Something about saying it out loud and hearing all of you say similar things made it easier to feel better.''

The group grew quiet, until Roger spoke up. "I wished I'd said more last week," he said slowly. "I'm going to try to talk more in here.''

"Me too," Susan added.

"Maybe we can help each other with that," Roger said to Susan rather eagerly.

"Okay," Susan agreed.

Speaking up with her with usual enthusiasm, Trina said, "I'm just glad to be here. It feels so normal, compared to spending time with my family, who are using and drinking, or with old friends who still drink. I feel like the oddball with them and get confused about right and wrong, too. I feel like I fit in more here, and I like it.''

"I have that, too," Michael said. "In this meeting and the Al-Anon ACOA meetings I attend, I feel more like myself.''

Nearly everyone echoed Trina's and Michael's sentiments. Sarah said, "I feel okay some places, with certain people, but something still feels great here. It's different. I never wonder if you think I'm exaggerating or making something up.''

Kathy nodded. "Even I feel some sense of fitting in, and that's terribly rare for me.''

Once everyone was done, Michael said, "These are the first places in my life where I have some idea of what fitting in and belonging feel like. I don't have it with my family or with people at work. Nowhere. You know, I thought about another 'I wish I had known.' I wish I had known about interventions when I was still close enough to my parents to maybe have done something about their drinking.''

Looking puzzled, Sarah asked, "What is an intervention?''

Michael responded, "Someone in my other group was telling us about an intervention he'd participated in. I hope I can remember just how he described it. He said that lots of people believe an alcoholic has to 'hit bottom' before going for help. That usually means losing everything, like your job, your family, your self-respect. An intervention is a crisis that is created for the alcoholic—some people call it 'raising the bottom.' The alcoholic is given a choice. Either go for treatment, or else. Those participating in the intervention define the 'or else.' The choice to go for treatment is usually more appealing to the alcoholic than the alternative.

"Sounds like that would be awfully tough to do," Sarah said.

"Well, they have help," Michael explained. "An alcoholism counselor trained in interventions meets them and plans the intervention. They figure out a way to all be together with the alcoholic and in a gentle, caring way tell the alcoholic about times his or her behavior hurt them. They each ask the alcoholic to go for treatment, saying what they'll do if the alcoholic doesn't go."

"Did it work?" Sarah asked.

"Yes, it did," Michael said. "It was this guy's father. And he went to treatment."

Anne added, "I've read that the success rate on interventions can be pretty high."

"And they say even if the alcoholic doesn't go for treatment that day, he or she may within several months," Szifra added.

Linda shifted uncomfortably on her chair. Talk of interventions, although familiar to her, made her feel tense. She wavered between wanting to disengage from her family and wanting to help them. It's a seesaw of emotions, she thought. After all I've been through with them, and their unwillingness to change, I know for my own sanity and well-being that it's best to detach like Al-Anon tells me to. But this talk of the success rate of interventions makes me feel guilty for not looking into it more.

A few moments later everyone grew quiet, ready for the transition into the evening's agenda. Szifra reached out to put a tape in the cassette player on her desk as she explained, "Tonight we're going to listen to a song written by Laurel Lewis. She is an ACOA and recovering alcoholic and cocaine addict. This song is from a release of her music, *My Way of Saying Thanks*, which she calls recovery music. She wrote these songs during her first year of recovery. I'm passing out a sheet with the words on it so you can follow along. Then we'll talk about what you thought and felt as you listened."

Everyone settled back while Szifra passed out the words to the song "One Day" and started the cassette player. The music began softly, with the first verse almost a whisper, then build to a hopeful climax.

If I would take a pill
If I would take a drink
I thought I'd understand
How my parents act and think

Maybe if I act like them
See the world as they do
They'll look at me in a different light
And know that I hurt, too

Right now I'm just twelve years
I venture to the past
When pain rose like the fear of war
And would last and last and last

If I would take a pill
If I would take a drink
I thought I'd understand
How my parents act and think

Maybe if I act like them
See the world as they do
They'll look at me in a different light
And know that I hurt, too

I saw my father angered by
The things that made no sense
And soon my heart was patterned by
Those ever lonely dents

I asked her why he drank so much
She said because he's sad
A pill was brought up to her lips
Not knowing that was bad

If I would take a pill
If I would take a drink
I thought I'd understand
How my parents act and think

Maybe if I act like them
See the world as they do
They'll look at me in a different light
And know that I hurt, too

Sometimes I think I miss those days
But I quickly, quickly look away
For there's so much more in living
There's so much more in giving
There is so much more in living
There's so much love in living
One day
One day
One day

As the song ended, Linda reached for a box of tissues. Sarah took some, too, taking off her glasses and wiping her eyes. The group remained quiet. Szifra didn't break the mood or rush them into conversation.

Kathy sat biting her top lip, avoiding all eye contact. Susan's hands were folded in her lap, but she was not relaxed. Anne looked pensive.

After several minutes, Michael began. "That was very hard for me, especially the line about her father getting angry about things that made no sense. It reminded me of the hundreds of times my father would get angry for no logical or apparent reason."

"My mother did that sometimes. My father, too," Roger said slowly. He brushed the tears from his eyes and sighed. "I still hate conflict. And I didn't know about my anger. In treatment my counselor always asked me where my anger was. I still don't know."

"Don't you think it was taken from us?" Trina asked. "If I got mad at my parents, I think I would have been killed. The only people I ever used to get angry with were my children. I heard a radio talk show once on anger, and the expert said if you don't express your anger as a child, you pack it away, and possibly you'll abuse your own children because you'll finally feel powerful instead of powerless, like most children. It's like you finally have a chance to express all the feelings you felt toward your parents.''

Trina's voice was softer than usual. She'd been deeply affected by the song. ''It's very scary, really, all those pent-up feelings you don't even know exist,'' she concluded sadly.

''I guess it's a good thing I'm not planning to have children,'' Michael said. ''I have so much anger stuffed away.'' He drew a deep breath, then added softly, ''I liked the last stanza of the song especially. It reminded me of my determination to change. There has to be a better way to live. I'm very sure there is. I just have to learn how to find that for myself.''

''I really liked one line in particular,'' Kathy said. ''When she sang, 'Sometimes I think I miss those days.' '' Her eyes filled with tears. ''I do miss those days. Even though they weren't terrific, they were what I knew. And sometimes I miss what never was, and wish it had been. It seems I'm sad when I hear sad things, and I'm sad when I hear happy things. The sad makes me feel hopeless; the happy, left out.''

She wiped her eyes before continuing. ''I shut it out to function. Some days are starting to be feeling days. I think I let feelings in in small doses, maybe when I think I can handle them or control them. Because my feelings are so unpredictable, though, I keep the lid on a lot. Sometimes I feel if I were back in those days, I'd make it different this time.''

She sat back, not giving in again to the tears that were still so close. After a minute she went on, ''For me, growing up in an alcoholic home meant always wondering, 'Will Dad be all right tonight?' We all knew Dad was an alcoholic, but we never admitted it or talked about it. We ignored it, so maybe it wouldn't be true. I concentrated on keeping everything fine—my grades, doing what Mom and Dad wanted, never starting any trouble. I just tried to keep things running smoothly.

''What makes it harder is that we did have good family times, too. Like breakfasts on the patio and special parties on birthdays and holidays. Mom even made working together fun. But there were those gut-wrenching times of fear, no matter how hard I tried to pretend otherwise.

"I would stay at the swimming pool in the summer until about the time Dad was due home. It was easier to be distracted there than to be at home, waiting, clutched up. Then I'd walk up the street, and as I got close to home, I'd hold my breath hoping Dad's car would be in the driveway, hoping he'd come straight home.

"When Dad wasn't home, I'd help Mom with supper and keep light chatter going so maybe she wouldn't notice how late it was getting. Lots of times I'd sneak a whispered telephone call to Tito's, the bar where Dad usually stopped. I never wanted Mom to know I called. They always said he wasn't there, but he always got home ten minutes after my call."

"Kathy, you are so much healthier," Szifra said softly after a few moments' silence. "A few weeks ago you would have had to joke in order to share such personal feelings. It's nice to see you share your feelings honestly, without trying to cover them up by joking around."

"Thanks," Kathy said, then looked away quickly.

"I felt a lot of hope at the end of the song," Roger said. "A lot of sadness during it, though. The line 'There's so much more in living' reminded me of my new relationships with my fiancée and my family, now that I'm sober.

"I feel sad because I tried to be different from my mom with my use of alcohol," he continued. "I tried to show her I could master alcohol like she couldn't. I never recognized how futile and destructive it would be. I want those years back and can't have them. Even though I feel cheated, I still question whether I have that right. I'm stuck in shame, but I hope time, and some hard work, will heal me."

"You sound very determined, Roger," Szifra said.

"I am," Roger confirmed.

"It's hard hearing about other people's sad childhoods," Kathy said. "Partly it confirms my nontrust and belief that it's never worth being involved with other people. Then the song ended positively, so that made me think maybe it is possible to find contentment."

"It helps me to hear someone else express the same thoughts and feelings I've had," Anne said.

"It never occurred to me that my parents might understand me better if I drank like Dad and used pills like Mom," Trina said. "But I did both alcohol and pills, anyway. Best of both worlds, I guess."

"I also really hooked into Laurel's line 'Now I'm just twelve years,' " Kathy said. "That put me back in the seventh grade, waking up in the middle of the night when I'd hear Dad up. I'd listen, hoping he wouldn't stumble. Hoping Mom wouldn't wake up.

"I remember so many times waiting in the parking lot at Tito's while Dad was having a drink. No matter what errand or time of day, we always stopped. I hated it when Mom would send Dad to pick me up after a meeting at school. We always stopped." Kathy paused briefly, then continued.

"After my senior year of high school, I was gone for the whole summer. It was pretty hard for me. I really missed Mom, especially. When I came home, Dad came alone to the airport to get me, and even after I was gone three months, I still had to sit in the truck and wait while he went in for a drink. Of course, Dad always asked me to come in, but after I was about eleven, I never did."

"I picked up on the line about pain rising like the fear of war," Linda said, crying. "I thought about myself as a child. I was filled with terror, lying in my bed. No one ever came to me to say, 'It will be all right.' I felt this overwhelming sense that I wouldn't survive the terrible loneliness. I wish someone had taken care of me so I would have felt safe. I had this immense longing, like an empty space. Today I'm still aware of that big space. The only thing in it is longing.

"I remember having so many questions. Always asking, 'What will happen next? What will we tell people this time? Why don't Mom and Dad come home on time? Why do they fight so much?' I always had questions, but never any answers." Linda started to sob. Szifra waited a moment, then invited her to say more.

"It was just so scary, so unfair. How could they have been so unaware of what we needed?" Linda said, still crying. Everyone sat quietly, not sure how to react.

"I really identify with you," Trina said, reaching out to Linda. "Questions were a big part of my childhood, too. I used to ask myself questions like 'Why am I alone? Why can't I be a kid? Why don't you love me?' I can't remember any good times. No happiness or love. I remember Dad beating Mom, then yelling at us because we were crying, and spanking us so we'd have something to cry about."

Trina sat back on her chair, her eyes far away now. "My first memory of my father is the day he and a neighbor got drunk and tried to drown a litter of newborn kittens in a bucket of water. The kittens still had the membrane on their fur, and the water was cold, but they swam about, meowing and searching for their mother. My father threw them up in the air, one at a time, and shot them with a rifle. Blood and guts rained down on us as we tried to stop him. I was four then. Mom locked the door and watched soap operas while Dad shot all the kittens. I felt like I could be next. If he got drunk enough, and there were no kittens available, he could use us kids for fun and games.

"The only way I survived was to start drinking," Trina concluded quietly. The group sat in silence a while before Michael spoke up.

"I survived by getting away," he said. "I'd walk down by a creek near our house after I felt hurt or had been punished. And I'd take my dog with me. I felt like he was the only one who understood me. I'd go to the creek a lot, to escape, I guess. I'd feel safe for a while. Then I'd go back home feeling somewhat better, but it would still be painful. They might still be fighting. If they weren't, the tension was there anyway.

"I always felt excluded and worried," he continued. "It's weird, too, because I realize now that I excluded myself. It makes sense, given the circumstances. The chaos felt so overwhelming, I never could relax totally at home. I guess I never knew when the war would start up again. Even though isolating myself meant missing anything good that might have gone on, I got to escape the bad. My goal was peace and quiet, to be left alone."

"When things were strange at home," Susan began, then laughed, rather easily for her. "When weren't they strange at home?!" A couple of others laughed a little with her. "I use the word *strange*," she continued, "because I never knew Dad drank. I just knew something wasn't right. Well, when things were too much for me to stay tuned in, I went into my imaginary world. I had my own secret world with wonderful brothers and sisters I would talk to. They helped me work out my problems.

"I guess I was lucky I did that instead of starting to drink," she concluded. "It can be very lonely, though."

Anne looked around, then spoke up. "I was struck by two lines in the song—'I asked her why he drank so much/ She said because he's sad.' In her way, my mom, too, tried to protect us from everything. But when we got older, we found out we had a father we didn't even know."

Trina looked pensive. Szifra asked her to share what she was feeling. As she spoke, Trina's voice trembled, although she didn't express her sadness. "That was one of the toughest parts of the song for me. For some reason, it made me sad wondering if my father's drinking was to cover his pain. I also thought about my drinking and behavior. Not because I tried to be bad, but because I was alcoholic and didn't know how to deal with feelings."

After a pause, Susan said, "I wanted to relate to what you said, Anne, about your mother protecting you. My mother smothered us. It made us really weak. Later in life we found ourselves asking, 'What are we going to do? How can we do this on our own?' That was really hard. Sometimes it seems Mom's protectiveness affected me more than Dad's drinking. I wish Mom had been able to be open and honest about Dad's alcoholism. I wish she had helped us learn people skills, too. I know she did the best she could, though."

"Oh, I have to say that, too," Anne said. "My mom was like a superwoman. I don't know how she did all she was able to do. I wish I had her energy."

With a strained look on his face, Michael joined in, "I remember as a kid I loved my dad, because he was my father. But I hated him so much because I got so hurt. It seems like maybe the song says that, too. I still feel guilty sometimes because I don't see my parents.

"Dad and I used to be close," he added. "I used to play tennis with him all the time. Then he started drinking so much. He stopped being with me and started hurting me."

"This song reminded me of so many unhappy times," Linda began.

Szifra looked around at the other group members as Linda spoke, paying attention to facial expressions and body language. It was apparent that some were apprehensive, probably thinking she would cry again. Szifra knew they'd all have a chance to talk about crying in a future meeting, so she decided not to make that a focus in tonight's group.

"One incident really stands out," Linda continued. "Mom and Dad were upstairs fighting and we were in the basement waiting until it was over. It's the only time I remember not being in the middle, trying to stop them. Dad said he was going to force Mom in the bedroom with a knife so she'd have to talk to him. I felt so scared and lonely that day. I never felt so helpless and frustrated.

"An ongoing war with intermittent peace. That was my childhood. Just like war, with battles you expect and surprise attacks. You just never knew. I guess the songwriter had that, too. I'm learning that lots of ACOAs experienced these things, not just me."

Sarah spoke up. "This reminded me of a story I'd like to tell. Laurel's mentioning being twelve years old brought this back, because I was twelve when this happened. My friend Elaine came to spend the night at my house. My dad's friend Dave and his five-year-old daughter came over. Dad told us to play with her, so we did. But when they left,

Dad was angry because we weren't more 'motherly' to the little girl.

"He yelled at us, making us sit at the kitchen table. My sister was at one end, and Elaine and I sat on either side of her. Dad gathered all the ashtrays in the house and started throwing them at my sister. There are still marks from them on the kitchen sink where they bounced. Then at one point Dad paused, looked at Elaine, and said, 'Don't worry, honey, I'm not going to hurt anybody.' "

After a slight pause, Sarah said, "Finally I got up my nerve and left the kitchen. I hid in a closet, crying and screaming."

"That makes me so mad," Trina said. "Damn them. Acting one way, saying something else. It's no wonder we have all these hang-ups, became alcoholic, or started other compulsive behaviors. We lived in a constant state of anxiety! Like I've said before, it was always, 'What did I do?' or 'Why me?'

"My father was an abusive drunk, taking out his anger on all of us. I could never understand the physical beatings or the emotional and sexual abuse he put us through. I always felt like I was walking on the edge of a knife. Getting nicked and cut no matter which way I turned, but trying to keep balanced so I wouldn't be cut in two.

"All I knew was that he was crazy, and I was scared to death of him. What I still get so mad about is that we are still so affected by them. Why can't we just say, 'They're crazy,' and be done!"

"Trina, as an ACOA, your allegiance, your loyalty, is to be expected," Szifra said softly. "Generally, the more dysfunctional our parents were, the harder it is for us to let go. It's very difficult to just 'be done with them.'

"What you can do is work to reduce how much you are affected by them and their crazy behavior. Even recognizing that their behavior was not appropriate is a big step in being able to reduce how deeply affected you are."

"Oh, I agree," Trina said. "And a lot of it is a matter of time, too."

"I remember the crazy actions, too. Just crazy," Michael said. "The confusion an being scared. It's funny, but until recently I would never have thought of myself as being afraid. But now I know I was and still am. I felt trapped.

"One very clear memory was a Fourth of July. Dad was drunk and Mom was high on pills. All the neighborhood kids, my brothers, my sister, and I were waiting to set off fireworks. My dad wanted to get more to drink, so I ran to the car and broke the ignition wire off so it wouldn't start.

"When Dad couldn't get the car started, he knew I'd done something, and out he came running, shouting, swearing. He was looking for me. I just ran toward the gas station up the street, but I don't remember where I ended up. I don't know what I did the rest of the night or when I came home.

"I feel like I've spent the rest of my life running," Michael said sadly. "I always wanted to get away from wherever I was. In high school, college, work, I wanted and still do want to get away from the people around me. I know it's not healthy for me, so I'm working on it, but the feeling's very strong. The urge to run. Like people will discover the real me, so I better leave before they do."

"I've felt that, too, Michael," Linda said. "It's hard to make friends because of it. I remember a lot of anger and things shattering like they'd never be put back together again. There was always fighting over money, sex, just everything in general."

"I remember many times watching my dad get mad, grab the keys, and head for the car," Susan said. "Those hours were horrible. Every sound of a car going by echoed through the house. Sometimes I really didn't want him to come back. My stomach still churns when people raise their voices."

"The more everyone talks, the more I remember," Kathy spoke up. "I remember Dad hardly ever called me by my right name. He always called me by my sister's name. It was a family joke, but not to me. This seems silly compared with what you experienced," she said, looking at Michael and Susan.

They reassured her that her pain was real, too, and not to be trivialized. "Not all of alcoholism's destructive pieces are blatant," Szifra added. "It's not just physical, sexual, and verbal abuse that undermines our self-esteem. It can be more subtle. In wealthy families, as an example, children may not miss meals or school events because someone is hired to take care of those needs. For these ACOAs the effects can be more insidious. They get mixed messages, an absence of consistency, warmth, and nurturing. It's even more confusing when alcoholism is done elegantly.

"Don't underestimate the pain you felt, even though your family wasn't blatantly abusive or destructive. The long-lasting effects, the losses, are very real for Children of Alcoholics regardless of the particulars. Of course, there are better and worse situations. But I doubt there are many children from alcoholic homes who have suffered no emotional losses as a result of alcoholism's effects."

Anne spoke up as Szifra finished. "I appreciate hearing this, Szifra. I tend to downplay my situation, saying, 'I'm just a baby. I should be grateful. Others had it so much worse.' "

"I do that, too," Kathy mentioned.

Szifra thought to herself, people are speaking up and sharing their feelings more easily tonight. Sitting back, she considered the goals set for the group members. Increased self-confidence, increased trust and less isolation were all things they wanted to work on. By letting go of pain and by sharing with one another, I can really see them moving forward, she thought.

Noticing the time, Szifra decided to move on. "I want to do something different to close tonight's meeting," she announced, giving everyone a legal pad. "Please take a few minutes to quickly write any reactions you have to this session. Don't worry about eloquent prose, just write whatever comes to mind in reaction to our meeting."

"Could you be more specific?" Linda asked.

"You can write about what you feel now, what feelings were stirred up tonight, what relief you might be experiencing. Try to write whatever comes to mind," Szifra replied. "Try to write spontaneously rather than thinking about what you're going to write."

Several began writing right away. Roger and Anne seemed stuck, though, not sure how to begin. Both looked to Szifra for more direction.

"If you would feel more comfortable with some structure," Szifra offered, "you might open your sentence with one of these." She walked over to a cardboard easel and wrote several sentences on the pad:

"After hearing about others' experiences, I feel . . ."

"I was surprised that others . . ."

"I learned that I . . ."

"I was saddened that . . ."

"I plan to change . . ."

"Use these to get started, if you'd like," she said. "There are no right or wrong answers here. I simply want you to write whatever comes to mind."

Anne watched Linda writing quickly and easily. She could tell by watching her that she wasn't worried about neatness or precision of words. Susan, on the other hand, was taking pains to write carefully.

I hate things like this, Anne said to herself. I always feel so stupid. I can't think of anything to write.

"After hearing about others' experiences, I feel . . ." she read silently. I never know how I feel, she thought.

"I was surprised that others . . ." she continued. Well, I'm surprised everyone else can write and speak so easily, she said to herself. I guess I'll put that down. She wrote briefly, then paused, panicked because she couldn't think of more. She glanced at the board again. "I learned that I . . ." Oh, I know! she thought. I learned that I can say some things about my family without falling apart. What a relief.

After a few minutes, Szifra asked everyone to finish the sentence they were working on and then stop. Then, smiling reassuringly, she asked Anne to read her reactions.

Anne looked stricken, and her face turned red. She began

slowly, her voice trembling. When she'd finished, she apologized because her comments were so short.

"Why are you putting yourself down?" Roger asked. "Writing something short doesn't mean it isn't good. Our parents and teachers put us down too much. We can't do that to ourselves, too! What you wrote was great!"

"It was, Anne," Sarah agreed. "Can you tell yourself you're pleased with what you've done? Don't I sound like Szifra?"

After the chuckling stopped, Roger chimed in again, "Yeah, we're here trying new things. We're experts at giving ourselves criticism. Let's practice the praise!"

Several of the group members smiled. They seemed surprised to hear Roger speak out that way. It sounded more like something Trina would say.

As the others read their reactions, Linda listened intently, relieved that others had shared incidents from their childhoods. It helped her feel less alone.

Susan said she felt confused but knew she was headed in the right direction. "This is the first time I've ever told anyone about my imaginary world. That was rather revealing on my part," she said. Roger gave her a thumbs-up sign.

Michael said he had mixed feelings of greater calm and greater tension. "My guilt is way up, I guess because I've talked about family secrets. Saying bad things about Dad relieves some pressure, I think, because I'm being honest about what went on instead of keeping up the facade. I'm so tired of pretending to be someone else, pretending my family's fine, pretending to be fine. I'm sick of it all. But when I openly admit these things, I feel tense. Yet, at the same time, I'm glad I said them."

"I understand what you mean by mixed feelings," Trina said. "That's pretty much what I wrote about, too."

"Well, the way I see it," Sarah began, "I lived this life for lots of years. It's going to take more than one night of talking about the past to sort it all out."

"You're right, Sarah," Szifra agreed. "I'm glad you

mentioned that. Resolution of your past will not happen overnight. With time, you'll remember more things, too. More time is needed for you to understand what happened and how you felt then in order to process how you feel now. The payoff, of course, is that it helps you overcome the problems you're experiencing today. Clearly we're not finished with these issues. I'd like to continue with more childhood experiences next week.

"Before we close," she continued, "I want to remind you to take time for yourselves this week. You're important. You count. Take time to call friends, take a walk, enjoy a bubble bath, read a book, play your favorite sport, do whatever will help you feel like you're treating yourself. Be gentle and kind to yourselves.

"Also, most of you have already read part or all of Claudia Black's book *It Will Never Happen to Me*. In a couple of weeks we'll be discussing the roles you took on as children, and it would be helpful if you finished reading her book before then. If you need a copy, I have several available to lend, or you may buy a copy from me."

She smiled at them all. "Keep up the good work! And have a good week," she concluded.

My Observations and Reactions to Meeting 4

Anne, 39, child care worker, lost child role in family, father died from alcoholism seven years ago.
Observations/progress noted:

Kathy, 33, secretary, mascot/responsible role in family, father died from alcoholism this year.
Observations/progress noted:

Linda, 36 nurse, responsible role in family, both parents are alcoholic, living.
Observations/progress noted:

Michael, 38, PR/advertising, responsible role in family, father is alcoholic, mother prescription drug–addicted, living.
Observations/progress noted:

Roger, 20, student, lost child/scapegoat in family, recovering, mother also recovering.
Observations/progress noted:

Sarah, 36, high school teacher, responsible role in family, father died from alcoholism five years ago.
Observations/progress noted:

Susan, 32, accountant, lost child/responsible role in family, father died from alcoholism two years ago.
Observations/progress noted:

Trina, 45, shipping clerk, scapegoat role in family, recovering, father quit drinking a few years ago.
Observations/progress noted:

Szifra, therapist
Observations:

Observations about me during this meeting:

My feelings during this meeting:

Issues I'd like to explore further:

My reactions to this meeting:

What I learned about myself during this meeting:

Realizing We Were So Often Alone

WHAT A GREAT day it had been! It was Ben's fourth birthday, and his party in day care had gone well. Anne felt great. The children loved the party favors, especially the hats she'd made. And the bubbles. Even though caring for preschoolers was physically draining, Anne loved her job and the children. She found caring for them rewarding. And she was so comfortable with children. Put me in a room full of adults and I freeze, she thought, frowning. Put me in a room with children, and I feel perfectly comfortable. Why is that? . . .

Oh, good heavens, here I go, thinking about ACOA issues. Next I'll be getting tense about group. I wish the aura of the party fun would stay with me a little longer. Ben was so darling telling his mom about the party when she picked him up. I felt like I'd done something important, like I'd made a contribution today. But when I try to interact with adults, I don't feel that I have anything important to talk about. I suppose that's why I prefer children. They accept me just as I am. I don't have to try to impress them.

Anne's long drive into town gave her plenty of time for thinking. If only the traffic didn't make her so nervous, she'd enjoy the time more.

She was glad to see Susan when she walked into Szifra's office. Susan had such a gentle manner; Anne felt comfortable with her. She waved hello to Trina and Roger, who were standing by the coffeepot.

Roger's fiancée had told him a couple of days ago that she'd like to know more about Alcoholics Anonymous and the ACOA group. Although she knew he was recovering, he'd kept that part of his life private. Not that he was ashamed, but this was where he went to keep himself together. He wasn't sure how he felt about including her in it. He had asked Trina what she thought.

"Have you ever taken her to an open AA meeting?" Trina asked. He hadn't, he said, nor had he given her anything to read.

"I know her interest is sincere," Roger said. "I don't think she'd be shocked by what she heard. I guess I'm not sure I want her there when I'm focusing on my sobriety. It feels private."

"Well," Trina said, "you must be focused on your sobriety more than just at AA meetings, or you wouldn't be making it. Don't you think you could be yourself at a meeting if she came?"

"I'm not sure," Roger said. "Maybe that's it."

"What if you told her that?"

"Oh, she'd understand. She's real accepting," he said. "Looking at it objectively, though, I can't find one good reason not to include her if she'd like to learn more about alcoholism."

"Don't discount your feelings," Trina cautioned. As an aside, she said, "I sound like Szifra, don't I? Last meeting Sarah was Szifra; tonight it's me!" Then she returned to Roger's issue. "You seem kind of uncomfortable. You just might not be ready for that, yet. After all, it's very personal to you." Laughing, she added, "That just reminded me of this ridiculous article I read several years ago. It was in some women's beauty magazine, telling women that some things must always remain personal to them and not be shared with their lovers. Believe it or not, the article said a woman should never let a man see her shaving her legs! She must create this mystique that her legs are always silky smooth!"

"Oh, right." Roger laughed, too. He wondered what Trina was even doing reading a women's beauty magazine. He wouldn't have thought she'd read stuff like that. She was an attractive woman, even though she never wore makeup and usually wore jeans and casual shirts. The article must have sounded especially silly to her.

"The story did have a point, though," Trina went on, "although it was almost lost in the nonsense about beauty secrets. The point is, not every single thing about ourselves has to be shared with our mate."

"I agree," Roger said. "It's an ACOA issue, though, trying to know when you're sharing a 'normal' amount. My relationship with her is too important to risk shutting her out. Have you ever taken someone really close to you to an AA meeting?"

"Not that close. Friends. Other drinkers. Your sobriety is something you have to do on your own, in your own time. Ask her when you're ready."

"Yeah," Roger agreed. "I guess I'll just be honest with her and tell her I'm not sure I'm ready for that. I'll encourage her to read about alcoholism. And go to an open meeting on her own. Maybe after a time I'll even take her to an open meeting."

Looking up, he realized everyone was settling in the circle of chairs in Szifra's office. "I didn't know everyone was here," he said apologetically when he and Trina walked into Szifra's office.

"They're not," Szifra replied. "Sarah is out of town on a school trip. She wasn't sure how late they'd return, so I wasn't expecting her. And Kathy left a message with the answering service that she wouldn't be here because she's sick."

Moving the extra chairs out of the circle, Szifra invited everyone to move in a little closer. "This will give our group a little different flavor, with only seven of us," Szifra said.

"Small numbers suit me fine," Susan said, laughing lightly. She sat down next to Anne. She was smiling a little more readily than in past weeks.

"Me too," Anne agreed, "except now I might be expected to talk more!"

Once everyone was seated, Szifra greeted them individually.

"Michael," she said, more softly than usual, "you seem very subdued tonight." She noticed that he was dressed carelessly, for him. Although he wore his usual name-brand casual slacks, his sweatshirt looked like one he'd wear to rake leaves in, not something he'd ordinarily wear out in public. "Is there anything you want to bring up before we begin with our regular agenda?"

"I don't think so," Michael responded. "I've been quiet all day. Thinking about a lot of things. But I don't feel like I want to process anything just now. Thank you, though."

"That's fine," Szifra said. "If any of you ever have something going on currently you feel is relevant to others in group, you're free to bring it up. I'd like this group to provide support. And we'd all benefit from the process of working through decisions, struggles, or everyday problems."

After a few moments during which no one indicated a desire to speak, Szifra nodded and went on. "It looks like we're ready to begin, then," she said. "In a sense, this is a continuation of our topic from last week. For many of you, the lyrics of Laurel Lewis's song triggered specific childhood memories. How many of you continued to recall incidents from your childhood during the past week?"

"Boy, I did," Linda said. "That song and everyone's comments started a chain reaction."

"For me, too," Roger said. Others agreed.

"Spending more time on this subject seems appropriate. Do you want to pick up where we left off or discuss reactions to last week's meeting?" Szifra asked.

"Let's just pick it up," Trina said. The rest agreed, and Linda volunteered to begin.

"I knew days ago I wanted to speak first tonight. Otherwise I figured I'd lose my nerve," Linda said.

"You?" Anne asked teasingly.

"Believe it or not, me," Linda said. "You see, I decided

not just to talk, but to share a poem I wrote. I've never done that before." She held her purse on her lap, snapping it open and shut as she talked.

"That's wonderful, Linda," Szifra said encouragingly.

"Well, I wrote this a few years ago," Linda said. "It's very personal. Our concentration last week on our childhoods reminded me of it, so I dug it out and brought it along. Here goes," she said, unfolding a paper she had pulled from her purse.

Wherever Can You Be?

Where are you, Mom and Dad?
Working to make ends meet?
But work has passed.
It's time for supper,
And time for the family to be together.
Mom, Dad, wherever can you be?

Supper!!!
Nancy ate at some friend's house.
Frankie and I stayed home and fixed our own.
Ann, she's eating with her boyfriend's folks again.
Mom, Dad, wherever can you be?

Frankie calls you, "Come home please!"
I pleaded, "I have no clean clothes for school tomorrow."
"The least they could do is come home and be parents,"
Nancy would often say.
"Ann, do you have anything to say?"
"I could care less. I have someone to take care of me!"
Mom, Dad, wherever can you be?

Could you love us
From that bar stool or the inside of that bottle?
It must be easier to love us from there,
Than to love us where we are.
Mom, Dad, here, over here we are!

As Linda read, her voice grew softer and more shaky. By the end, tears were rolling down her cheeks, but she continued. When she had finished, she set the paper in her lap and sat crying quietly. The others sat very still. No one seemed ready to break the silence.

Anne's eyes had filled with tears, also. She thought how much harder Linda's childhood had been than her own. How lucky she was that her mother had worked so hard to keep family life intact.

Linda's poem hit Michael especially hard. He felt it was such an injustice to bring children into the world for a life like that. Even though he wasn't planning to discuss it in group, his thoughts were consumed with child issues. He'd just learned that his wife might be pregnant. They had decided not to have children—at least not in the foreseeable future. Neither had taken a permanent step to prevent pregnancy, and now he didn't know what they would do. Hearing Linda's poem underscored his fear of dealing with this crisis in his life.

After a few more moments of silence, Szifra thanked Linda for sharing her poem with the group and asked her how she felt.

"I'm glad I brought it in. It was difficult reading it. But it says what I wanted to say."

"It was beautiful, Linda," Trina said. "I hope you know what I mean. Beautiful in the way you were able to express your feelings."

"Thanks," Linda said. "I know what you mean."

"I couldn't write anything that well," Anne said. "Nor would I be brave enough to bring it in here to read. I think it's great that you did."

Linda smiled at Anne. She knew it was hard for her to speak up, especially when she wasn't responding to a direct question. Anne's words meant a lot to her.

"No doubt Linda's poem has sparked more memories," Szifra said. "How about moving on to sharing your experiences and memories?"

Roger began. "I remember staying in my bedroom by

myself. I was very lonely as a child, even though I had lots of toys to play with.'' He appeared more reflective than usual. He sat still, not alternating between stretching out his legs and sitting up straight, as he usually did.

"I never felt comfortable bringing friends home because I didn't want them to see my mother,'' he continued. "I would only have friends over when I knew she wasn't drinking or before she'd get completely wasted.

"I'm angry about this,'' he said suddenly, "because I didn't deserve to be alone. I didn't know how to reach out and tell anyone what I needed.'' He sat rigidly on his chair, obviously trying to control his feelings. "I feel so sad, I could almost cry. But I never cry in front of people. I haven't since I was a little boy. My parents didn't let me cry. I guess because I'm a boy.''

"Bull,'' Trina said quickly. "My parents didn't let me cry, either. They'd scream things at me, like 'I'll give you something to cry about.' And if I ever got mad, I'd get killed.''

"Anger and crying are both current adult issues we'll need to spend more time on. And we will at another meeting,'' Szifra promised. "What other childhood memories have been stirred up in the last couple of weeks?''

"I remember always feeling there was something wrong in my home,'' Trina began. "There was terrible yelling almost all the time. In winter, Dad was too lazy to go to the bathroom, so he kept a bucket in the dining room, where he went to the bathroom. And sometimes he left it there. That was so disgusting. And embarrassing. No wonder I was so reluctant to have people over.

"I built a fantasy world, too, like you did, Susan,'' Trina continued. "I spent a lot of time in a corner of my room. I didn't have my own room, so privacy was unheard of. But I'd sit in that corner, holding my pillow to feel secure. I listened to the radio a lot. The music blocked out most of the crap. I created my private world.

"I also spent a lot of time in the attic by myself,'' she added, smiling grimly. "I guess that was the only place I ever found where I could be alone. It was hotter than heck in the summer and freezing cold in the winter, but I could be alone. I had my private silence of pain that nobody knew." Trina spoke easily, as was her custom, even when the sharing was very personal. Her strength in group was an inspiration to the other members.

"I had a hard time expressing my feelings and making friends. I withdrew into myself more all the time, feeling lonely, different, quiet, and shy." Trina laughed a little, using the word *shy* made her realize how much she'd changed. "I covered up being shy by drinking," she said.

Roger leaned back, rocking his chair on the back two legs. How sad these childhood stories sounded, he reflected. How would his fiancée react, hearing them, if she ever did? It's a sordid part of life, he acknowledged to himself. Do I want her to know how sordid?

"I never felt close to my parents," Trina continued. "I thought something was wrong with me. I felt hurt, angry, lonely, and worthless. I had a lot of hate toward my dad."

"I spent a lot of time alone, too," Anne said. "I simply didn't want to be with anyone. It hurt too much. I asked myself time and time again, 'Why does he do this?'"

" 'When will all this craziness stop?' was what I always asked," Trina said.

"Has it stopped, Trina?" Michael asked.

"Not really. He quit drinking a while back, but he never got sober. He's stayed almost the same as if he were still drinking. Only now he can't beat me. I have my own home and can get away."

"How do we get through it?" Michael asked, then answered his own question. "I got through it by pouring myself into school and outside activities. I tried so hard to succeed since I couldn't improve the situation at home."

"I think that's what my older sister did," Anne said. "She had a million friends and belonged to every club. Then there was me, just tagging along when Mom made me get out of the house, even though I didn't want to."

"I tried running away," Trina confided. "Then I'd get

lonely or homesick. I couldn't understand why, but I'd go back. I hated their screaming and telling me what to do, but I came home anyway."

"It was what you knew," Szifra said. "So many ACOAs can intellectually realize their home life was horrible, but they were tied to it emotionally nevertheless. It takes a lot of work to separate from our parents."

"I think it'll be the last to go for me," Michael said. "Living with an alcoholic was like a nightmare for me. Only I never woke up. Every time my father picked up a drink, he abandoned me. I get angry and hurt thinking about it. How could they be so irresponsible? They had us. They stayed children. If I ever have kids, I hope they realize what a commitment I've made. I hope I don't shirk it like so many of our parents did. Some of us had one parent who tried to keep our needs in focus. I just don't get it. How could you not realize your kids would be hurt if you weren't there for them, predictably and consistently?"

"What we're saying," Linda said, "relates to one issue. We lost our childhoods. And that's sad for me to think about."

"Whether you were hiding in attics, blocking your memories, taking on your parents' roles when you were kids, or feeling rejected because they abandoned you, many ACOA's lose the chance to be children," Szifra agreed.

"I think the last time I was a child was when I was five years old," Linda continued. "That year I remember the anticipation and excitement of Christmas. Looking forward to presents and fun, and guessing with my younger brother and sisters what we'd get. Then in a minute, it was over. Dad came to me and told me Mom was sick. 'There's no Santa Claus,' Dad said, 'because Mom is sick—you'll have to take care of Christmas for the rest of the kids.' From that day on, I was always taking care. My strongest memory, though, is always trying to agree with both of my parents at the same time," she concluded.

"Now that would be pretty difficult," Trina said.

"It was." Linda laughed a little. "I was good at making

each parent believe I was on their side, though. I always tried to keep them separated. I would make one go to the kitchen and the other stay in the living room. They would argue, but at least that way I could keep them from hitting each other. I'd stay right in the middle."

"Hearing this makes me realize how lucky I was," Anne said. "I feel guilty being here because my dad was never violent. He never got into screaming matches or was mean to us. He was more of a happy drinker. I know Szifra said we all still experience plenty of loss."

"That's right. Don't discount its impact on you, Anne," Michael said. "Even though Dad would get crazy sometimes, most of the time our family looked pretty normal. It was that unspoken tension, wondering when it would happen again, that made it so unbearable. And never knowing what would happen if you said something. I guess I learned pretty early not to state my needs or wants to Dad."

"Actually, I do have a few memories of Mom being mad at Dad. I suppose because he'd had too much to drink," Anne responded. "There's so much I don't remember, though. My sister who first started sending me ACOA material remembers much more than do I. She talks about things that happened when I was still living at home, and I just don't remember a thing about them."

"I wish I could forget what I remember," Linda said. "So much of my childhood was spent dealing with things other kids took for granted, like having toilet paper and clean clothes."

"My parents didn't have a washing machine, so I was the one who went to the Laundromat to do the wash—when there was money for it," she continued. "While I did the laundry, my dad would sit across the street in a tavern. We often had to plead with Mom and Dad to come home because we didn't have clean clothes, like I said in my poem. Many times when they didn't come home, I'd go through the laundry and dig up what I wanted to wear, then wash it by hand and iron it dry.

"I remember one time we spent months without a hot

water heater. Dad bought two large kettles, and we boiled and carried water to take a bath or do dishes. But they always had the money to go to the bar.'' Linda's voice hardened as she spoke.

Something clicked for Anne as Linda spoke. That's probably why she's so meticulous about her appearance now, because she always had to struggle just to have clean clothes as a kid, she thought. That became a real priority for her. Looking at her now, you'd never know she once had to scrounge for clean clothes. Tonight Linda wore a skirt and jacket in this season's new colors. Her bags and shoes matched. She had on delicate earrings and eyeshadow that picked up the colors of her outfit. Everything seems just right, Anne thought, realizing she was a much more practical dresser—she liked nice clothes, of course, but she was conservative in both spending and tastes.

Linda continued, ''My parents still drink. I see their car at the bar when I drive by, and I think, What will they buy their next water heater with? Money for booze always came first.''

Susan decided to go next. Looking back at her childhood was not easy. Speaking without crying will be a miracle, she thought. ''Since I never saw my father drink,'' she said slowly, ''I had very different experiences. Dad was always distant, uninvolved. At report card time Mom made a ceremony of us appearing before him. It was a terrifying event. I was lucky because my grades were good, but I knew my brother's and sister's weren't perfect enough, and Dad would disapprove. I'd feel guilty and sorry and afraid for them. For me it was, 'Go on being good so I can continue to be proud of you and ignore you.' ''

''The password was tension, right, Susan?'' Trina asked.

''Good way to put it.''

Michael pushed his up sweatshirt sleeves as he began to speak. ''I remember feeling odd because my dad was different from the other kids' fathers. He wasn't as nice as their fathers. But I didn't want to tell anybody I didn't have a really great dad. I never had kids over from school. I didn't want anybody to see what he was like. I wanted them to think I had just as good a dad as they had.

"When I was around eight or nine, Dad was drinking heavily," he continued. "I remember when I went to school, I wouldn't really think about it. But as soon as it was time for Dad to come home, I would start getting afraid and wondering, Is he going to be drunk tonight? Is he going to start yelling tonight? And whenever he was drunk, everybody but Dad got away. We would leave the house, just because he was there.

"I felt alone most of the time. Whenever weather permitted, I would walk the countryside or go swimming in a nearby lake, just to get away from the oppressive atmosphere. Having close friends was impossible because of the secrets and just plain bad manners, so I rode my bike or walked in the woods alone, dreaming of a better day. I didn't tell my friends at school because I thought they'd think I was strange."

"I never told, either," Linda said. "We kept so many family secrets. Who could have lived with that embarrassment?" She shook her head, remembering.

"One of the most difficult things that I still deal with was the verbal belittling I got from my parents," she went on. "They told me I was a mistake, not to mention a girl. I felt alone for years regardless of how hard I tried to fit in a family or a group."

Michael groaned inwardly when he heard Linda say she was a mistake. How could parents ever tell a child that? He wondered if subconsciously he was thinking the same thing about his wife's possible pregnancy. What a horrible thought—that a person's life was a "mistake." He fidgeted nervously, anxious for the meeting to end. He looked up as Szifra asked Anne if she had anything else she'd like to share.

"I feel funny because I remember so little," Anne said. "My sister gets angry with me because I don't remember things. She'll call me with what she thinks is a great piece of news about someone, and then I can't even remember the person she's talking about. She screams at me, 'How could you forget?!' It makes me feel dumb.''

"I hope you can understand, Anne, that what you did was block those feelings and memories," Szifra said. "It was all part of the role you took on as a child to survive. We'll be talking more about roles in this group. When you consider you survived more effectively by blocking memories, and your sister by going to club meetings, it only makes sense that you two would have different memories."

"There are a few things I remember," Anne said. "There was a man who lived down the road from us. He was a drunk. That's what we always called him. I never thought of him as an alcoholic. My father was pretty young then, and his alcoholism had not progressed too far, so at that time I didn't think much about my dad's drinking.

"Anyway, this man, Unc, would come down and disturb the whole house. I hated it when he came down. He'd usually show up when we were trying to play a game or cards, and he'd stay and talk and talk and talk. It made me want to vomit. We could never get him to go home. I think later I was afraid Dad would turn out to be like Unc."

"Do you think because he didn't it's made it easier for you?" Michael asked her.

"Oh, probably in some ways. Dad wasn't a public drinker, like Unc. He didn't go visit all the neighbors. He'd stop at a bar after work, but otherwise he mostly would drink at home, very covertly, and then just go to bed when he'd had too much to drink."

"It's interesting that you called Unc a drunk instead of an alcoholic," Trina said.

"I know. I never thought much about that. But I was a child when we lived near Unc. And that's what everyone called him. Now when I think about Unc, I feel sad, kind of sorry for him. No one ever thought about how he felt."

Szifra said, "I'm glad you could remember some early memories. And glad you told us about them, Anne.

"It seems like you've all been able to remember several distinct incidents from your childhood," she continued.

"Does thinking about them with the new information you have help you better understand what went on?"

"Oh, sure," Trina said. "But it would have been better if I'd had that knowledge sooner."

"Sure, that would have been great," Szifra agreed. "Hopefully your new knowledge will help you resolve some of the history that cannot be changed. As adults, we can add data, change our perceptions, and grow past some of the pain."

"I guess that's why the Serenity Prayer is so helpful," Trina said.

"Good point," Szifra said. "Why don't you share it with those who may not be familiar with the verse?"

"Sure," Trina agreed. " 'God, grant me the serenity to accept the things I cannot change, courage to change the things I can, and wisdom to know the difference.' "

"I really like the Serenity Prayer," Sarah said.

"It helps me gain perspective," Linda agreed.

"Exploring these earlier times is one step in understanding how alcoholism affects the entire family," Szifra said, "and how it continues to affect you even today, although your alcoholic parent may have died or may live miles away. We'll be learning more about this next week when we talk about the roles you took on as children. Please try to finish reading Claudia Black's *It Will Never Happen to Me* by next week. She discusses the roles in depth. Think about what role or combination of roles you took on and how much of that you may still be playing today."

Checking her watch, she said, "It's week five. Each of you made a six-week commitment. Is anyone thinking about leaving?"

Michael responded, "The first two or three meetings, I really thought I could quit at six. Now I can't imagine quitting. It'll probably be a while for me. These meetings really help me."

Others responded to Michael's comment. Trina summed it up by saying, "It's hard. It hurts. It helps. We're ACOAs.

We're tough, and we're finding out we like the support we get, too.''

No one could imagine leaving after only six meetings. They agreed to let the group know at least one meeting beforehand when they did decide to leave. It would give everyone a chance to say good-bye.

"Anything else before we stop?" Szifra asked, looking around. Everyone seemed finished, ready to stop for the night, so she smiled and stood up, wishing them all a good week.

As the meeting broke up, Roger told Trina he'd like to walk out with her. "Great," Trina said. "I've got a few minutes, if you'd like to chat some more. Let's sit outside."

"Gosh, that was a hard meeting," Anne said to Susan as they walked out. "How everyone survived those rough times is beyond me."

"I know what you mean," Susan said. "Things in my home were usually so quiet and orderly. I never even knew Dad drank. I can't imagine living with the chaos and physical violence."

"I'm not sure I'd trade with you guys, though," Linda said. "At least I knew what was causing my parents' craziness. I knew they were alcoholics. I would find the unspoken, hidden tension and terror more frightening and difficult to deal with."

"Well, neither way is the ideal situation, obviously," Anne said. "I just hope I'm not doing these things to my kids. I want it to be better for them."

"Don't you think awareness is helping you make it better?" Linda asked. "I know with my daughters, we have our ups and downs, but I try to be open so we can discuss things."

"I'm not confident enough about my parenting skills. But I'm sure trying," Anne said emphatically. "Well, I better get going. See you next week." As she walked briskly to her car, she reflected that she wasn't much for small talk, but she was starting to feel more comfortable with the group members.

It's been a full day, she thought, realizing how tired she was when she sat down in the car. But a good one. This is the most comfortable I've felt since I started coming to group. Now wouldn't I be surprised if this got easier?!

My Observations and Reactions to Meeting 5

Anne, 39, child care worker, lost child role in family, father died from alcoholism seven years ago.
Observations/progress noted:

Linda, 36, nurse, responsible role in family, both parents are alcoholic, living.
Observations/progress noted:

Michael, 38, PR/advertising, responsible role in family, father is alcoholic, mother prescription drug–addicted, living.
Observations/progress noted:

Roger, 20, student, lost child/scapegoat in family, recovering, mother also recovering.
Observations/progress noted:

Susan, 32, accountant, lost child/responsible role in family, father died from alcoholism two years ago.
Observations/progress noted:

Trina, 45, shipping clerk, scapegoat role in family, recovering, father quit drinking a few years ago.
Observations/progress noted:

Szifra, therapist
Observations:

Observations about me during this meeting:

My feelings during this meeting:

Issues I'd like to explore further:

My reactions to this meeting:

What I learned about myself during this meeting:

Taking on ACOA Roles

"HOW DO YOU want your hamburger?" Michael asked Roger.

"Medium, thanks."

"Medium it is. So, how are classes going this semester?"

"Not too bad," Roger said. "Much better than last. I especially like my class on expert systems."

"Oh, that would be interesting. I've read a little about expert systems. One of our clients sells computer software. I don't know too much about it, though. What is your class covering?" Michael asked.

"Right now, pretty introductory. Kind of an overview of the different types for mainframe and microcomputers," Roger explained, and continued on enthusiastically about his favorite topic.

Earlier in the week, Michael had invited Roger to have supper with him before group. He'd decided it was time he got to know some of the people in group. After all, he'd said to himself, I'm sharing some rather personal stuff with them! He usually had supper alone on Tuesday nights because his wife, Sharon, had a class.

Roger had been surprised by the invitation but pleased. He was a little nervous beforehand but reminded himself that he was much better at socializing than he used to be. I don't need to be overly nervous, he told himself.

They continued their conversation on technology while eating hamburgers and chips. Michael was impressed with Roger's computer background. Perhaps getting to know more about his work and studies would make it easier to relate to him on personal issues as well. Who knows? Michael said to himself. I might as well try it. I guess all of us ACOAs are learning how to be comfortable discussing personal issues.

This week more than ever before Michael had realized how much he wanted to have someone he could talk to. Sharon had put off going for a pregnancy test He still had no idea what they would do if she was pregnant, but having the possibility hanging over his head kept him from thinking about much else. Still, he didn't bring it up with Roger, and the diversion of other conversation helped.

Roger and Michael arrived at Szifra's office as Sarah pulled up. "Where were you last week?" Michael called out.

"Oh," Sarah said, "be glad you're not a high school teacher. Remember class trips?"

"Big-time fun, sure, I remember. What are they like from the teacher's side of the fence?" Michael laughed.

"Just as you'd think," Sarah said. "The highlight was getting home."

They walked in, talking about this year's spoof-the-teacher prank. Nearly everyone was already there. Linda came rushing in just as the group moved from the waiting room to Szifra's office.

"Oh, we have audiovisuals tonight," Trina commented as she walked in. Szifra had set up posters depicting the various roles Children of Alcoholics take on.

"Just a few props," Szifra said. "I thought they would help point out the common characteristics of ACOA roles."

"Cue cards," Anne said. "I love it. When I don't know what to say, I'll just glance at one of these!"

Szifra was pleased to see Anne's sense of humor emerging. Obviously she was feeling much more comfortable in group. "Well, I had no idea how much attention the artwork would generate," Szifra said, laughing. "I should try this more often." When everyone was seated, she resumed. "Hi. Good to see everyone here. We missed you last week, Kathy and Sarah.

"Before we begin, I'd like to announce that two people have asked to join our group. Unlike the ACOA drop-in meetings, we've decided on a more formal structure, so I want to ask you before accepting any new members.

"These ACOAs are both men; they've been working on ACOA issues for several months. Both said I was free to tell you they are recovering—one from alcoholism, the other from drug dependency. How would you feel about two new members next week?"

"It's fine with me," Kathy said.

"I'd like to see a few more men in here," Trina said. "I suppose Roger and Michael would, too."

Susan voiced some concern; she felt her discomfort would increase with a larger group but said she was willing to risk that. "These six weeks have helped me," she said, "so how could I justify someone else not being able to get help, too?" Most seemed eager to have new members join, although Linda wondered if it would affect the rapport they were building.

"It could make us all back off a little," Michael agreed. "It seems we're just starting to get to know each other and open up more. But I think we should include them."

After some more discussion, the group agreed that Szifra could let them know they were welcome to join the group beginning next week.

"Anything else before we begin with tonight's topic?" Szifra asked. When no one offered anything, she turned to Kathy.

Kathy nodded. "I feel a little silly, but Szifra suggested I tell the group. So I will. I've finally decided to try to do what I went to school for: write."

The group sat in silence, not sure what Kathy's announcement meant, even to her. Kathy continued, "I always wanted to be a writer, but I would never take the risk.

Instead I took no-risk jobs I'd end up hating in a few months. So, twelve years after getting my degree in journalism, I'm going to try writing something.''

"That's great, Kathy," Linda said. "Good luck!"

"Really, Kathy," Trina said. "I had no idea you wanted to be a writer. You kept that secret locked away!"

Szifra, too, was enthusiastic and encouraging, saying she felt a little like a proud mother. "I'm excited for you, Kathy, and proud of you. And I believe you'll be good," she said.

After allowing time for the group to react to Kathy's announcement, Szifra asked, "Does anyone have any comments or reactions to last week's meeting or something else you want to bring up?"

No one had anything to say, so Szifra asked, "Did you think of other childhood incidents during the week?"

"Oh, I did," Trina said. "They just flash into my mind, with no connection to what's going on or to what I was thinking about. All of a sudden, boom. I remember Dad starting a big fight over nothing. Or dragging us all on a picnic, but then not letting any of us get out of the car when we got there."

"For me," Linda said, "once I start remembering, I keep on remembering things until I make a real effort to switch it off. It's fine now, though."

"I'd like to thank you again for bringing in your poem," Michael said to Linda.

"What did I miss?" Sarah asked.

As Michael explained, Linda reached in her purse for copies she'd made for Sarah and Kathy. "I figured my poem might come up and you'd feel funny not knowing what we were talking about," she said as she handed Sarah and Kathy copies. "Now I feel funny giving them to you," she added, blushing.

"This is off the subject," Trina said, "but maybe I should mention that my dad isn't doing very well. The doctor doesn't expect him to last much longer. I just thought I'd mention it in case I'm not here next week."

The news shocked everyone but Szifra, who had spent time with Trina earlier in the week talking about this.

"I'm sorry to hear that," Sarah said. "Are you doing okay?"

"Well, I think so," Trina said. "After all these years of hating him and wanting him out of my life, it's scary to think it may happen soon. I've reached out to everyone I know for support, though. I'm not going through this one alone. In fact, after meeting with Szifra, I was able to talk to Dad alone about some things, and I feel good about that."

"Do you want to say anything about your talk with your dad?" Szifra asked Trina.

"Well, I told him I wished we'd been able to have a closer relationship," Trina said. "I asked him some questions about how his father and mother treated him. I cried and told him I'd miss him."

"How did he respond?" asked Sarah.

"Well, he said more than usual," Trina replied. "He told me his parents had 'whooped him pretty hard.' He told me he loved me. It's the only time in his life he told me that." Her eyes filled with tears. "It was pretty hard, but it was okay. He was also himself—three minutes of close stuff was it. He began to talk about my brothers and sisters. I started to feel hurt about that. Then I talked to myself about it and got more comfortable. . . . Anyway, I'm ready to go on with the agenda now," she concluded.

"We'll be thinking of you, Trina," Linda said, and everyone else nodded in agreement.

Szifra waited a few moments, then introduced the topic for that evening. "As you all know from reading and the discussions we've had individually, various roles have been identified as those Children of Alcoholics take on to survive living with their families. Claudia Black calls them the responsible person, the acting-out child, the adjuster, and the placater. Sharon Wegscheider-Cruse has also worked extensively with Children of Alcoholics. She attributes similar characteristics to the roles of family hero, scapegoat, lost child, and family mascot.

"What happens," she continued, "is that Children of Alcoholics carry these same coping skills and behavior patterns into adulthood. Not because they necessarily work optimally. Or because the ACOAs like them. But because they don't know any other way." She glanced around the circle to make sure there were no questions, then stood up.

"Well, enough lecture. Take a few minutes to look these posters over and then we'll talk."

The group spent some time examining the material, then Szifra asked, "Okay, who's ready to talk about what they discovered?"

"I am," Roger said. "Since I got involved with alcohol so young, I guess I would be the acting-out child, or scapegoat, in the family. Neither my brother or sister ever got in trouble. I didn't get in much trouble, but I was a very young alcohol abuser. And even defiant at times. I think I also have parts of the lost child, like being alone a lot and being timid. I'm a mix of scapegoat and lost child."

"What traits do you think you continued as an adult, Roger?" Szifra asked.

"For a while, the acting-out child. Now that I'm recovering, I'm working on everything that goes along with that. I think loneliness and rejection are still strong, but I'm battling the wall of defenses. So, I think I'm well on my way to giving up the scapegoat role.

"Now, the lost child role is another story," he continued. "In some ways, giving up alcohol contributed to my lost child characteristics becoming stronger. I used alcohol partly to cover up shyness and discomfort with people. I think I'm afraid to take risks. I'm quiet, and I keep up a wall of defense by being independent of people. That's a big part of why I'm in this group, to work on those very things that seem to be lost child patterns."

"I think you've done a great job, Roger, of both recognizing behavior patterns you want to change and working to change them," Szifra said. "Your progress in here has been significant. When you first thought about coming to this group, would you have imagined yourself speaking first tonight?"

"Not really." Roger smiled. He liked Szifra's encouragement. Even though he felt self-conscious, it felt good to hear that he was making progress.

Szifra asked Anne to go next.

"Oh, gosh," Anne said. "I'm not really ready, but I probably won't be ready later, either. This is so confusing. I kept rereading these chapters, trying to make my family fit into these different roles. Then every time I thought I had it figured out, I'd think about it some more, and decide I was wrong."

"Maybe it would help if you didn't think of these as rigidly defined roles," Szifra offered, "but as general behavior patterns. Perhaps your family members took on two or more roles. What behavior patterns did you recognize in yourself?"

"Well, I'm timid and a follower. I'm withdrawn. And I usually go with the flow rather than speak up about what I want. Those are all the adjuster or lost child." Anne shrugged almost apologetically. "I don't think I have any of the acting-out characteristics. I'm not defiant, I didn't misbehave as a kid. I do think I'm responsible, though. I always focus on performance and try to be perfect. But I'm not independent, so I don't have all the pieces of the family hero."

"I would agree that you are responsible, even overresponsible sometimes," Szifra said. "You take your job and raising your family very seriously. I also agree with your assessment of your adjuster behaviors. It seems you do have pieces of both. How do you all see Anne?" she asked the group.

"I think you do seem a lot like the lost child," Linda said. "But instead of being invisible, you've also become very responsible. You even said tonight you wanted to be sure to do this right."

"Oh," Anne said. "I guess I did."

Susan added, "I understand. I wanted to do this perfectly, too."

"This was very eerie reading," Kathy began. "I literally saw my whole family right there in the book. I had this sense Claudia Black had to have met us; she was writing about us." Kathy frowned in concentration as she strove to express her feelings.

"So, let's start at the top. The family hero. That's my oldest sister. Graduated from college with a degree in math, went to work for a big computer company, did all the kinds of things you get awards and recognition for.

"Next, my second sister. Quiet, rarely expresses her opinions. I read a description of the adjuster that blew me away." She pretended to pick up a photograph from a table, acting as a friend of the family and looking shocked. "Who's that? I didn't know there were six kids in your family." Setting the pretend photo back down, she said, "That fit my sister perfectly. People just didn't know she existed.

"My younger brother was used as the model to define scapegoat, I'm sure," she continued, grinning. "And then there's me, the placater, the mascot. I tried to keep everything fine. Even if I had to act funny to lighten the situation. I was real short as a child. Well, not just as a child." She laughed. Most people doubt the five feet one inch Kathy claims.

"Anyway, my older sisters were both tall, then five years later little Kathy was born. People always commented about what a cute little thing I was; and when I was young, I thought I was cute. That probably contributed to my 'cute' behavior. After my older sisters left home, though, I took on a lot of the family hero characteristics."

"It seems like it was pretty easy for you to see your family," Linda commented.

"Right from the first reading," Kathy said, nodding. "I also have a younger sister and brother who were adopted after my two older sisters left home. So there was lots of shifting of roles in our family. My sister, who is ten years younger than I, was probably another scapegoat. And then my youngest brother, the baby of the family, was another mascot. I guess I passed my cuteness on to him.''

''It wasn't quite that easy for me to identify my family's roles,'' Linda began. ''I first decided about me. Because I was the oldest and involved in caring for my brother and sisters, I fit mostly into the responsible role. One of my sisters was a mascot, and another was always in trouble, so she'd be the acting-out child. Maybe my brother was the lost child. But he was so good, he was sort of a hero, too.''

''Tell us a little more about your early behaviors, Linda,'' Szifra encouraged her.

''Well, I was helpful. I managed everything, the house, the laundry, meals once I could cook. I made sure my brother and sisters got their homework done.''

Szifra nodded, then looked to Susan to see if she was ready to speak.

Susan began hesitantly, ''I don't think there's any doubt I was the adjuster. And still am! Just tell me where you want me to be, what you want me to do. I'll oblige. I think that's why you also related to the responsible child, Anne. We both are so obedient.

''Mom was the hero, we all followed her. I did take on some hero characteristics, though. I work hard to be perfect. I think in many ways my brother and sister were lost children, too. And there weren't many characteristics of mascots, in the sense of being funny or providing humor. Our family was too proper for that. We were more like porcelain dolls on display.''

''You express yourself so eloquently, Susan,'' Kathy said. ''I can visualize these three kids all dressed up, sitting quietly on the sofa, behaving so properly.''

''You're not too far off,'' Susan agreed.

Sarah waited a minute to make sure Susan was finished, then spoke up. ''I recognized myself as the family hero, because of my independence and achievements,'' she said. ''But I didn't like reading that those were covers for feelings of inadequacy and confusion. I feel like I'm being labeled. If I admit to one thing, then the other gets thrown in automatically. This seems too black and white for me.''

"I think I know what you mean," Szifra said gently. "Would it help if you imagine the posters I've made as being gray and the circles very uneven? These are only meant as an aid in learning to recognize how you might have behaved in your family of origin. I'm not asking you to buy the concept as it is if pieces don't fit. Can you use what fits?''

"You make me sound like I'm on the defensive. I'm not. I just don't think I feel inadequate," Sarah replied, obviously frustrated. "How could a high achiever feel inadequate?''

"Many ACOA experts believe that sometimes children are superachievers as a reaction to never being able to accomplish what they'd really like to—having healthy, happy parents," Szifra explained. "As with other codependents, children believe they can make their parents happy, if only they try hard enough. So they try hard and they do bring the family esteem and pride from their accomplishments. It feels very good to them, not only because it makes their parents happy, but because the individuals, too, get good feelings about themselves. But nothing they do ever feels like enough. Once the goal is accomplished, they're on to the next challenge, never having really recognized that they have indeed accomplished something. It doesn't feel like a choice to go on or to take a break. It's a trap. The only way they feel good is when they are accomplishing. That you are able to give yourself credit for achieving something is wonderful. Congratulating ourselves is important. That's a very healthy sign.''

"Well, I don't like these labels," Sarah said, "and I don't buy it, either.''

"Use what fits, Sarah," Szifra told her. "There's no need to buy the whole package if it doesn't fit. But it's equally unproductive to throw it all out because you disagree with some part. Perhaps pieces here and there can help you understand yourself and your family better. I'm asking only that you let yourself be open." Szifra could tell that this was touching a "hot button" for Sarah. She decided to wait and see what emerged.

"Well, perhaps," Sarah said after a slight pause.

"There was a lot of crossover in my family, too, Sarah," Trina said. "Of course, there were so many of us, there had to be a big mix. Reading some of the characteristics, though, caused all kinds of things to click in my head." She snapped her fingers. "Perfect. That was my oldest sister. Fun. That was my little brother. Acting out and defiant. That was most of us! The lost child. That must be the kid that was always under the bed. I don't even remember his name!" Trina laughed. "That's not exactly true, but it's truer than I'd like to admit. I didn't try to make up a list and plug in names with roles. But I could see lots of these characteristics were true for us."

"How did I end up being last?" Michael asked after Trina sat back and crossed her legs, her usual sign that she was through. He looked teasingly at Susan and Anne.

"This book was enlightening," he began. "I had some of the same sense you had, Kathy, that the author knew me. I felt exposed, reading it at home, alone. I couldn't read much at a time. It brought up too many feelings.

"As for the roles," he continued, "I think there were two heroes in my family. My brother was hero major, and I was hero minor, with lots of lost child thrown in. We were both very responsible and focused on performance. I saw the garbage he went through, so I decided to go off on my own a lot and stay out of my parents' way. I didn't make my own needs known. My sister is probably the scapegoat. She bucked my parents a lot on the rules and would stand up to them when she wanted something badly enough."

"What about today?" Szifra asked. "How many of these characteristics are you continuing?"

"Quite a few," Michael replied. "I haven't learned how to relax or play. I have unbelievably high expectations of myself, so I'm still focused on performance. And I've remained pretty isolated.''

"How about you, Susan? What behaviors do you think you may have kept as an adult?'' Szifra asked.

"Being timid. I'm terrified of everything, it seems!'' Susan responded. "And I feel I'm unimportant. I get angry with myself about this, too. I don't understand why I have these particular personality problems. How did I end up so scared, with so much lost child?''

"Try not to blame yourself, Susan,'' Szifra said gently. "I believe our role is determined by what we need to do to survive, what mask we need to wear to survive. It isn't a conscious choice. It's not our fault. Sure, at some point, if we become aware we have choices, we can change. I'm trying to get you to put away the whip, Susan. You did what you did, became who you were, to survive in your family. You are no longer there. Now you have two options. You can change.''

"And I will,'' Susan said hesitantly.

"Can others share what you've kept as adults?'' Szifra asked.

"What are we going to do once we get our label tags on our chests?'' Sarah asked, still not willing to buy into the role issue.

"How about switch them around?'' Trina said impationtly and rather sarcastically. "I'm sorry to be so testy, Sarah, but you seem to be fighting this.''

"I hate generalizations and labels.''

"Who doesn't?'' Trina responded. "But the fact is, sometimes I blame others for things I should take responsibility for. It's not a label. But it's something I sometimes do. The labels are a shorthand way to talk about these issues, no more than that. If I want to recover, I figure I've got to know what I'm doing before I can figure out how I'm going to change the parts that still get in my way and trip me up.''

"I can see your point, Trina,'' Sarah said. "I turn a lot of these problems over to my Higher Power. That works for me.''

"I'd never challenge what works for you, Sarah," Trina said, more softly this time. "Just let the rest of us use what might work for us."

"Okay," Sarah said, "as long as you don't try to label me."

"No problem," Trina said. "I've got enough to handle trying to work on me! To borrow an AA term, 'I'm not trying to take your inventory.' I hope you believe that."

Sarah nodded and said, "Someone else can go now."

"I am finding this helps my self-awareness," Linda said. "I have to admit I do feel inadequate. Even though I think I'm a high achiever, not much feels like successful achievement to me. I'm like you, Michael, I set higher standards for myself than I do for anyone else. I didn't realize that until I read this book."

"It's incredible," Kathy said. "I lived my life in what I thought was my unique way, but now I know that it was almost predictable at the same time. It's a little humbling!

"I know I've kept pieces of both roles," she went on after a moment's pause. "I'm still the mascot when things get uncomfortable. Since reading this book, I've noticed it several times. When I pull on the mascot mask, people laugh and enjoy it, so it encourages me. But when it's appropriate to be serious, I'm trying not to bring in inappropriate humor.

"I especially notice my mascot behavior when I'm around my two older sisters. We're not together often, but recently my oldest sister flew in and the three of us drove several hours to our aunt's. Without planning it this way, my oldest sister drove, with my other sister in the front next to her, reading the map. Then I climbed in the backseat and acted like a kid. Right in the middle of being funny one time, I thought, here comes the mascot! It felt very strange.

"Of the family hero characteristics," Kathy concluded, "I impose high goals on myself, too. Szifra says 'unreasonably high,' although I don't see that. And even though I'm incredibly responsible and efficient, I'm big-time emotionally dependent, especially in relationships." She laughed, "You can verify that with my ex-husband."

The group laughed with her, despite their awareness that she was deflecting pain by being funny. She put so much humorous body language into her speech, it was hard not to laugh.

The group grew quiet after that. Szifra knew Anne had not yet taken a turn, but she wanted her to speak up on her own.

Yet the longer Anne waited the more uncomfortable Anne got. Wouldn't it ever be all right to just sit here and learn from others? she wondered. Why do I have to talk myself to get anything out of this? This is too much pressure for me. Her eyes filled with tears.

At last Trina broke the silence. "This was kind of fun. I'm thinking about learning more about psychology. The human mind is pretty interesting."

"And how much our minds control our behavior, even without us realizing it," Michael added.

Szifra glanced at her watch, a signal that time was running short. Recognizing Anne's discomfort, she looked encouragingly at everyone. "Does anyone else want to add anything to our role discussion? Sarah? Anne?"

"I'm sorry I was so outspoken," Sarah said. "I've started to feel so good, I don't want to sabotage my program. Or my good feelings. Even though it's not related to the role discussion, I want to share something."

"Go ahead, Sarah," Linda said.

"I have a date!" Sarah blurted out. "It's been three years since I got divorced, and I'm finally going to get out again."

"Good for you," Trina said, and the others agreed. Sarah's good humor helped them all feel better about her earlier challenges. The conversation rambled on about what it was like to date after being "out of circulation," as Sarah put it, for so long. Without a formal announcement that group was over, several conversations sprang up among the members.

Szifra recognized a rapport was building among the group members. She hoped Bob and Mark would fit in and the group would continue the connections that were being forged.

Roger waved good-bye to Michael, thanking him for supper.

"Speaking of supper," Trina said, "does anyone want to go eat?"

"Maybe next time," Kathy said. "I can't tonight."

"Let's plan on that," Trina said.

Kathy nodded. "Call me."

"I don't have your number."

"Oh, that's right. Here. . . ."

"I could go for a quick soft drink," Linda said to Trina.

Anne left quietly, feeling foolish because she hadn't spoken up. Well, that's just me, she told herself, trying to rationalize away her first feeling. She did feel better when Trina gave her a thumbs-up sign from across the parking lot.

"Thanks, Trina," Anne called, and waved back, smiling. After all Trina has been through, her positiveness is amazing, she thought. It's also catching. Anne smiled to herself. Next week . . . I always have next week to be the super-performer. What's that saying Sarah uses all the time? "One Day at a Time." I guess I better realize I'll change one day at a time, not overnight.

My Observations and Reactions to Meeting 6

Anne, 39, child care worker, lost child role in family, father died from alcoholism seven years ago.
Observations/progress noted:

Kathy, 33, secretary, mascot/responsible role in family, father died from alcoholism this year.
Observations/progress noted:

Linda, 36, nurse, responsible role in family, both parents are alcoholic, living.
Observations/progress noted:

Michael, 38, PR/advertising, responsible role in family, father is alcoholic, mother prescription drug–addicted, living.
Observations/progress noted:

Roger, 20, student, lost child/scapegoat in family, recovering, mother also recovering.
Observations/progress noted:

Sarah, 36, high school teacher, responsible role in family, father died from alcoholism five years ago.
Observations/progress noted:

Susan, 32, accountant, lost child/responsible role in family, father died from alcoholism two years ago.
Observations/progress noted:

Trina, 45, shipping clerk, scapegoat role in family, recovering, father quit drinking a few years ago.
Observations/progress noted:

Szifra, therapist
Observations:

Observations about me during this meeting:

My feelings during this meeting:

Issues I'd like to explore further:

My reactions to this meeting:

What I learned about myself during this meeting:

Recognizing Our Feelings

BOB WAS USED to running things. He was a recovering alcoholic and an alcohol counselor in private practice. He was his own boss, and that was how he liked it. He never liked working for other people, although he had to when he was in the army. He made sure, though, that his squad did things right. Right, according to Bob, was his way. He'd recognized this trait in himself a while ago. He wondered, as he got ready to leave for his first ACOA group meeting, how he would feel participating as a client. After all, he said to himself, I run groups. Am I going to be able to handle not being in charge of this one?

He thought about it a few minutes. He really wanted to get over that need to control. Perhaps he'd tell the group that was one of the things he needed to work on. I have such a need to be right, to do things my way. It makes me so rigid, he thought. I'd like to get comfortable being more flexible. I wonder if I'll have the guts to tell them all that. I can choose to give up some control. I know my role in this group will be much harder since I'll be the client. I won't be as comfortable talking about myself. When my self-disclosure is for my client's benefit, it's easier. He laughed to himself. I'm a good family hero! Self-disclosing to people other than clients makes me feel weak.

Bob had agreed to attend group a minimum of six weeks, as Szifra asked. It seemed like a big commitment, though.

After all, he said to himself, I've been recovering six years. I've gone to AA regularly. My wife and I even got into counseling for a while. And I read everything I can on alcoholism, as well as see all the new alcohol films. I wonder if I'll need that long to get what I want out of the experience. He could almost feel denial creeping in.

Bob's original interest in the ACOA group was to get information for his clients, many of whom had grown up in alcoholic homes. After several months of encouraging his recovering ACOA clients to deal with these issues, he began to wonder if his own ACOA issues might be adversely affecting his adult life.

On a brave day, he had called Szifra, and after speaking with him individually, Szifra thought her ACOA group would be helpful to him. He told Szifra that he felt ready to work through his feelings about his alcoholic mother and nonalcoholic father. He knew he had unfinished business about his childhood, he'd told Szifra, as well as unfinished business from all those years of drinking.

As everyone gathered in the waiting room this Tuesday night, the ease of interaction that had begun to develop in previous weeks was missing. The group seemed mildly off balance. Some obviously felt shy meeting strangers. Others had trouble trusting people they didn't know. Many in the group were thinking, What will these two new guys think of me? or, What will this be like?

Roger was glad to have more men in the group. He introduced himself to Bob and Mark, the other new member. Susan and Anne also smiled a welcome, but more hesitantly.

Mark's composure told others he had probably been in groups before. He walked into the waiting room, said hello to everyone, then headed for the coffeepot. He looked around for ashtrays but found none.

An hour and a half and no smokes! he thought. Hope it's worth it.

Mark had seen Szifra a few times individually. He liked her. His style made him appear quite open sometimes, but he usually kept private issues private. Even though he talked a lot, it wasn't very personal. In treatment, Mark had held back. Tonight he was undecided about how much to disclose.

Bob and Mark discovered from the group's interactions that they were the newcomers. They sized each other up, looking for common ground. Physically, they were very different.

Mark was stocky, medium height. He'd dressed in jeans, a pocket T-shirt, and boots. He paced back and forth in the waiting room, returning to his coffee cup on the counter now and then.

Bob noticed Mark's nervous habits—pacing and flicking his hair back a lot. He tried to be clinical, moving into his counselor mode. Mark must be very nervous about being here, he thought. I wonder if he's always this fidgety. Then he realized he was being a therapist again, as a way of distancing himself from his discomfort.

Bob himself was dressed casually but professionally in brown slacks, loafers, and a plaid sports shirt. His blond hair was short, and he wore aviator glasses. He looked as if he could be Mark's father.

Other members of the group chatted lightly. Watching the easy interaction between them all, Susan wished she were more outgoing. She wanted to say more than "Hi" but found her anxiety rising and her mind shutting down, so she backed off. Linda, she noticed, was quite comfortable visiting with Kathy.

Once everyone had settled in and was ready for group to begin, Szifra announced that Trina had called. Her father had died, so she would not be coming in, but she would be back next week. "Trina said he didn't suffer long," Szifra reported. The group received the news with obvious sadness. Szifra knew many of them thought of their own parents and the losses they had already suffered or knew were to come. She had planned to address feelings in tonight's group, and discussing how everyone felt hearing the news about Trina's father would be appropriate . . . except that

Bob and Mark didn't know Trina. In the end she decided to trust her instincts and move on.

Szifra had told Bob and Mark, as well as the other group members, that they would be asked to introduce themselves briefly, to share their family backgrounds and current family situations.

"I'd like everyone to introduce themselves to Mark and Bob, and Mark and Bob to introduce themselves to the rest of the group," she said, beginning the meeting. "Please say a little about yourself, then close by telling us how you're feeling."

Linda spoke first. "Hi." She smiled warmly at Bob and Mark. "I'm Linda. Both of my parents are active alcoholics. I have two sisters and one brother; two use and abuse drugs and alcohol. I'm married and have two daughters. Right now, I feel kind of nervous."

"Nervous about what?" Bob asked.

Linda was caught off guard. "I don't know exactly," she replied.

"But you must be nervous about something," Bob prodded her.

Most of the people in the group were stunned—not so much by Bob's words, but by the force with which he said them. Mark and Roger both recognized this was probably Bob's style. They'd been similarly confronted in other therapy groups while in treatment. Susan and Anne were extremely uncomfortable. Anne reacted physically, jerking her head back and literally backing away. Any semblance of conflict distressed and alienated her.

Susan felt herself numbing out, something she'd learned many ACOAs did as a mean of self-protection when they were feeling anxious. Sometimes they even became sleepy during fights or other high-anxiety times.

Szifra understood Bob wasn't trying to put Linda on the spot; he didn't intend to be critical. She knew, though, that Linda felt criticized. "Linda, we'll have time, if you'd like, to address Bob's interaction with you," Szifra said, acknowledging Linda's feelings without letting the focus of the group change. "I can tell it's made you uncomfortable. Is it okay if we finish the introductions first? Then you can have the time if you want it."

Linda nodded, relieved that Szifra didn't pressure her for immediate processing.

Bob felt confused, unsure why Linda had backed off. He saw no connection between what he'd said and her reaction. He decided she was overly sensitive.

Roger introduced himself next. "I'm a recovering alcoholic," he said. "My mother is recovering, too. I feel kind of uncomfortable right now. It's still a little hard for me to talk in new situations."

Szifra thanked him for his input and asked Mark to go next.

"I'm Mark," he began. "I'm thirty years old. I'm a recovering heroin addict." He was surprised at how easy it felt sharing such personal information in this group. He felt that they cared, even though he was meeting them for the first time. He decided to continue.

"I only recently realized that being a Child of an Alcoholic might have something to do with my life today," he said. "My father was an alcoholic; he's gone now. I'm divorced, no children. I'm feeling okay telling you about myself, probably because I was in groups while in treatment."

Mark talked on, longer than most ACOAs ordinarily would this early in group. He explained that for many years he'd seen no connection between his chemical dependency and his father's alcoholism. Only recently had he done some reading that led him to believe the ACOA issue was something he should look into. He spoke in almost reverent tones about his dad, making it clear that he thought highly of his father and would not want to change that.

Kathy spoke next, introducing herself to Bob and Mark. "My father, too, was an alcoholic," she said. "He died less than a year ago. I'm the third of six children. Of the ACOA roles, I'm a blend of the family mascot and the responsible child. Right now I'm feeling nervous because I'm talking about issues that are very personal to me."

Bob decided to plunge in. He introduced himself, then continued, "I'm fifty, a recovering alcoholic, now an alcoholism counselor. I'm married for the second time. My first marriage was destroyed by my alcoholism. I have two children from that marriage. I'm here to explore the ACOA issues I'm starting to recognize in myself, issues like control and rigidity."

"Thanks, Bob," Szifra said. "How are you feeling right now?"

"Pretty comfortable," he replied, nodding.

Kathy thought he seemed less comfortable than he said he was. He sat erect; his jaw seemed tight. Observing him, she realized the progress she was making. In the past she would have been so focused on her own anxiety and discomfort, she wouldn't have even noticed Bob's. She recognized she liked being more aware of others, acknowledging their feelings more. She also decided she was no longer so self-focused and self-conscious—a real change from how she'd been at the start of therapy. It felt good to acknowledge how much she'd already accomplished, rather than how much more work there was left to do. And she was giving herself more credit, which felt good. *I guess there really is hope,* she thought, smiling.

As the group members finished introducing themselves, Szifra passed out a long list of words. In an earlier workshop, she had learned how much ACOAs seemed to benefit from the "Feelings List," as it was called.

"Please take a few minutes to look over this list of words," she said as she passed out the papers. "Tonight we're going to talk about feelings and learn how to identify and understand them. It's one more tool for your toolbox."

The Feelings List

abandoned	admired
acceptable	affectionate
accepting	afraid
adequate	agitated

alive
alone
amazed
amused
angry
animated
annoyed
apart
appeased
appreciated
astonished
at a loss
at peace
attentive
attractive
bad
beautiful
bewitched
bored
bothered
bubbly
buoyant
burdensome
caged
callous
calm
capable
captivated
cared for
censored
cheerful
childlike
cold
comfortable
competent
composed
concerned
confident
confused
considered
contented

controlled
cordial
cornered
cozy
creative
curious
dead
defeated
dejected
depressed
delighted
delirious
deserving
desirable
disappointed
discouraged
disgusted
disinterested
distressed
disturbed
dull
eager
ecstatic
effervescent
elated
embarrassed
emotional
emphatic
enamored
enchanted
endured
energetic
enjoyment
enlightened
enriched
enthusiastic
entranced
envious
euphoric
exhausted
excited

expressive
failure
fascinated
fearful
feminine
fidgety
flabbergasted
fortunate
frantic
free
friendly
frightened
frustrated
fulfilled
fuming
furious
gay
generous
giddy
glamorous
gracious
grateful
gregarious
grief
guilt
handsome
happy
hateful
healthy
held back
hopeful
horrified
hospitable
hostile
hurt
hysterical
ill at ease
immobilized
immoral
impetuous
important

imposed upon
impressed
inadequate
included
indifferent
inferior
insecure
inspired
intelligent
interested
in the way
intoxicated
invigorated
irritated
jealous
joyful
jubilant
left out
let down
lively
lonely
looked up to
loved
lovely
lucky
lukewarm
managed
maneuvered
manipulated
masculine
masterful
meddlesome
melancholic
mixed up
morose
mortified
naughty
needed
negative
numb
optimistic

outgoing
out of control
overjoyed
overworked
pain
paralyzed
passionate
passive
patient
peaceful
pensive
perturbed
pessimistic
pestered
picked on
placated
pleased
posed
positive
powerful
pressured
productive
prosperous
protective
proud
purposeful
put down
put upon
put up with
quiet
receptive
refreshed
rejected
repelled
repugnant
repulsed
resentment
resigned
respected
responsive
restless

restrained
revitalized
romantic
sad
safe
satisfied
scared
secure
seductive
seething
sensitive
sentimental
serene
shaken
shamed
shocked
sincere
sociable
spiritual
stifled
stimulated
stubborn
stunned
subdued
submissive
subversive
successful
supported
surprised
susceptible
sympathetic
tactful
talented
tenderness
terrified
thankful
thoughtful
threatened
thrilled
tired
tolerated

tormented
tortured
transported
tranquil
trapped
triumphant
troubled
trusted
trusting
uncared for
uncomfortable
unconcerned
undemonstrative
understanding
understood
uneasy
unencumbered
unfair
unfeeling
unhappy
unloved

unreasonable
unwanted
unwelcome
unworthy
uplifted
upset
used
vibrant
victorious
virile
vivacious
vulnerable
wanted
warmed
weak
weary
wild
worried
worthless
worthy

As the group glanced through the list, Szifra continued, "These are only a few of the words that can describe how you are feeling."

"I can't believe this!" Michael commented. "There must be a couple hundred possible feelings on this list! I usually think in terms of being either happy, sad, or neutral."

"That's exactly what many of us do," Szifra confirmed. "I worked with a woman who had successfully blocked her feelings throughout childhood and throughout a twenty-year marriage to an alcoholic man. In therapy, I tried to help her get in touch with them. Whatever the situation or incident, her response to how she felt was, 'I was humiliated.'

"When I tried to get at other feelings she might have been experiencing, she could not understand what I was asking for. She felt she could only have one feeling at a time, and humiliation was the one. Finally I said, 'Pretend that ''humiliated'' does not exist. You cannot feel *humiliated*. Now tell me what you feel.'

''After a time, she was able to recognize she felt hurt, sad, let down, and scared. It was a tremendous breakthrough for her; she was able to understand that part of her reaction to what was going on included feeling hurt and scared. She was surprised to learn that, but once she did, she was able to move beyond the humiliation that had immobilized her.''

''When I first came to see Szifra,'' Kathy said, ''I told her my goal was not to feel anymore. Getting this list is a bit frightening! It makes me want to back away. My goal was to get rid of my depression. For that, I told Szifra, I was willing to sacrifice any possibility of good feelings. Not feeling at all would be wonderful, I thought.''

''I'm glad you brought that up, Kathy, and were willing to share it with the group,'' Szifra said. ''Would you say a little more about how you realized 'depressed' was not the only feeling you were experiencing?''

''Okay,'' Kathy said. ''Thinking about how I felt was not something I had ever done, needless to say! I always reacted to outside situations, things that were going on at work or with my family. When there was something troubling happening, I got through it fine. Afterward, I would be what I thought was depressed. I never really thought about it that much, I was just aware of it. After I accepted the fact that I couldn't find a permanent state of no feeling, I agreed to try looking closer at my feelings.

''I recalled several incidents when I had been recently depressed. I scrutinized the situations, trying to identify my feelings. One in particular was when one of my family members was arrested. In looking more closely at the incident, I realized I had felt angry, scared, and embarrassed, too.''

Kathy felt good that she was able to share what felt like a lot of personal information. This is sure new to be able to talk about such private issues, she thought.

''What did realizing that do for you?'' Szifra asked.

''Well, knowing more about how I felt gave me some tools to resolve my feelings,'' Kathy replied. ''Since the incident was in the past, I decided not to do anything about that particular time. Had I been able to identify my feelings at the time, though, I would have had several options.

"For instance, if I'd known I was angry, I could have chosen to let the family member involved know I felt angry," she said. "Being able to express it would have helped me. And chances are it would have helped that person, too, to know that I could not condone the behavior.

"If I'd known I was embarrassed," she continued, "I might have been able to help myself understand that it was perfectly normal to feel embarrassed when a family member is involved with the law. If I could have told myself, What another person chooses to do is no reflection on me, I could have let go of some of that 'depression' I thought I had."

"Wow," Roger said. "You've really said a lot. I don't mean in taking a lot of time, but in expressing how valuable it is to understand ourselves. Although I spent a lot of time in treatment working on issues like that, I sure can use more."

"There's a good book about this," Bob offered. "It's called *Feeling Good* by David Burns. Kathy, you were discussing self-talk, talking to yourself about a situation. Burns does a good job in his book on that issue. I recommend it."

"Thanks," Kathy said. She read a lot of self-help books and would no doubt read this one.

"I love all those positive feelings," Sarah said, scanning the list. "Who would have thought we could have this many different good feelings!"

"It is amazing," Linda said. "I'd love experiencing some of these—like 'I feel understood.' What an incredible feeling that would be. Or 'deserving.' That's one I don't feel much."

The group continued glancing at the list, laughing at words they found humorous or commenting on feelings they found desirable. Szifra asked them to think of an incident in which they had at first identified one feeling, then recognized a number of concurrent feelings.

After taking a couple of minutes to think, Sarah said, "Well, most of what I've felt in the last several years has been anger toward my ex-husband. When he left me, I let him and the rest of the world know I was angry. I'm still angry. But if had to be honest and admit to some other feelings, I'd also have to say I feel lonely, rejected, scared, and unloved."

She paused, trying to control her tears. "But being angry is easier for me. I can direct it at my ex and make him take the responsibility. Saying I'm lonely and scared is so self-revealing. It's like ripping my clothes off for the world to see everything about me. I don't like doing that. Now I guess I could add embarrassed."

"I can understand how you would feel vulnerable, Sarah," Szifra said. "Can you see that looking at and dealing with those other feelings could also give you some power back? If you can recognize that you are lonely, you can reach out and do something about your loneliness. Knowing you're scared might free you to evaluate the things you're feeling scared about and then work to overcome them."

"Putting it that way helps," Sarah agreed. "I like the idea of getting some power back. That guy has wiped me out once too many times. It's time I felt I had some control over my life again. Thanks."

"Who else has thought of an incident to share?" Szifra asked once she was sure Sarah had finished.

"I have," Linda said. "A few weeks ago, my oldest daughter announced out of the blue that she wanted to live with her father. When Lynn told me, I was totally overcome by this feeling that she didn't love me anymore. That was really all I could feel. Unloved and rejected by her.

"As the day and night wore on, I started to realize I was also feeling jealous that my ex-husband had a good relationship with her. I felt scared that my life would be thrown off balance if she did go live with him, that I wouldn't know how to cope with her being gone." She glanced at the list in her hands.

"Looking at this," she said, "I can find several other feelings that were going on. I felt confused. Disappointed that she'd rather live with him. Guilt. Maybe if I'd been a better mother, she wouldn't want to leave me. Hurt. I wanted her to like me best. Insecure, unsure of myself. I was worried. I can't believe how many of these feel-ings I can now recognize were going on for me that day and night.''

"Does it help knowing now?" Szifra asked.

Linda nodded. "I think so. It feels more normal to see a more complete picture. I mean, for a mother to instantly think her child doesn't love her anymore because she wants to live with her father is a little black and white. Knowing that I was feeling these other things makes it seem like I wasn't being so rigid or narrow in my focus, and that feels good. I guess I'm thinking it would be very normal for a person to experience all kinds of feelings in a situation like that. It's less 'Adult Child-ish' to see the bigger picture. That's growth for me.''

"So you feel better about yourself?" Sarah asked, pleased to find that she was able to listen empathically.

"Yes, I think so.''

"Linda, I'm really glad that you can say, 'It would be very normal for a person to feel what I felt,' '' Szifra said warmly. "That is a nurturing, comforting thing to tell yourself, as opposed to the critical messages we're more used to giving ourselves.''

Linda was pleased with Szifra's comment. "It helps me when you say things like that,'' she told her, "because I don't always see myself the way you see me. I guess I don't see the changes in me as easily as you see them. I keep thinking I'm the same, just as self-critical as ever. I like knowing I'm getting somewhere.''

"And I like being able to tell you. Keep up the good work,'' Szifra said, then asked who else had thought of an incident to tell the group about.

Susan laughed a little as she began, "I'm laughing because I've thought of many instances, and they all have the same feeling—'terrified.' No matter what's going on with me, I can usually best describe it by saying, 'I'm terrified.'

If I have to speak before a group, I'm terrified. I have to sit in here, I'm terrified. I think I need to do what you did with your client who was humiliated," she told Szifra. "I have to ask myself, 'What would I be feeling if I weren't feeling terrified?' I can think of feelings like frustrated, worried, embarrassed, and nervous. I'm so used to thinking in such high intensity about my fear, I forget I might be experiencing a normal amount of feeling for the situation. Truthfully, whenever I feel much, regardless of the feeling, I feel scared. As I say this, I realize it's even true for good feelings. If I get really excited about something, often I confuse that with fear or panic. I was so used to shutting down feelings, trying to be feeling-free, now when I let myself feel, it's pretty confusing."

Suddenly Susan felt self-conscious. I've gone on and on, she thought. She was used to censoring her words, measuring them out. She wondered if she sounded silly, saying she didn't know how to tell the difference between positive and negative feelings.

"I understand what you're saying, Susan," Anne said softly. "I've never thought it was a good use of time to worry about how I was feeling. It just didn't seem important or productive. My time was better spent getting something constructive done. Even now, getting into feelings doesn't feel very comfortable. It stirs up so many things I think I can't handle, I decide I'm better shutting them off. What difference would it make how I felt about a situation? I couldn't change it." She was surprised at how opinionated she'd been. But she became impatient with people who processed and reprocessed things they had no control over, anyway.

"That's where you have to be careful, Anne," Roger cautioned. "When you think the result might be changing someone or something. If you think that, you're setting yourself up for failure. In treatment they pounded it into my head that I couldn't change a darn thing about this world, but one. Me. I could change how I felt or what I did about something."

"So, I'm not supposed to let things bother me?" Anne asked, a little sharply for her.

Roger felt the slight sting in Anne's tone, and underneath he felt a bit tense. Then he decided to give himself a little time to think of what he'd like to say. A couple of months ago in an individual session, he and Szifra had discussed how he got stuck in conversations, which caused him to tense up and withdraw. This time he decided not to withdraw, despite his discomfort.

"I'm a little stuck, Anne. Let me think a second," he said calmly, leaning back and looking up while he thought.

"I guess I'd say if something happens that you couldn't have prevented or changed, you can decide not to let it beat you," he explained after a slight pause. "You can accept that it happened, that you couldn't have prevented it, but you have control over how much you will let it affect what you do. Will you give up and never try again if you fail once? Or will you come back with renewed determination?"

"That's an excellent way to phrase it, Roger," Szifra said encouragingly. "I want to add that we often may not have control over how we initially feel, though. Whatever we feel initially is okay. It's understandable, probably quite normal! Once we're aware, though, it helps to also be aware that we have choices. We have some choice over how much we'll let it affect what we do. Anne, how do you feel about what Roger said?"

"Well, since you said it was excellent, I guess I will say so, too, being the good adjuster," Anne said, smiling and bringing out her usually hidden sense of humor. "Really, though, I understand what Roger is saying. Carrying it out sounds awfully difficult to me. I guess I don't want to give up my practice of just blocking all feelings and keep on keeping on."

Michael spoke up. "Anne, I recently realized I do that, too. Letting myself feel anything is very new to me. In the past, if feelings started to surface, I kept busy. The first time Szifra brought up my feelings, she might as well have been speaking in another language. I had no idea what she meant.

Frankly, even though I'm beginning to understand, it's still hard for me. I'm tempted to use my old, reliable, runaway strategies.''

"What keeps you from doing that?" Bob asked.

"Because I end up physically ill, over and over," Michael replied. "I end up in bed for a few hours to a few days, wiped out. It also never helped me break the cycle. I watched myself go from the feelings to being sick over and over. It's been one too many times. I'm also noticing that it's not working well in my marriage," he added.

"You reminded me of my old pattern, Michael," Bob said. "Instead of keeping busy to block feelings, though, I'd drink. I told myself I was entitled to a few drinks. After all, everyone should be able to relax after work. When I was wound up after a high-stress day, a few drinks helped me relax. I was able to play with my kids, help with dinner preparations, talk calmly, and be involved with the family. I rationalized that anyone would do that. It seemed perfectly normal. But after years of running from my feelings with booze and trying without success to drink responsibly, I finally realized I had to abstain. No drinking. Period."

He paused briefly, then continued. "I thought I was doing great with feelings. After all, I'm a counselor, I go to AA and to alcoholism conferences about therapy and feelings. But when I read a book recently about Adult Children of Alcoholics, I realized I had a long way to go. I still want things to fit into neat little packages, black and white. Even feelings."

"That's my story, too," Mark admitted. "I altered my feelings with chemicals. The feeling I never could shut down for very long, though, was anger. I still don't know how to deal with anger. Either I swallow it and feel awful, or I get more angry than makes sense. I explode about it. When I used, I would go on verbal tirades. It was incredible. I never thought about the impact on others. I went from feeling anger to expressing it like crazy. It was a tremendous release, a release I haven't replaced since I've been straight."

"What do you do with your anger now?" Bob asked.

"Nothing much," Mark responded slowly. "Sometimes I'm overly sarcastic, or get on my soapbox. Maybe I need to find a physical release, a sport of some kind. You know, when I was younger, I used to play basketball for hours, all by myself. I'd stay out way past dark, and Mom would be calling me in. I'd forgotten about how much I played basketball until just now. Maybe that was a kind of release then."

"Is it something you'd think about trying again?" Bob asked.

"With the shape my body's in," Mark said wryly, "I doubt I could play long. But it would probably feel pretty good. Yeah, I'd give it a try."

"I used to get into fistfights when I drank," Roger said to Mark. "That rush of adrenaline felt good. Powerful. I'm so passive when I'm sober, I think I swallow my anger a lot. In fact, most of the time I can't tell when I'm angry. Like I'm so used to sitting on my anger, I can't even recognize it.

"This talk about feelings has reminded me about something else, too," he added. "I talked to Szifra about my father and his stern manner and emotional coldness. Even though Mom's the alcoholic, sometimes I think I've been more affected by Dad's behavior. Anyway, Szifra suggested it seemed like I was feeling both disappointment and understanding. That was the first time I realized I had mixed feelings. And that it was okay to have more than one feeling. I always thought I had to have one clear feeling. I spent so much time bouncing from one feeling to another, trying to choose. Do I feel angry? Do I feel sorry for him? As soon as I settled on one, 'Yes, I'm angry,' then the 'feel sorry' part would nag at me, so I'd focus on that. Then the angry part would haunt me, and on and on it would go.

"Finally, I realized I could feel both instead of either one or the other," he concluded. "It's helped me a lot. I don't feel like there's a civil war inside so often. And I feel less urgency to take action. I try to make decisions about my behavior, incorporating the mixture of feelings.''

''That hits home for me, too,'' Sarah said. ''When my dad was drinking I'd get so mad that I thought I hated him. Other times when he was kind and caring, and calling me 'kitten,' I knew I loved him. It was confusing, feeling love and hate for the same person. Especially my father. I guess I loved him and hated him both. Now, I realize I can love him and hate his alcoholism.

''I resent what I missed. I feel a little guilty for feeling that way, then I resent that he didn't rise above the addiction. I wanted a dad, and I never really got one. I'm mad at my mom, too. She was so smart, she should have gotten us help, and gotten Dad to AA or treatment.'' She spoke with more harshness than usual.

''It's amazing how much blame we put on the nonalcoholic,'' Linda observed.

''It's useful to note how much blaming there is,'' Szifra added. ''I don't want to minimize your feelings of loss, of having been ripped off. You did miss out on a lot. You did not have the childhood you deserved. Again, though, steering away from black-and-white thinking will be useful in the long run. Blaming the alcoholic or the nonalcoholic for everything is nonproductive. It will keep you stuck in either-or thinking.

''For most of us, there are multiple reasons for our losses,'' she explained. ''I don't want you to ignore the impact of losses you experienced as children and remaining effects today. I'm concerned, though, that as you blame others, you may also blame yourselves. 'It must have been my fault' is the slogan of too many ACOAs.''

''That's true for me,'' Susan said. ''When anything goes wrong—if there's a conflict with my husband, my boss, anyone—I always assume I did something wrong.''

''The perfectionists among you may also have a motto, 'It's okay for you, but I have a different standard for myself,' '' Szifra said. ''That makes it very difficult to accept 'normal.' ''

"I do that, too. Isn't that normal?" Linda said jokingly.

The group chuckled a bit about everyone's perception of "normal" and desire to be normal, whatever that was. "I never thought about the blaming that way," said Bob. "It's like if I'm judgmental about others, I'm more likely to be judgmental about myself. That really makes sense. Better to find a way to accept without so much fingerpointing, without having to establish if it was 'your fault' or 'my fault.' It seems pretty difficult, though."

Szifra agreed that it was difficult, then asked, "Has this discussion of feelings triggered anything else for anyone?" Glancing around the circle, she noticed that Michael seemed preoccupied, out of sync with the relaxed mood the group had taken on. "Michael, how about you?" she asked.

Michael looked up, undecided about whether to speak. He had been thinking about his wife's possible pregnancy and decided that he felt comfortable enough with the group to bring it up.

"I have some feelings I guess I'd like to mention," he began. "I think I've mentioned before that I planned not to have children. A few weeks ago my wife told me she thought she was pregnant. I was pretty upset and didn't know what to do. I just kept hoping she wouldn't be pregnant. I tried to avoid thinking about it, but it crept in. I was really nervous. And I didn't want to deal with my feelings about her being pregnant."

He spoke slowly and carefully. It was apparent the issue was a serious one for him, not one he could handle casually. "Today I found out she isn't pregnant." He sighed sitting back on his chair. "I would have given anything for that news at first, but now I don't feel relieved. I can't believe it, but I think I feel disappointed. I'm really confused because I was sure I knew what I wanted."

Linda reached out to Michael, telling him she understood. She'd experienced those same mixed feelings, she said, and they had caused her to doubt herself. "I've learned, though, that I often have mixed feelings, but in the past I buried them, only allowing myself to have one at a time.

When the others crept out, I was blown away. It was just too confusing. It really is hard at first, but it does get more comfortable once you're used to it and recognize what's happening.''

"Maybe you're not as certain about having or not having children as you once thought, Michael," Kathy said. "You're entitled to reevaluate your feelings or even change how you feel."

"I guess I'm going to think more about that," Michael said.

For a few minutes the group continued discussing Michael's issue in particular and mixed feelings in general. At the end of discussion Michael thanked everyone for their assistance. He was glad he'd brought the issue up, although he'd felt uncomfortable. It was new for him to open up about how he was feeling, and especially when he was unsure about how he felt. It was only recently that he'd begun even to talk about feelings, and that was only when he felt in control of the situation. Discussing an emotional issue that he hadn't worked through at all was new.

Szifra would say, "Pat yourself on the back!" Michael thought. Increased trust, increased risk, increased intimacy. Hmmm—progress! And to top it off, I feel lighter, too, not so weighed down. Maybe there is something to all this! And maybe if I learn to get comfortable talking about these things, it'll relieve some internal pressure and I won't get so depressed and immobilized. Boy, that would be great!

Szifra told Michael she was glad he felt comfortable enough with himself and the group to bring up an issue that was troubling him. Then, as the meeting ended for the evening, she thanked everyone for sharing, mentioning how pleased she was with Bob's and Mark's participation in the group.

Sarah said, "I'm surprised how well you guys fit in so early. I felt very comfortable having you here. No wait, let me check the Feelings List! Maybe that's not exactly the right word. I felt effervescent? No, not really. Inspired?

Well, that's going a little far! I think I'll stick with comfortable," she said.

"Me too," Susan said, laughing. "I was afraid I'd be terrified with two new members, but I felt relatively comfortable."

"I'm glad you joined the group," Michael said, and others nodded in agreement.

My Observations and Reactions to Meeting 7

Anne, 39, child care worker, lost child role in family, father died from alcoholism seven years ago.
Observations/progress noted:

Bob, 50, alcoholism counselor, scapegoat in family, recovering, mother alcoholic, now deceased.
Observations:

Kathy, 33, secretary, mascot/responsible role in family, father died from alcoholism this year.
Observations/progress noted:

Linda, 36, nurse, responsible role in family, both parents are alcoholic, living.
Observations/progress noted:

Mark, 30, welder, scapegoat role in family, recovering, father died from alcoholism six years ago.
Observations:

Michael, 38, PR/advertising, responsible role in family, father is alcoholic, mother prescription drug–addicted, living.
Observations/progress noted:

Roger, 20, student, lost child/scapegoat in family, recovering, mother also recovering.
Observations/progress noted:

Sarah, 36, high school teacher, responsible role in family, father died from alcoholism five years ago.
Observations/progress noted:

Susan, 32, accountant, lost child/responsible role in family, father died from alcoholism two years ago.
Observations/progress noted:

Szifra, therapist
Observations:

Observations about me during this meeting:

My feelings during this meeting:

Issues I'd like to explore further:

My reactions to this meeting:

What I learned about myself during this meeting:

MEETING 8

Rewriting Our Family Rules

IT'S TUESDAY NIGHT again—sometimes the weeks just speed by, Sarah thought. Lately it seems like it's always Tuesday night!

She thought back three years. Divorce time, when each hour seemed a week long. Yet when a year had passed, she recalled thinking it couldn't have been a whole twelve months. Time was such a paradox: an hour could feel like a week, yet a year could somehow speed by.

She thought about her ex-husband, who was still drinking. How different her life was now that it didn't revolve around his moods, his needs, his alcoholism. Although she still had rough moments, she realized how little stress she had now compared with the last several years of her marriage.

I can't imagine tolerating the inconsistency and putdowns from him, she thought. I couldn't do it today. I *wouldn't* do it today.

Sarah used to wonder what was wrong with her. Her ex-husband so often told her she was strange, even crazy. She used to think he was probably right: she did act crazy at times. Now she knew much of her behavior was in reaction to his. Without his drinking and associated behaviors, her emotions were on a much more even keel.

I liked being married, though, she thought with a hint of regret. I guess I liked knowing my role.

Now Sarah found she had to make more of an effort socially. I was used to going along, based on what he was up to. It's hard to be the captain of the ship, she reflected, thinking co-captain was a more comfortable, familiar role. Then she realized she actually had been a passenger, following his program for her.

She thought about her recent date and how good it felt to go out. She worried, too. It's new, she thought. I hate beginning again, trying to establish familiarity and comfort. I'm just not feeling confident in those areas.

Sarah's divorce had shattered her trust. Learning that trust and intimacy were often ACOA issues, she knew now she had gone into her marriage handicapped. She'd never had good role models for marriage, never learned to share feelings, be assertive, or negotiate differences. Her "never rock the boat" style only perpetuated the problems. Of course, she hadn't realized that during the marriage.

Sarah liked group. Maybe it met some of her social needs, although it was more than that, she knew. She felt safe there; she was able to share more of herself.

As Sarah dressed for group, she remembered an article she'd read in the paper about protesters getting arrested. For some reason she had immediately thought of Roger. He'd said a few things before and after group that had led her to believe he was active in social issues. He took strong stands on human rights and wasn't afraid to verbalize them. Interesting, Sarah thought, he's really pretty quiet. But when an individual's rights are threatened, it lights a fire in Roger. At the end of the article, she'd noticed that a Roger somebody was reported as having been arrested. She didn't know his last name but thought it might have been Roger.

I could ask him, I guess, Sarah thought, then laughed to herself, realizing how strange that felt to her. Sometimes in group she wasn't sure when to speak up and when to "mind her own business." It was hard to know how to strike a good balance.

When she held back, she felt powerless, unassertive, even wimpy. When she spoke up, she felt guilty, pushy, as if she were invading someone else's space. Her ex-husband used to tell her she was domineering. But recently people complimented her on her gutsiness, saying they wished they were able to speak up the way she did. Sarah was confused by the conflicting messages.

Szifra had suggested that perhaps she should update her sense of herself. Maybe the "pushy" label was out of date, belonging to the era with her ex-husband. Maybe she'd reached a balance between being aggressive and passive. She wondered if her ex-husband had felt threatened by her assertiveness and experienced it as pushiness. It was not unusual for active alcoholics and untreated ACOAs, too, to feel pushed around when others told them how they felt or what they needed. They frequently lacked the ability to respond nondefensively. Instead they felt attacked, mowed down. Sarah remembered feeling like that at times, too. Probably an ACOA issue, she thought.

As she arrived for group, Roger was filling everyone in on his arrest.

Well, I don't have to worry about him, Sarah thought, smiling to herself. She listened as Roger explained that he had never expected their protest to get the attention it did. The media and the police had played it up more than his group had expected. Although he wanted the issue to come to the attention of the public, he admitted the arrest was distasteful.

"I guess it's part of doing what I believe in," he said. Sarah wondered if Roger was changing. At first she'd thought he was quiet but he hadn't seemed quiet lately.

As Roger talked, Mark remembered his younger years and his defiance of what was called "the Establishment" back then. He felt a longing for the days when he didn't have to worry so much about the rent getting paid, when he could pursue more idealistic avenues. He congratulated Roger for standing up for his convictions.

As group began, Sarah noticed that everyone seemed eager to begin. Trina was introduced to Bob and Mark. It turned out Bob and Trina were already acquainted through AA.

Szifra suggested they postpone any reactions to last week's meeting and asked Trina if she could use some time to share her feelings.

"I could," Trina said. "Dad's dying was rough, much rougher than I would have guessed. Not just being with my family, which would test anyone's patience. The rough part was how I reacted to losing my dad. I was surprised at how intensely I felt it. So many times I'd wished he was dead, and now that he was, all I could do was cry. There was no relief in his death; at least I haven't felt any yet. The rage and anger and hurt I've felt about all his abuse seems to be gone. I feel like I'm left with a big, empty hole.

"I guess it's finally accepting I can never have the relationship I wanted to have with him," she continued, "a relationship where I could be closer to him, understand him, where I could talk about my feelings and be heard and understood. A relationship in which he'd tell me he loved me and I'd know he meant it."

Trina choked on her words, sharing her emotions openly. The group felt her sadness and disappointment.

Kathy's eyes filled with tears. Anne was crying, too. The room was quiet. Roger's face reflected his thoughts, as he wonder~ if he would ever have a close relationship with his father. He felt sad, too. Since his mother had begun recovery, his relationship with her had gotten increasingly close. But his emotional distance with his father had stayed the same.

Szifra reached over, touching Trina's hand to let her know her tears were okay. Trina continued talking about her father and her feelings now that he was gone. She continued to cry, not even trying to hold back the tears. She ended by saying, "I'm feeling very self-conscious because I'm not used to showing my emotions, but it also feels good to let this hurt out. I feel better. I know you guys care. I can feel it. And that part feels good. It still is real hard to let feelings out in front of people, though." She looked around the circle, smiling her appreciation through her tears.

Anne asked if there was anything she could do to help.

"I don't know right now, but if I think of something, I'll let you know," Trina said. "Thanks for offering."

Bob spoke for a few minutes about the loss of his mother. "I went through all kinds of phases. First I felt guilty, then I went through my regret stage. I regretted we never had a close relationship. I regretted that our lives had been so busy with unimportant things. Then I went through an angry stage, when I was really angry she drank herself to death. I blamed her for not taking care of herself, which could have prevented her early death. Then I went through a period of feeling hurt. Now I'm mostly reconciled, but there are times when I feel so ripped off because of Mom's alcoholism and its devastating effects." Bob sighed and sat back, letting his voice and body language reveal his disappointment.

"Generally, though, I think Mom was a victim, too," he concluded. "We both lost out because of alcoholism."

"I feel a lot of those same things, too," Mark said. "I'm probably not as far along in accepting Dad's death, though."

Susan surprised everyone by saying that she mostly felt relief when her father died. "I rarely think of Dad positively, and I almost never miss him," she said quietly.

"How do you feel about sharing that with us, Susan?" Szifra asked.

"I feel badly having said it to others. I feel exposed," Susan answered. "And I wonder what others think of me now."

"Are you okay with others telling you?" Szifra asked. Susan replied that she was.

Without prompting, Mark offered, "I think Susan's feelings are perfectly reasonable." Turning to Susan, he said, "I'm sure not judging you."

Szifra noted to herself that in earlier weeks, most group members had spoken mostly to her. Now, instead of talking about each other to her, they generally addressed each other directly, as Mark had done with Susan.

Sarah echoed Mark's thoughts, adding, "Frankly, I feel

envious. I wish I felt more pure relief. It would probably be more healthy, given the circumstances. I guess I must still believe there's a law that says, 'Never say anything against your parents.' "

Michael nodded. "Frankly, I think I'll feel like you do, Susan, when my dad dies. I hope I can be honest and healthy enough to tell people, too. I respect your ability to do that."

Kathy said, "It makes me feel sad, too, that so many of us have incomplete or even empty relationships with one or both of our parents. All any of us really wanted was a warm, caring, consistent relationship with the two people who matter most. Then we learned to turn off those wishes. We built walls to survive. Now, as adults, those walls don't always serve us well. In fact, they can get in the way of developing and maintaining good relationships. It's all pretty sad to me."

Susan thanked everyone for sharing their reactions and said it helped.

"I'm pleased you were able to be open, Susan," Szifra said, and pointed out how much progress Susan was making.

"Sarah's remark, 'Never say anything against your parents,' is a good opening for tonight's topic, family rules," she remarked, turning to the agenda scheduled for the evening's group. "I would like to explore some of the family rules you grew up with. These rules may have been spoken or they may have only been implied. Somehow, you knew the rules dictating your actions. Today, you may continue to honor these without even realizing it. Without trying to make any judgments about their appropriateness, let's take a few minutes to recall what rules guided your family."

Getting up to pull an easel closer to the circle, Szifra explained, "I'll jot down the rules as you say them. Let's go ahead and write Sarah's down," she said, and wrote "Never say anything against your parents."

Turning back to the group, she continued, "Say anything that comes to mind. Jump in free-style," she encouraged them. "Who's thought of another family rule?"

"The biggies in our family were 'Don't rock the boat' and 'Don't make waves,' " Bob said. "And, no, my father was not a navy man. I'm not sure why both rules have to do with the sea," he joked.

" 'Don't upset Mother,' " Linda said. " 'And don't do anything to make Dad angry.' "

" 'Don't talk. Don't tell anyone,' " Sarah offered, stressing the word *anyone*.

" 'Family business is family business,' " said someone else. Szifra wrote quickly to keep up with the group.

Mark said, "Along that same line, 'Family comes first' and 'Be loyal to your family.' "

"That reminds me of a needlework instruction book I saw this week," Kathy said. "The book had a pattern for a sample with the saying, 'Family is everything.' I couldn't believe the significance of that."

"Wow," Trina said. "Get that done up in needlepoint and hang it on the front door. And while you're at it, add 'Stick up for your family no matter what.' And, right with that one, 'Don't make friends outside the family.' "

" 'Nothing is wrong,' " Susan suggested next.

" 'Everything is fine,' " Kathy said, expanding on Susan's rule.

"We had a general rule that implied 'Don't feel,' " Michael said. "That included 'Don't laugh, don't cry, don't touch, don't trust.' "

" 'Do as I say, not as I do,' " someone else tossed in.

"How about 'Don't ask for explanations, just do it'?" said Roger.

" 'Don't wear out your welcome,' " Anne said. "And 'Be quiet and stay out of the way.' "

" 'Don't talk back,' " Michael said.

Szifra's poster board was getting crowded. She started to write smaller, sensing that the group was just getting warmed up.

" 'Your problems are not important,' " someone said harshly, imitating a stern parent.

" 'Children have no rights,' " Trina said.

"Speaking of right," Linda said, " 'Parents are always right.' "

" 'Be thankful for what you have,' " said Kathy.

" 'Don't want anything, either,' " Michael emphasized. As he spoke, he realized how big this was for him. Don't want anything, he thought. Don't hope for anything. This is it in life. If you let yourself want anything, you'll crash, because you won't get it. For him this applied to wanting material things as well as emotional support, he realized.

Michael had only recently become aware that he kept himself from hoping out of fear and mistrust. He still was unsure about how he planned to change this, if at all. He vacillated between thinking, I'm right. It's just smart to be the way I am, and, What's wrong with hoping and trying to effect change? What's wrong with asking for what I need and want? He realized it was a big job, because right now it was difficult to identify what he needed and wanted.

Tuning back in, Michael heard Bob saying, " 'The good host pushes the beer. The good guest drinks it.' " The group laughed at his rule, realizing at the same time how seriously some people took it.

" 'Keep your feelings and thoughts to yourself. Bury them if you have to. Just don't feel,' " Susan said.

"That's right." Trina laughed. " 'Don't even have feelings. If you do, don't tell me about them. Never discuss them. Period.' "

Roger was quieter than usual. He spoke up during a pause. "I think a rule in my house was, 'Your feelings aren't right unless I approve them.' "

The group grew quiet as several reread what Szifra had written. It seems like a lot of rules, Kathy thought. A lot more than the Ten Commandments.

"Does anyone remember anything about anger?" Szifra asked.

"Oh, heavens, yes," Trina said. " 'Don't get angry'!"

" 'Or be angry,' " Sarah added.

"Certainly 'Never express anger,' " Susan said in a chastising tone.

" 'Life is too short to be angry,' " Anne spoke up.

"Unless you're the parent, of course," Trina added. "One set of rules for the kids, another for the adults."

" 'Don't fight,' " Mark added.

" 'Always maintain control,' " Bob said. " 'If control is not possible, exert more effort!' "

The group laughed a little as Szifra wrote down Bob's last rule. It seemed so ridiculous, yet it was all too true for many of them.

" 'Don't get too close,' " Linda said.

"Oh, that's going to make us think of all kinds of rules," Michael predicted as he offered his own: " 'Don't show affection for each other.' "

" 'Don't say "I love you," ' " Trina said.

" 'Don't cry,' " Roger added.

" 'If you don't quit crying, I'll give you something to cry about,' " Mark said. "I heard that one a lot. It was a rule often spoken in my family."

" 'Shut up or I'll give you something to cry about' was how it was said in my house," Bob said.

" 'Put a smile on your face,' " Kathy said.

"You're kidding," Sarah said, almost laughing.

"No, I'm not," Kathy said.

Trina had turned quite serious. Now she spoke up. "In my home, it was 'Quit crying,' sometimes accompanied by the belt. When my dad got real mad and was beating us, he wouldn't stop until we'd stopped crying. Great way to get you in touch with feelings, isn't it?"

Kathy and Anne said, as they had at other times, how sad they felt at hearing such stories. "I feel guilty even being here," Anne said.

In past weeks Szifra had reassured them that their losses were important, that they had been affected by alcoholism, too. This time Trina said it for her. "Look, you guys, it was no picnic! It really stank. But don't downplay the hurt you experienced, too. Both of your fathers cut their lives short because of alcoholism. You lost out, too."

After a minute Trina suggested they get back to the rules.

Sarah said she remembered hearing "People should solve their own problems."

"How about, 'Be responsible'?" Michael asked.

"Oh, and 'Do your best,' " Kathy continued.

" 'If it's worth doing, it's worth doing well,' " Mark said. "Gosh, I can hear my mom saying that. It makes me feel kind of sad."

After a pause, Bob said, " 'Be the best you can be.' "

" 'Do everything perfectly or you are worthless,' " Linda added.

" 'Perfection is the norm,' " Susan said. " 'Anything less is unacceptable.' "

" 'You must superachieve to be valued,' " someone else offered.

" 'Don't expect too much from life,' " said Trina. "And I didn't. Not for years and years. I followed that rule very well."

"Yeah, me too," Michael said.

By this time Szifra had filled the poster board. "Time out," she called as she leaned the poster against the filing cabinet where everyone could see it. Reaching out for another blank board, she said, "Okay, any others?"

" 'Work before play,' " Mark remembered.

"For us, too!" Kathy said. "I mean, reading the funny papers in the daylight hours was not a good use of our time."

" 'If you see something that needs to be done, do it,' " Sarah said shaking her finger to emphasize her words.

" 'Don't just stand there, do something,' " Mark said.

" 'Be productive with your time,' " Roger threw out.

" 'You must always have something constructive to do,' " Anne said, smiling rather self-consciously. "I feel funny giving that rule. I have to admit I still adhere to it."

"It's good you recognize that," Szifra said, writing rapidly to catch up.

" 'Don't relax or you'll get lazy and worthless,' " Trina said. "I can't believe how quickly we thought of all these!" Waving her arms, she asked the group, "What a bunch of cruddy rules, don't you think? No wonder we're messed up about feelings. So many rules against normal feelings.''

Michael nodded. ''It makes me mad,'' he said. ''I have so much new stuff to learn, and so much old stuff to 'unlearn.' It's a lot of work, and so hard to do. It's difficult changing these old patterns.''

''Especially because we're not always even consciously aware of still following these old rules,'' said Sarah, somewhat bitterly. This discussion had dredged up some very uncomfortable feelings. ''Parents should have to get permits before they're allowed to have kids. Who cares about marriage licenses? Childbearing licenses are what should be required, and only after being certified competent.''

''I understand what you're saying, Sarah,'' Anne said. ''I worry so much about that with my own children. How do I know what I'm doing is right? How much am I hurting them without even realizing it? All my ACOA issues are being handed down!''

As the group moved into a discussion of parenting skills, Szifra sat back down, facilitating only when the discussion seemed to need her input. She felt good about the group's response tonight; everyone seemed involved in the topic. She noticed, though, that Kathy had grown quiet. She seemed to be off in her own reverie.

And she was. As the group discussed how the rules were affecting their lives today, it dawned on Kathy that a good part of who she was stemmed from the rules she followed in her family. Because of that, she was realizing, her adult relationships had been affected.

It's like I was programmed, she thought. Not enough of who I've been resulted from my own choices. Too much of me has been reaction, rather than active choices. I married someone who wasn't raised by the same rules. No wonder it didn't last. Although if he had been raised by the same rules, that would probably have been disastrous, too.

Gradually the group's discussion died down. Looking at those early family rules had prompted all kinds of feelings and thoughts. Szifra took advantage of the lull in conversation to suggest, "Let's take some power here!"

She rose and picked up the two poster boards. "You don't have to live by these rules any longer," she reminded them. "You are the adults now. You can write your own rules. Let's start by rewriting these."

She propped the first poster back on the easel. "Let's go through these one by one and decide whether we'll keep, reject, or modify the rule. Don't forget, you may not all want the same rules."

As the group shouted, "Kill it off!" "Get rid of it!" and "Out!" Szifra drew red lines through those no longer appropriate. A few were modified, such as "Be thankful for what you have, but know it's okay to want other things." Only "Be responsible" was kept without alteration. When the review was finished, she propped the posters against the file cabinet and pulled out a third, setting it on the easel.

"How about some brand-new rules, more appropriate for today?" she asked.

Trina began, "It's okay to say Dad was an alcoholic."

"Or Mom," added Roger.

"It's okay for children to speak their minds," Bob suggested.

"It's okay to make my own decisions," Anne said.

"It's okay to talk about my feelings. All feelings are valid," Susan offered.

"My family is not superior," Linda said. "We have much to learn from, share with, and enjoy with other families."

"It's okay not to hang on to relationships that don't hold enough rewards for me," Mark said.

Anne suggested, "It's okay to speak up. It's okay to discuss issues."

"Well, since you're being so brave"—Susan smiled over at Anne—"I'll say, 'It's okay to have my own opinion.' "

"Hooray for you guys!" Trina shouted enthusiastically.

"I'd like to add, 'It's okay to argue,' " Sarah spoke up.

"Oh, I'm not sure about that," Anne teased.

"And it's okay to be sad sometimes," Kathy added. "I don't have to smile all the time."

"I like the shift you made, Kathy," Szifra said, "to 'I don't have to . . .' "

"It's okay to be angry and talk about it," Michael offered. "Healthy, happy people get angry. It's okay for me to get angry. I hope I can learn this one."

Szifra wrote more slowly than when she had written the early childhood rules. And it took the group longer to decide about rules they felt were appropriate. After a lifetime of too many rigid rules, they were putting a great deal of thought into this exercise.

"It's okay for me to have feelings," Roger said, "and it's okay for me to share them. I feel like you, Michael. I hope I can do it! Even though I know it's okay, it's still very hard to do."

"It's good, healthy, and life-giving to have feelings and express them," Sarah added, embellishing Roger's suggestion.

"That was a pretty fancy one, Sarah," Trina teased.

Everyone laughed, especially Sarah. "Highfalutin, huh?" she said.

"How about, It's okay to like myself?" Michael asked, and everyone nodded. "And," he added, "it's okay to have wants. Or let's say, It's okay for *me* to have wants."

"It's even okay to ask for my needs to be met," Trina suggested.

"It's okay to ask for help," Roger said.

Mark teased, "Yes, but is it okay for *you* to ask for help, Roger?"

"All right," Roger said, laughing, "It's okay for *me* to ask for help!"

"I have a right to ask for what I need," Bob said.

"It's okay to buy myself special treats or just something I want," Michael suggested. He decided he liked saying these out loud and hoped he could get more comfortable living the new rules as well.

Linda asked Szifra to write, "It's okay for me to work

toward dreams and wishes and expect to get them fulfilled.''

"It's okay for me to cry," Susan offered, and the group gave her affirmation for that one. "Well, then while I'm on a roll," she said, "I'll add, I don't have to be perfect.''

"Right on!" Mark said and added, "It's okay to be myself and have fun.''

Szifra noticed that the more the group got into this, the more permission they were giving themselves to do all kinds of things. She loved watching them break the rigid family roles, replacing them with permission to be themselves, to share their feelings, and to have fun.

"It's okay to play," Kathy said. "Now, if someone would only teach me!''

"It's okay to be silly!" Sarah said, enjoying herself. It was fun coming up with such extravagant ideas.

"I think we should say we not only think it's okay to play and relax," Anne suggested, "but that play and relaxation, enjoying life, can be very important. Although I'm with you on that one, Kathy, I need help in this area, too! A lot of help!" She laughed.

"The flip side of fun," said Susan, "would be, I don't have to be a workaholic.''

Mark nodded. "And even it's okay not to be successful monetarily. My family would never be surprised that's one I thought of!" he said, laughing.

"I decided we needed to modify the 'Be responsible' rule, too," Trina said. "It's okay to be responsible to others if we are also responsible to ourselves. I mean, it's okay to have a balance between work and fun. That's responsible, too.''

"I agree, now that you mention it," Sarah said.

"This has been great," Szifra said, pleased. She pointed to the poster, which listed the new rules the group had come up with. "I hope you are all proud of yourselves for replacing the rigid rules, which constricted you, with new rules, which offer you freedom," she said.

"Actually, it's been fun," Kathy said. "A conscious effort to look at the rigidity I maintained, but a real opportunity to break out of it.''

The others agreed. They all felt excited about the opportunity the new rules gave them.

"One last one before we stop," Trina suggested. "It's okay not to clean house. Crud on the rug has never killed anyone!"

My Observations and Reactions to Meeting 8

Anne, 39, child care worker, lost child role in family, father died from alcoholism seven years ago.
Observations/progress noted:

Bob, 50, alcoholism counselor, scapegoat in family, recovering, mother alcoholic, now deceased.
Observations/progress noted:

Kathy, 33, secretary, mascot/responsible role in family, father died from alcoholism this year.
Observations/progress noted:

Linda, 36, nurse, responsible role in family, both parents are alcoholic, living.
Observations/progress noted:

Mark, 30, welder, scapegoat role in family, recovering, father died from alcoholism six years ago.
Observations/progress noted:

Michael, 38, PR/advertising, responsible role in family, father is alcoholic, mother prescription drug–addicted, living.
Observations/progress noted:

Roger, 20, student, lost child/scapegoat in family, recovering, mother also recovering.
Observations/progress noted:

Sarah, 36, high school teacher, responsible role in family, father died from alcoholism five years ago.
Observations/progress noted:

Susan, 32, accountant, lost child/responsible role in family, father died from alcoholism two years ago.
Observations/progress noted:

Trina, 45, shipping clerk, scapegoat role in family, recovering, father quit drinking a few years ago.
Observations/progress noted:

Szifra, therapist
Observations:

Observations about me during this meeting:

My feelings during this meeting:

Issues I'd like to explore further:

My reactions to this meeting:

What I learned about myself during this meeting:

Feeling Powerless

TRINA RESTED a minute in her downtown apartment. She sat back, collecting her thoughts and looking around her. Her home was small but neat; money had been tight the past several years, so furnishings were sparse. Even though she owned relatively little, she felt good about how far she'd come. Her small color television was her most expensive possession, but her sobriety was by far her most valued.

Trina had grown up in poverty. Often there'd been barely enough food to get by, and she'd known many hungry days and nights. But she hadn't gone without money since she'd left home years ago. There were times in her drinking days when she'd forget to eat, of course. And as her alcoholism progressed, her hangovers would sometimes be so bad that she couldn't eat. Then she'd developed ulcers and other stomach problems.

This old body has tolerated a lot of abuse, she thought. I'm surprised I'm still alive! The last time she'd been tempted to drink again, she'd discussed her feelings with Szifra. Together they had played out a scenario of her liver talking to Trina: "C'mon, Trina, you're killing me! You know I've held up better than most, given the level of abuse. There's only one of me. I'm wearing out. Why do you want to hurt me?" It had seemed like an absurd little play, but it had increased Trina's concern for her physical health.

As she learned more about physiology and what her body had been through as a result of alcoholism, poor nutrition, and lack of exercise, Trina realized she had continued the abused child cycle as an adult by further neglecting and abusing her own body. It had made her feel sad, but it had strengthened her sobriety, too.

Checking the time, Trina decided she'd better head out for group. Get another fix of support, she thought, laughing to herself. Even in recovery she often used dependency terms. Humor helped her deal with the serious issues.

The evening's session began with Szifra announcing that neither Linda nor Roger would be there. They had both called to say that they were sick. Then she asked for reactions to last week's discussion of old and new rules.

"I liked last week a lot," Sarah said cheerfully. She was in an especially good mood. She'd met Susan for coffee before group and had really enjoyed their one-on-one interaction. She had called Susan on impulse to see if she'd like to meet and was delighted when Susan had agreed.

"I liked throwing out the old rules and writing new ones," Michael said. "I know it will take a long time to incorporate them automatically in my life, but I like knowing what I'm aiming for. Before this group, nothing felt okay if it had to do with feelings."

He paused a minute, deciding whether to bring something up now or wait to see what the agenda was going to be. Finally he indicated he was through by sitting back in his chair and looking over at Szifra.

"Thanks, Michael," Szifra said, and paused, sensing his indecision. "Anyone else?" she asked when it was clear he had finished.

"I was glad I spoke up so much," Susan confided. "Once I got the first rule out, it seemed pretty easy, so I kept on. Also, so many were popping into my mind, it wasn't like I had to think very hard about what to say."

"I'm glad you spoke up, too, Susan," Szifra said. "Your contributions were valuable. And it was nice watching you break old 'invisible Susan' patterns."

"Even I spoke up without being asked," Anne said, feeling a little silly, as though she were asking for recognition, but also feeling like she deserved it. "I liked being able to."

"I'm glad it's getting easier, Anne," Szifra said, acknowledging her efforts. "You have so much to offer."

"You did speak out more, Anne. It was great," Sarah affirmed.

"I got a lot out of realizing so many of us had the same or similar rules in our families," Bob said. "I had to give up feeling I was unique, of course, but it helped in lots of ways, too."

Mark agreed with Bob, and a discussion followed about how strange it felt to share so many similarities with people you were just getting to know.

"Does anyone else want to add anything?" Szifra asked during a lull.

Michael decided it was now or never. He couldn't wait for any more appropriate moments. "I have something," he said hesitantly.

"Go ahead, Michael," Szifra encouraged him.

"Well, it's not a reaction. It's something I need some help with. It may not be a group issue, though. I guess I should have checked this out with you ahead of time, Szifra. It came up so suddenly, and I've debated about whether to mention it at all, so here I am unprepared."

"Michael, if it's something you feel comfortable bringing up in group, I want you to," Szifra said. "A big part of our purpose is to provide support for each other. If it seems rather like an individual issue, one the entire group could benefit from, we can address that and schedule an individual session if you want one. I'd like each of you to feel free to bring up anything, and as a group we can decide if it is a group or individual issue. None of you have to check it out with me ahead of time. Do you feel comfortable continuing, Michael?" Szifra asked.

"I think I want to. I'm not especially comfortable, but I've got to talk to somebody." Michael sat forward on his chair, looking down at his hands as he spoke.

The other group members sat quietly, sensing something serious. Kathy felt scared, afraid to hear what he might mention. Anne sat rigidly, expecting something very heavy.

"Begin when you're ready, Michael," Szifra said softly.

He looked up at Szifra, his eyes filled with tears. "I got a telephone call last Wednesday night from my sister who lives in Florida. She was drunk and feeling down. I've had little contact with anyone in my family, so I was surprised to hear from her. She called to tell me she needed me." He wiped his eyes and went on, "She told me Dad had sexually abused her when she was young."

Michael sat quietly. He could hear "sexually abused" echoing over and over in his mind. Where did I get my nerve? he wondered to himself. How could I have brought this up?

Kathy sat stunned. This is bigger than I ever would have guessed, she thought, and glanced at Szifra. After a long silence Szifra took the lead. "Michael, do you want to say more?"

"Does it seem like something I should wait and talk to you about alone?" he asked.

"I think it's relevant for group. There's so much sexual abuse in alcoholic families, I think it would be appropriate to process it here," Szifra responded. "How do the rest of you feel?"

"I've wanted to bring it up," Trina said softly. "I was just waiting for the right time."

"It's okay with me," Bob said. The others agreed without saying too much.

"I can tell I've dropped a bomb," Michael said. "We've never been this quiet. Steph called me Wednesday night. She's been abusing alcohol a while, so I wasn't surprised she was drunk. But I was surprised when she told me about Dad. At first I didn't want to believe her. I thought it was the liquor talking. Then I started to listen better, and I felt she was telling me the truth. After I hung up, I said, 'No, it's a lie.' Now I don't know what to think.

"I had no idea anything like that was going on," he continued. "I was still living at home when it happened. She was twelve the first time, she said, so I would have been thirteen. How could I not have known what was happening in my own house? I was devastated when I hung up the phone. I didn't work Thursday or Friday. I felt physically sick, like I had the flu. I worried a lot. And mostly I felt scared to death." He fell silent, staring at his hands. At last he looked up.

"To find out my sister had gone through such hell was awful," he said. "Sexual abuse, I thought, only happened in terrible places, not our middle-class home, even though it was an alcoholic home. Worse, though, was finding out my father was capable of such monstrosities. No, I can't say which side of it was worse; all I know is I feel the deepest pain of my life. I wish my father had been killed in the war so none of us would have been born."

Michael's voice became firmer as he spoke. His pain was evident, but now his anger was surfacing. "I hate my father for this. I feel awful. And I don't know what to do now. Should I confront Dad? Should I write or call her? Could she have been making it up? Could she have been in an alcoholic blackout and not remember telling me?"

"I know this is really hard," Szifra said softly. "It's understandable that you're not sure what's the best thing to do at this point. It's a major shock. You have only started to think about it and feel through it. Perhaps talking in here tonight will help you resolve what you'll do next, if anything. I know you felt uncomfortable. It's really hard to open up about such personal issues."

Michael appreciated her words. He no longer felt confused about whether he should have brought the matter up. And that helped him focus on the real issue.

"Michael, my ex-wife was abused by an uncle," Mark said as he flicked back his hair, revealing his nervousness. His voice reflected his sincerity as he continued. "Since he was a stepuncle, not really her uncle, she told me, she thought that was the reason he did it to her. She never dreamed he would do something to one of her half sisters, his real nieces, too, but he did.

"She never told anyone because she thought they'd say she was causing trouble again. She thought no one would believe her and it would hurt a lot of people. She'd be the cause of it, she thought. There was no one she could tell. She figured he knew she was bad. That's what she'd always been told by her family, and that's why she thought he abused her—" Mark's voice broke, and he had to clear his throat to continue.

"Later, she found out he molested her younger sister. Then her problems with it really began. She decided if she had told, he wouldn't have gotten the chance to do what he did." He talked rapidly now, as though he were trying to distance himself from his words.

"I guess I'm telling you this because I saw what keeping it a secret did to her. It was years before she told a counselor. She lived with that secret, that guilt, those horrible feelings for years. I saw her struggle a long time to overcome that abuse."

"Are you suggesting Michael or his sister should blow the whistle on their father so he won't molest someone else?" Sarah asked.

"I don't know what I'm suggesting," Mark replied. "I mostly wanted to let Michael know that it happens. Not just in his family. And that I saw what it did to one person, so I can understand in some way what he's going through." He shook his head and shrugged, indicating he didn't know what was best.

Anne sat on her chair, crying visibly but not making a sound. She was clutching the arms of her chair. Szifra realized she was identifying personally with the discussion and gently asked her if she would like to say anything.

"I want to, but it will be so hard," Anne said, now crying audibly. After a few moments she continued.

"My sister called me one day, after I had left home and was married. She was fifteen. She told me Dad had attempted to sexually abuse her the night before. He had been drunk. I can remember exactly what I was doing when she called, where I was standing, and the horrible rush of fear and nausea I felt while we talked. It was also a shock, because we never talked about these kinds of things.

"I was very supportive over the telephone, gave her good advice, and confirmed emphatically that she should stop him from coming near her." Anne cried harder for a minute, then went on.

"But when I thought about doing more about the situation, I couldn't. I never told another person or brought it up with my father, even though we lived in the same town. I never even asked my sister if it happened again. I decided instead to believe she had made it up."

Anne was overwhelmed, feeling exposed before the group. Through her hurt and shame, though, she felt—and acknowledged—a touch of relief at having broken the silence. That helped her calm down, and she remembered to breathe deeply. Szifra reached for Anne's hand and thanked her for sharing her experience with the group.

"Thanks, Anne," Michael added. "I know that was hard for you. It helped me, though, to know I'm not all alone with this. It occurred to me to pretend she never told me; that's what I'd really like to do. But I'm so angry at my dad, I'd like to hurt him. I just don't know what I'm going to do."

"You'll never be able to forget it, Mike," Trina said. "Never. And neither will she." She spoke firmly, bitterness coming through. Leaning forward on her chair, she said, "I've wanted to talk about this for a long time, but I didn't know how or when to bring it up. . . . I was sexually molested by grandfathers, a grandmother, uncles, my own father, and 'friends' of the family. I never gave myself the right to question their right to assault me as they saw fit to do. I don't know why, but I didn't feel free to tell them to leave me alone. It never entered my mind to tell my mother. I don't know why. I remember the sexual assaults started with Grandpa. He had sex with me quite frequently from the time I was three years old until I was five. Others took his place throughout my childhood and adolescence.

"It's only in the past year that I've begun to deal with it," she continued after a slight pause. "We're talking about things I kept secret for almost forty years. Just because your sister didn't tell you for a long, long time, I wouldn't doubt what she's saying. She may have wanted to reach out long ago, but couldn't.

"I've never trusted men. I always thought they wanted something from me. When a man was nice to me, I was sure it was because he wanted something sexual." Trina's belligerence softened as she felt the sadness.

"I always felt naked around my father. It seemed he could see right through me and the clothes I had on. Sort of like I had no hiding place. I was always in danger of some sort of physical, emotional, and sexual abuse from him and other family members. It was commonplace. Like lightning, I never knew where it was going to strike next. Physical abuse seems like an almost continuous roll of thunder, going on forever, starting when I was two and not ending until I left home at the age of fifteen and got married."

"Where were our mothers during all this?" Sarah asked. "Didn't they know or suspect? Why didn't they stop this?"

No one seemed to have an answer. The group sat in silence. Szifra let them take a few minutes to reflect, sensing their need for quiet. She wanted to say a few more things about codependence but didn't think this was the time.

Finally Michael spoke up. "My sister always chose men who abused her physically or verbally. I never understood it. I used to be so annoyed with her for her dumb choices in men. Now I'm beginning to understand why her life's been the way it has."

"Fortunately, I never suffered any sexual abuse," Bob said. "I'm sure I can't grasp how horrible that must have been. In our family, we suffered from another kind of abuse, though. Physical. My father was the most violent and physically abusive person I've ever known, and he wasn't the drinker. He would slap, hit, punch, literally beat us. For the slightest infractions. If the phone rang late at night, we got it because we didn't have friends who knew not to call late. If one got it, we all got it. 'Just for good measure,' he'd say.

"When we got a little older, we'd try to run away, but that only inspired him to pick up a broom or a belt and inflict more serious injuries when he did catch us. The worst part was, we never knew what would set him off. Now I wonder sometimes if Mom's alcoholism or even her sobriety set him off." Bob seemed subdued as he stopped talking, but then he drew himself up, looked around the circle with angry eyes, and said, "I hate him for doing that to us all those years."

Trina said, "They did such awful things. I remember when I was ten my father locked me in a hole under the basement stairs for a couple of hours. He and a friend were drunk, and they told me they wanted to hand me some things to store in there. When I climbed in, Dad locked the door and they stood there laughing while I pounded on the door and screamed to get out. There were spiderwebs and bugs all over. I was bitten and bruised and covered with dirt and cobwebs when he finally let me out. It's amazing I'm as okay as I am," she said.

"I knew it was time to move out several years later when my father wanted me to go out with a bartender he owed fifty dollars to." She spoke with obvious disgust. "If I'd go out with him, Dad said, he wouldn't have to pay back the fifty dollars."

Bob asked, "How did we ever survive this stuff?"

"I don't think I could have," Kathy said quietly. "I never realized how common sexual and physical abuse is in families. When my dad had too much to drink, he would just go to bed. I don't think he ever hit me. I had no idea others lived through such horrors. I'm feeling a little like Ann; how can I feel like I suffered from living with an alcoholic when at his worst Dad drank too much and went to bed early?"

"I know what you mean, Kathy, and yet you still suffered the absence of nurturing," Szifra said. "And the inconsistency of not knowing, as you have said before, 'if Dad will be all right tonight,' 'if Mom will be mad.' ''

Kathy nodded. "True. But I was never afraid of Dad or what he might do. He never got mad. It was Mom who would get mad. That was always my fear. Sometimes Mom wouldn't talk to us for days if she was mad. And that tore me up. I couldn't stand for Mom to be mad, to be hurt."

"It's important to be aware that abuse can come in many forms," Szifra reminded the group. "As Michael, Trina, and Anne have shared, it can be sexual. Or, as with Bob and Trina, it can be physical. In your case, Kathy, I'd term it emotional neglect. Your father and mother didn't set out to neglect you, but your father's absence as an involved parent created an emotional void in your life. And your mother's codependency left her unable to meet your needs effectively. You ended up becoming your father's mother in some ways. That kind of cross-generational behavior often leads to dysfunction later, in adulthood. It also means you got too little time for an appropriate childhood and adolescence.

"Sometimes ACOAs refrained from asking their parents for what they needed," she continued. " 'I can't upset Mom, she's got too much already,' they'll say. Or, 'I can't be late getting home, Mom will be worried. She has too much to worry about without having to worry about me.' Or, 'My pain doesn't really count, because hers is so much worse.' Your nondrinking parent may have been consumed with worries about the alcoholic and repercussions from the drinking, like too little money. You couldn't consistently get what you needed from your parents.

"Another form of abuse is verbal, where a child may be subjected to hurtful degradations. Too many clients have told me their parents would repeatedly tell them they were stupid, useless, no good. In many families the abuse is far more insidious. It's covert. An example might be the parent who controls the children with guilt. Or the effect on the children of a parent who doesn't see them because it rocks the boat with a new spouse. The feeling the child is left with may be, 'I'm not important enough to my mom or dad for them to stand up for me. They must not really care about me.' The net result for most of these children is, 'I'm not really lovable.' They end up measuring their self-worth and too often come up with 'inadequate, not worthwhile.' All these behaviors can be seriously destructive, whether they're sexual, physical, emotional, or verbal.

"Try not to minimize your feelings and losses," Szifra concluded. "Each of you suffered plenty. You have the right and responsibility, too, to grieve your losses."

The group was silent for a minute. Susan straightened her skirt, shifting on her chair. She wanted to speak up but hesitated.

"Everyone has been so open," she finally began, her voice cracking. "It's been hard listening to everyone talk about their early childhood abuses. I was feeling lucky until Szifra mentioned verbal abuse. I hadn't thought about my father's tirades as abusive. I thought they were his problem. But thinking about it, I realize they were my problem, too, because they hurt me.

"Dad never struck out—except with his tongue. He would say cruel things, often at the dinner table. He'd be in a good mood, then suddenly he'd flip into a mean, angry mood. He often told me I was ugly, and that trying to use makeup to look pretty was a waste of time and money. He lashed out at my brother, telling him he was dumb. Once he started in with his demeaning words, he'd continue until there was nothing left to us. I felt worthless. And I guess he felt powerful."

"I hate admitting it," Sarah said, "but I guess there was verbal abuse in my home, too. Not so much hurtful things being said as the tone of voice and lack of kindness. It was like I never could do enough to warrant a compliment. Good things I did were not noticed, only the minor flaws in them were pointed out. Like I'd get almost all A's on my report card, but Dad would ask why I got a B in something rather than complimenting me for the A's. That did hurt me, even though it wasn't scary, like so much of the abuse that's been shared tonight. Good was never enough.''

"This is a good example of the covert emotional abuse I referred to earlier,'' Szifra said. "The Welfare Department couldn't ever press charges, but this kind of communication makes it hard to feel good about yourself. This communication erodes your self-esteem. We continue feeling less than whole in adulthood. Many messages we hear from others in our childhoods are ones we hear internally in our adulthoods.

"I also want to address covert sexual abuse,'' she continued. "Many of us never think of this as an issue. These days we hear a lot about 'good touch,' 'bad touch.' We tell our children they'll be able to feel the difference. Some of us were never sexually abused in the standard sense, but we felt like someone was sexually inappropriate with us. The touching that was presented as affection felt sexual to us. We, of course, thought it was our problem. We were making it up. Jealousy by our fathers or stepfathers or our mothers or stepmothers when we began dating, or sexual innuendos by family members or friends of our parents— these are all examples. When we felt like our parent was undressing us with his eyes, staring at our breasts. When they walked into the bathroom or our bedroom unannounced. Or our fathers giving us long kisses on the lips, even after we asked them not to. These are covert forms of abuse, which can cause lingering problems in adulthood.''

"I'm not sure our family had much that was covert,'' Bob said. "My dad was quite overt, like Sarah's . . . verbally abusive, along with the physical abuse I mentioned earlier. My old man was mean. There's no other way to put it. He'd beat the heck out of me and my sister, for the smallest things. I actually wonder if he didn't enjoy it.

"One of my earliest childhood memories is of Dad making me stand in a corner of the room for a whole day because I'd snuck a banana right after breakfast. I hadn't asked, and that was a big mistake. I'm sure that if I'd asked, I would have been told, 'No.' When he caught me with that banana, he said he'd teach me a lesson I'd never forget. He was right. I never forgot it. I can't stand bananas today. Every time I smell bananas, I remember my terror that day."

"This makes me so angry, hearing about this," Kathy spoke up. "Children are so powerless. How can parents be so cruel?"

"The key here is just that, Kathy," Szifra said. "Children are powerless. The feeling of having no power may be what keeps the cycle of violence and abuse going. At some point, I wish children who had been battered or abused could claim their power, refuse to be abused by anyone. But, as children, unfortunately, you had no power to stop the abuse.

"As adults it's essential to find ways of working through what happened to you. To resolve a past you had no control over. And, slowly, you learn to take control today. To learn you have control over much more in your lives today. You can interpret how you feel. No one can tell you that you must feel happy or feel sad. Or feel bad because you ate a banana.

"Resolving early abuse is a tough job, I won't try to minimize that," Szifra added. "Uncovering these old secrets is a good beginning. Secrets can fester and get more infected. Bringing them out in the open, looking at them, and figuring out what you can do today are steps in overcoming the old horrors. Each of you who opened up tonight took big steps. And I'd like to know how you're feeling now, after having opened up such personal issues."

"I feel relieved," Michael said. "I came in thinking this would be so embarrassing, never dreaming that others in the group would have experienced the same kinds of things. I'm still not sure what I'm going to do about my sister or father, but hearing others tonight has helped me realize that I shouldn't decide in one night, or even one week. This issue is going to need some time."

"Time is right," Trina said. "I've resigned myself to

that. In a year, I've made some progress, but it still hurts like hell.''

"Trina, how do you feel having shared with the group?" Szifra asked.

"Okay," Trina said. "I trust you guys. I couldn't imagine a safer place to discuss an issue like this."

"I'm feeling sad for everyone," Kathy said. "I wish I could wave a magic wand and take away all this hurt. And I'm feeling fortunate, too."

"Me too," Mark said. "I got spanked a lot, but I never felt physically abused. My dad teased me a lot, and sometimes that hurt, but it was never as verbally abusive as others have described. It's pretty strange to suddenly feel lucky."

"I never really thought that much about Dad's verbal tirades as being abusive," Susan said. "It was such an everyday fact of life for us, I didn't think it was especially unusual. I didn't like them, but I didn't recognize his pattern as being different, I guess. I suppose I figured that's what all fathers did."

"I'm feeling more guilty," Anne said. "Like I buried my head in the sand when I should have helped my sister. Now that I've heard how sexual abuse is repeated and repeated, I doubt if my sister suffered just once. And I feel guilty for not having done something to help her. I'm going to work up the courage to talk with her about it sometime."

"This talk has kind of fired me up," Sarah said. "It's made me angry. Like Dad got away with one more thing. He not only abused alcohol—he abused us. It's just not fair."

" 'Not fair' is an understatement," said Mark. "It's unjust. It's disgusting."

"But we don't have to suffer this unfairness, or injustice, anymore," Trina reminded them. "I guess that's part of the reason we're in this group. Gosh, I needed tonight's meeting. I'm so glad I'm here."

As group broke up, Trina walked over to Michael, offering to talk more with him if it would help. Michael thanked her. "I'll probably take you up on your offer," he said. "I'm still in shock."

"Call me sometime," she said, giving him her number.

There was less chatter as everyone headed out. The session had been very heavy, and most preferred silence as they headed home.

My Observations and Reactions to Meeting 9

Anne, 39, child care worker, lost child role in family, father died from alcoholism seven years ago.
Observations/progress noted:

Bob, 50, alcoholism counselor, scapegoat in family, recovering, mother alcoholic, now deceased.
Observations/progress noted:

Kathy, 33, secretary, mascot/responsible role in family, father died from alcoholism this year.
Observations/progress noted:

Mark, 30, welder, scapegoat role in family, recovering, father died from alcoholism six years ago.
Observations/progress noted:

Michael, 38, PR/advertising, responsible role in family, father is alcoholic, mother prescription drug–addicted, living. .
Observations/progress noted:

Sarah, 36, high school teacher, responsible role in family, father died from alcoholism five years ago.
Observations/progress noted:

Susan, 32, accountant, lost child/responsible role in family, father died from alcoholism two years ago.
Observations/progress noted:

Trina, 45, shipping clerk, scapegoat role in family, recovering, father quit drinking a few years ago.
Observations/progress noted.

Szifra, therapist
Observations:

Observations about me during this meeting:

My feelings during this meeting:

Issues I'd like to explore further:

My reactions to this meeting:

What I learned about myself during this meeting:

Looking at Our Own Addictive Behaviors

"YOU GUYS REMIND me of my mother!" Mark practically shouted. "No matter what the problem was, she always found a way to turn it around to alcohol. Alcohol is legal, for crying out loud, and a few drinks don't make you an alcoholic."

Mark was irritated. He felt as if Bob had put him on the defensive and everyone was on Bob's side. "Just because some people have problems with alcohol doesn't mean everyone does," he said as he stood up.

He paced around his chair, waving his arms in frustration. I'd really like a cigarette, he thought, but he sat back down instead, apologizing for his outburst. "I think we need to be careful about coming up with universal truths here and lumping every drinker into the alcoholic category," he said to sum up his feelings.

"I agree," said Bob. "I wasn't trying to ban alcohol. I know there are plenty of people who can drink responsibly. I know I can't. And all I was asking you was, are you sure you can?"

Bob's confrontation had felt like an attack to Mark. He pegged Bob as an AA type who couldn't handle a heroin addict. Pure drinkers always think they're one up on druggies, Mark thought bitterly. Well, I was addicted to heroin, but I'm not addicted to alcohol.

Szifra was surprised at Mark's intense reaction to what

seemed like an uncritical inquiry on Bob's part. Mark's explosion was unexpected and quickly took the meeting out of the slow pace of the first half hour.

Michael wasn't there that evening. He had called to say he would be out of town presenting an ad campaign to a new client. Szifra wondered whether he had avoided the meeting because of his personal discussions last week about his sister. Sometimes ACOAs felt overexposed after sharing personal issues. Many times the overexposure caused shame, and the old coping styles emerged. For Michael, the old coping styles meant avoiding people and situations, isolating himself. Szifra knew she'd explore this with Michael in an individual session scheduled later in the week.

When Szifra asked about reactions to last week's session, Sarah suggested they wait for Michael to come back before they responded. Anne agreed and the others did, too, almost too readily for Szifra's comfort.

"Do any of you feel overexposed after last week?" she asked. Sarah asked her to explain what she meant.

"Well, are you feeling like you said more than you wish you had," she elaborated, "or more than you were comfortable saying?"

Anne said she had. "I took a few steps beyond what you'd call my comfort level, Szifra."

"I was surprised at how uncomfortable I felt the next day," Trina said. "I guess I was thinking I'd let too much out. I suppose some of the 'old tapes' started playing, making me feel more vulnerable. All those stupid, old rules come at me. Instead of drinking, at least now I have a voice that can come in and argue the side of the healthy, new rules. But it's like living a debate. Sometimes I think the old rules will win. They always used to."

Trina looked up, nodding with her usual enthusiasm. "You know, though, they almost never do anymore. But I do feel like I was put through a wringer. I know I did the right thing last week, but it still feels scary. That fear of talking about my family and what I'd get if I did is still very strong. It's a relief, though, to know I can handle it. To know I have a nurturing, confident, more healthy part of my self that assures me I'm okay. It's like having a built-in, nice mother. What I always wanted deep down.''

The group spent some time discussing the feeling of having said "too much" that comes from overexposure and talked about ways to quiet the sabotaging voices on the old tapes.

"You need to build emotional muscle slowly and patiently," Szifra explained. "We do not develop great physical muscles in a week, or even in a month. We have to work at it."

Szifra had planned to focus on fun and play during this session—not as the content of the meeting, but as a Children of Alcoholics issue. She knew from her work that having fun and playing were low priorities in many ACOAs' lives. Many had difficulty relaxing, especially playing. She had proposed they discuss what they did for fun, so they might get ideas from each other on how to break out of their rigid routines to enjoy lighter moments.

Then, just when it seemed the group was comfortable with admitting that, for the most part, they didn't know how to have fun, Mark had suggested that a few beers and good conversation were one way to have a good time. Bob had been direct with Mark in questioning his drinking, and it had felt like an attack to Mark.

Szifra gave Mark a minute to relax and the others time to refocus before she continued.

"We all know that alcohol is an important issue for ACOAs," she said. "Should we continue this discussion?"

"I think I pretty well ruined the subject of fun," Bob said.

"Oh, take the blame, Bob!" Trina said, laughing but meaning it seriously as well.

"Okay, you caught me, Trina," Bob replied with a sheepish grin. "I'm thinking it would be hard to get back on the subject of fun now. Our moods seem much too serious to handle that well. I move for talking about fun next week and tossing this drinking issue around some more."

Kathy agreed it would interest her but wanted to know how Mark felt about it. Mark admitted it would be uncomfortable for him, but he could handle it. Anne surprised everyone by speaking up on her own, saying she really wanted to talk about drinking.

Not sure how she wanted to direct the discussion, Szifra took a minute to collect her thoughts. No one seemed willing to jump in, so she decided to reestablish a cooperative mood rather than have Mark and Bob resolve their earlier conversation now.

"Perhaps more than most subjects, discussing your drinking could be something you easily become defensive about," she said. "Our other topics may have been easier because they didn't seem like conscious adult choices, which drinking appears to be. I encourage each of you to be open and honest about your feelings and thoughts on your use of alcohol. As you've learned to do with other topics, be open-minded about others' feelings, recognizing each person's right to choose what's appropriate for him or her. . . .

"So, who feels comfortable sharing their feelings on alcohol use?" she concluded.

"I do," Sarah said willingly. "My feelings are a mixture of me, Al-Anon, and my church. How's that for an odd combination?" She chuckled. "First, Al-Anon. In Al-Anon, I heard so many horror stories about alcohol abuse, I couldn't imagine why anyone who wasn't already addicted would even want to take the risk. That was at first. After a while, as I worked the program, I realized it was an individual choice, so I heartily endorse Al-Anon's motto, 'Live and let live.' It's a choice each individual has to make.

"Then, there's my church," she continued. "Drinking alcohol is absolutely forbidden. It's a sin. They don't recognize alcoholism as a disease. I've even heard preachers say it's the devil at work. For a long time, I touted that same belief. But as I learned more about alcoholism, the 'me' part of my three-part system took a stronger hold."

Sarah paused a minute as she collected her thoughts. "I respect my church's instructions that I may not drink. I have no real desire to drink. But neither do I judge those who do. Nor do I believe alcoholics are sinful. I do believe alcoholism is a disease. I know what's right for me, but I leave the choice for others to them.'' Her objectivity sounded sincere, and by their reactions several other members obviously agreed with her.

"I can't afford to focus on anyone's drinking but my own," Roger began. "Alcohol is poison to me. What it is to or for other people is none of my business."

"Isn't that a little self-centered?" Kathy asked. "I always understood AA followed slogans like 'Pass it on.' Doesn't the fellowship believe in reaching out more?"

"Reaching out in response to a request for help," Roger said quickly, "not getting on a soapbox and deciding what's right for others."

"That sounds a lot like waiting for an alcoholic to hit bottom," Kathy said. "How does AA feel about interventions?"

"I'm not really sure," Roger admitted. "I'm still in the early stages of my sobriety where I have to focus my energy on my own recovery."

"There's a movement of acceptance for interventions in AA," Bob said. "As a counselor, I've seen many that were successful. Years ago, AA members felt someone had to come to AA entirely voluntarily. That's still true to a certain extent. Like Roger said, AA will never become a preaching organization. It's there to help those who want help. The rise in the number of employee assistance programs and treatment centers is changing the way some people get help, but the basic philosophy of AA will always remain the same, I believe."

"Kathy, how do you feel about drinking?" Szifra asked, wanting to shift the focus back to personal sharing.

"I'm in a new stage, I guess I'd say," Kathy answered. "When I was young, I thought Mom was too much against it. Even though I knew Dad was an alcoholic, I didn't think alcohol itself was bad. And when Dad wanted to build a bar in the room he'd added on for a pool table, I couldn't understand my mom's distaste for it. I even bought him bar accessories for Christmas one year.

"Then, after Mom died, Dad's alcoholism progressed rapidly, and I found myself becoming impatient with his drinking," she continued. "I sure understood Mom's feelings better. As far as my own drinking goes, during my twenties I did some drinking. I got married pretty young and didn't drink much during those years. After I got divorced, I did some partying, and I went along with the crowd. I remember sometimes talking a little about my father and why the drug and alcohol scene made me uncomfortable. But I was so wrapped up in a new relationship, I compromised to stay in it.

"Now, I've come full circle," she said. "I've recognized how much hurt and pain has come from alcohol consumption, and I want no part of it. I don't drink at all, and I don't like to be around people who have been drinking a lot."

"You and I sure agree on that one," Anne said. "I used to drink every now and then. I never could drink too much because it made me feel so woozy."

Roger laughed. "That was the idea, Anne."

"Oh," Anne said, a little embarrassed. "It burned my lips to drink it. My husband used to laugh at me when I told him that. Neither one of us ever drank very much. We'd serve alcohol for company dinners. But, like Kathy, as I learned more about ACOA and alcoholism issues, I decided I never needed or wanted to drink."

"I've done my share of drinking," Susan spoke up, "especially in college. I still drink now. I enjoy wine with dinner. I don't see how my social drinking relates in any way to my father's dependency."

"I think I would still be drinking if I could," Trina said. "I always loved both the feeling and the taste! Funny how that worked out, isn't it?" She made light of her dependency, a fact she'd long ago accepted.

"I'd like to add something," said Sarah. "I don't want Mark or any of you to think I was judging him. Even though I've chosen not to drink, I want you to know, if you choose to drink, that's your choice. I won't judge you either way."

"Thanks, Sarah," Mark said. "I didn't feel judged by you. And I know Bob's intentions were good, even though they were expressed pretty strongly. Right now I'm just trying to take this all in. I'm not sure where it will lead. But I want to hear what's going on with others."

Szifra let Mark know she was glad he could keep an open mind. Then she asked, "Linda, what about you?"

Linda shrugged. "I feel like I don't have an original idea. I went through pretty much the same process as Kathy. After my divorce, I went to the bars a lot and did a lot of drinking. It was what all my friends did. That's how we had fun. That's how we met guys. I continued to drink for a couple of years after I started learning about alcoholism and its effects on me. Then one day I said, 'I don't want to drink anymore.' It's been over a year since I drank, and I have no intention of ever drinking again."

"Why?" asked Mark.

"One time I spent an evening out, drinking only soft drinks," she replied. "I looked around and realized I didn't want to keep spending my time this way. The more knowledge I gained, the more I couldn't justify my own drinking. I'm especially interested in the hereditary aspects of alcoholism. Even though research hasn't said for sure yet, I've read a lot that says there's at least the predisposition for alcoholism. With an alcoholic mother and father, I can't take the risk. I won't take the risk."

"One thing bothers me about this discussion," Mark said. He seemed relaxed again. "My studies in addiction make it clear that if you're addicted to one substance, that doesn't necessarily make you addicted to another. I can't go near heroin, that's clear. But I'm not an alcoholic. So why should I be concerned about a drink now and then?"

"Maybe because your father was an alcoholic, and you don't know what predisposition you may have," Linda said, surprised at her boldness in answering Mark so directly. "You're still pretty young. You could become alcoholic if you kept up a steady drinking pattern."

"Are you referring to the 'drug of choice' issue?" Bob asked Mark.

"Not really."

"What's that?" asked Sarah.

"Well, I'm a beer drinker," Bob explained. "That's what I was addicted to; that's what I got drunk on. When I tried to prove I wasn't an alcoholic, I quit drinking beer. Instead, I drank vodka. But that didn't last long. I hated the stuff. It was better than doing without entirely, though, because it 'did the trick.' Then I switched to gin. 'See,' I said to everyone, 'I'm not an alcoholic.' I thought because I could go without beer, I wasn't an alcoholic. Beer was my drug of choice, but if that choice was gone, I could find a substitute."

Without warning, Trina found herself feeling flushed and nervous. She'd been okay during the drinking discussion, but this drug-of-choice talk brought a new picture to mind: her prescription drugs.

She had been able to rationalize that her ulcer and stomach problems forced her to take these medications. Her physical symptoms were real, and a doctor had prescribed them. But she had a nagging thought every now and then that maybe she liked taking them more than she admitted. Maybe I'm just being paranoid, she told herself, thinking that if I take anything, it's wrong. Surely I'm entitled to medicate an illness!

As she listened to the discussion, Trina grew more and more uncomfortable. Finally she said, "I'm sitting here going nuts."

Everyone looked at her with surprise.

"I've tried not to think about this too much," she said, "but I can't get it off my mind. I have some physical problems I treat with prescription drugs. Am I taking them because I need them or because I *need* them?"

"Do you mean you wonder if you're addicted to them?" asked Linda, the nurse. "Have you checked to see if they are addictive substances?"

"No," Trina admitted. "But I could be psychologically addicted without being physically addicted. Either way, I hate to admit it, but it may be a problem for me. I've denied it big time up until tonight."

"Do you think that's what I'm doing?" Mark asked her.

"I have no idea," she replied. "I've got enough trouble figuring out what *I'm* doing. I've never tried to go off the medication and see if my stomach could handle it. I suppose that's something I should do before I find myself in real trouble."

"I'd take a look at it, Trina," Bob said with concern.

"Just like you want me to take a look at it," Mark said.

Oh, no, thought Anne, Here we go again.

"No, Mark," Bob said bluntly. "I'm not suggesting that. Earlier, I asked you to look at that possibility. But I'm in no position to suggest anything to anyone. I've got my hands full with my own sobriety. I'm not taking your inventory."

"But you counsel other recovering alcoholics," Sarah reminded him.

"True," Bob said. "But I've tried to leave my counselor hat outside this room. I'm here as an ACOA."

Mark was getting tense again. He still felt the group was putting the drinking issue in a black or white category, as ACOAs tended to do with so many issues. Either you're alcoholic, which makes you the bad guy, he thought, or you're a smart ACOA who doesn't drink, which makes you the good guy.

Mark had had drug counselors who'd told him it was okay for him to drink. He'd never thought too much about it. But this discussion was getting to him. It felt too much like his own family situation, where he couldn't really talk to his brother and sisters. The discussion brought to mind some writing he had done while in treatment. Paragraphs and phrases crowded into his consciousness.

"I wish I'd never met Sister Morphine or Brother Heroin," he remembered writing. "Not until my entire life and those around me were almost totally destroyed was I granted my last reprieve. It's no small miracle I'm even alive today."

He shuddered, recalling the feelings he'd had then. He remembered the denial and wondered if he was doing some of the same with alcohol now. Not a conscious denial, perhaps, just the predictable pattern of someone who wanted to keep using. He felt scared; maybe he did depend on alcohol to help him through some situations. Will I really have to deal with this? he thought miserably. I've had enough. I only drink now and then, anyway. Mostly it's to be sociable. Why should I give that up?

He remembered his compulsive, burn-it-out style of doing things, remembered a counselor once saying, "Let's look at your family history. Your father abused alcohol; he died from complications of his alcoholism. His body just couldn't take any more. You have many relatives who abuse alcohol. The genes have conspired against you. Your role modeling taught you to normalize excessive dependency on alcohol. You also do many things compulsively. Why take the chance?"

Mark decided he'd discuss the matter with Szifra individually. Nevertheless he felt almost panicked, thinking beer might have some hold over him that he'd never been aware of. He'd never thought he'd need to consider giving it up.

As he broke out of his reverie, he realized he had no idea what the others had been talking about. Szifra was discussing "fun" again, and Mark groaned. He knew where that topic had led them the last time.

"I'm not sure if our diversion tonight was so much out of a need to discuss the drinking issue, or because it would have been even more difficult to discuss fun," she teased. "I'd like you each to spend some time this week making a list of things you do to have fun. Anything you enjoy. Then I'd like you to list some activities you might like to try. Many ACOAs have to make a sincere effort to fit leisure activities into their lives. It's important to your physical and mental health," she reminded everyone.

Linda promptly wrote down the task in the small notebook she carried in her purse. She enjoyed these homework assignments. They helped her focus on the issues and learn more.

Bob, on the other hand, thought they were juvenile. He preferred adult conversation and thought the assignments gave Szifra an authority she really didn't have over him. He never worried about doing them. If he wanted to fool her, he could, because he thought so quickly on his feet. Let the rest of them pretend this is school, he thought scornfully. I'm here as an adult.

As group broke up, he decided to risk one more conversation with Mark. He'd grown quite fond of the younger man, although he knew Mark felt threatened by him. He offered his hand to Mark. "No hard feelings?" he asked as they shook.

"Of course not," Mark replied. They walked out together chatting amiably about the game that was to be on television that night.

My Observations and Reactions to Meeting 10

Anne, 39, child care worker, lost child role in family, father died from alcoholism seven years ago.
Observations/progress noted:

Bob, 50, alcoholism counselor, scapegoat in family, recovering, mother alcoholic, now deceased.
Observations/progress noted:

Kathy, 33, secretary, mascot/responsible role in family, father died from alcoholism this year.
Observations/progress noted:

Linda, 36, nurse, responsible role in family, both parents are alcoholic, living.
Observations/progress noted:

Mark, 30, welder, scapegoat role in family, recovering, father died from alcoholism six years ago.
Observations/progress noted:

Roger, 20, student, lost child/scapegoat in family, recovering, mother also recovering.
Observations/progress noted:

Sarah, 36, high school teacher, responsible role in family, father died from alcoholism five years ago.
Observations/progress noted:

Susan, 32, accountant, lost child/responsible role in family, father died from alcoholism two years ago.
Observations/progress noted:

Trina, 45, shipping clerk, scapegoat role in family, recovering, father quit drinking a few years ago.
Observations/progress noted:

Szifra, therapist
Observations:

Observations about me during this meeting:

My feelings during this meeting:

Issues I'd like to explore further:

My reactions to this meeting:

What I learned about myself during this meeting:

MEETING 11

Having Fun

OH, THEY'RE GOING to see what fun is all about, Bob thought, laughing as he headed for group. He loved times when he could be as silly as he wanted, and tonight was going to be one of those times.

I hope I can make it sound like I know how to have fun, Susan thought as she headed for the meeting. She hated being forced into situations where she was supposed to be having a good time but wasn't, and tonight was going to be like that.

Imagine trying to have fun without booze, Roger said to himself as he headed for group. I'm just learning to be okay without it. Expecting me to have fun without drinking is asking a lot. He hadn't had much practice at having a good time without alcohol, but maybe tonight would be one of those times.

"Tuesday night and time for fun!" Sarah announced as she walked in. "Who would have ever thought we'd be saying that?"

Everyone burst into laughter when Bob walked in with a big smile on his face and started handing out helium-filled balloons, one for each of them. "You want to have fun?" he asked as he passed around the balloons.

"What a different way to start group," Szifra greeted everyone, accepting her own balloon from Bob. "What a great idea!"

Several conversations were going on simultaneously as everyone crowded into the circle of chairs. The balloons had taken the edge off much of their anxiety. Strings were tied to chair arms and wrists. Roger let his float up to the ceiling, where it just missed the overhead light fixture.

"You obviously remembered tonight's topic, Bob," Sarah said, teasing him.

"This is wild!"

"This is fun!"

"Really!"

Even though Linda tried to get into the spirit of the fun, she didn't feel comfortable. She felt removed from the group, as though someone other than herself were participating in the fun. It was a common feeling for her. She tried to join in, to keep up with the spirit of the group, but she felt phony.

Just as everyone seemed to be settled on their chairs, Bob pulled packs of bubble gum from his shirt pocket and started handing out pieces. "Hey, we're really going to have fun," he said.

"Oh, my gosh, I wonder if I can still make a bubble?" Anne said. Like Linda, she felt uncomfortable. Her outward appearance seemed calm, but inwardly she was very nervous. Playing was so unfamiliar to her.

"And make a bubble without getting it in your hair!" Linda laughed, feeling good that she was able to join in even though she knew her laugh wasn't sincere.

The room filled with the overpoweringly sweet scent of pink bubble gum.

Someone finally explained what was going on to Michael, who hadn't heard about the agenda. Even though he was enjoying Bob's antics, he'd been wondering what Bob was up to.

"It's been years since I did anything like this," Trina said. "This is great, Bob."

"I think we should have a bubble-blowing contest," Sarah suggested. "Biggest bubble wins."

"Give me a minute to soften this gum up," Trina said, chewing rapidly.

"One, two, three . . ."

Szifra watched the group. She loved seeing them let their guard down, interacting with such childlike joy. This is one of the most rewarding things about counseling ACOAs, she thought. Seeing the progress. It seems like a little bit of knowledge and encouragement sends them soaring to heights they never thought they could achieve.

She sensed Linda's and Anne's discomfort, however, and she also wondered about Susan. How was she feeling? Clear progress, though, she said to herself. A few months ago Anne would not have been able to join in this situation at all because she would have felt so tense.

Linda, too, had come a long way. There was so much heaviness in her past, she seldom played at all.

Szifra let the fun continue uninterrupted. This kind of spontaneity was so good for them, she knew; besides, she was enjoying it, too. She blew bubbles and laughed along with them.

Finally Bob confessed that he had no more toys or tricks, and the room settled down.

"I'm delighted," Szifra said. "With you, Bob, for being so willing to be courageous and outrageous, and with the rest of us for jumping at this splendid opportunity for fun. Congratulations!"

"It was a great idea, Bob," Kathy agreed. "Even if I'd thought of it, I wouldn't have had the nerve. But I'm glad you did."

"It was neat," Anne said. "But I do have to get rid of this gum. I remember now why I gave it up years ago. It's so sweet!"

"Well, Bob, since you've been such a great initiator tonight, how about initiating our discussion of fun?" Szifra asked.

"Fine," Bob replied, nodding. "As I remember, I'm supposed to share ways I have fun. Well, since there's some family mascot in me, I can get into fun a little easier than ACOAs who took on other roles. What can I say, I like attention! And being silly.

"I wasn't always this way," he continued. "In fact, when I was drinking, I sometimes got very morose. I was cynical, too. Even though my snide remarks were funny, they weren't fun, so I had deteriorated into a mostly no-fun life. I was too busy being a victim.

"After I was sober a while, I had to consciously find ways to enjoy some fun; I had to give up my 'poor me' humor. Every now and then I've been known to show up at an AA meeting with balloons or pull some other childlike antic."

"How else do you relax?" Szifra asked.

"Funny you should ask," Bob said. "I suppose reading professional journals doesn't count."

"No," Szifra agreed.

"Oh, no," Michael moaned. "That's a big part of my fun, too!"

"Well, that's not to minimize your enjoyment of reading work-related material," Szifra said. "But I'd like to know what you do for sheer fun."

"As you suspected last week, Szifra," Bob said, "I don't do a whole lot just for the fun of it. Getting other people to laugh is fun for me. But other than that, I don't enjoy pure leisure activities. If there's some end to it, like good conversation with friends, I'm okay about it. But my work is most of my life. I know that's not good. It's too 'ACOA-ish.' "

Linda was glad group had settled down to the structure she was accustomed to. Seeing everyone have so much fun had made her feel sad. She wished she'd enjoyed it as much as everyone else seemed to. At least I wish I had been more comfortable with it, she thought, instead of feeling left out.

"Work is a big part of my life, too," she heard Kathy say. "That's why for years, in addition to my full-time job, I kept working evenings and weekends at the bookstore. That was most of my social life. Then when I decided to try free-lance writing, I gave up the bookstore so I'd have the time to write. Since then I've become sort of a recluse, home either reading or writing."

"Is that fun?" Anne asked.

"It is for me," Kathy replied. "I love to read. I don't always find writing fun, but it's what I want to do, so I stick it out in the grueling times. And I'm involved in a lot of volunteer work that is very rewarding to me."

"What do you do to play?" Szifra asked.

"Needlework. I love counted canvas work."

"I'm sure I heard you use the word *work*," Sarah said, laughing.

Kathy shrugged. "Well, it's fun to do. I enjoy it. When I really vegetate, just play for the sake of play, I spend time with my cats, Kitty Kitty and Meow Meow."

Szifra remembered how surprised she was the first time Kathy mentioned her cats' names. Kathy seemed more earthy, not prissy or sweet as her cats' names might imply.

As if mirroring her thoughts, Trina commented, "Those are pretty amazing names for cats, Kathy. Did you pick them out?"

"Actually, I did," Kathy admitted, laughing.

"Well, I'm glad you enjoy your cats," Trina said. "For me, one of the best days of my life was when I got rid of a cat I'd sort of adopted. Playing with a cat just isn't my idea of fun."

"What do you do for fun?" Szifra asked.

Trina made a face. "Oh, I shouldn't have spoken up. What do I do for fun? Would going to AA meetings and this group qualify as fun?"

"Not for me!" Susan said. She'd been very quiet so far, and it pleased her that she could feel comfortable enough to tease Trina. She hated it when she hung back for most of the evening.

"You know, it's fun for me," Trina said. "Especially when I connect with someone outside of group. Or go for coffee after an AA meeting. Those are important social interactions for me. And I also enjoy spending time with my grandchildren. Not a lot of time, but some time," she added, laughing.

"I enjoy children, too," Anne said. "My own children,

of course. Young children really steal my heart away, though, especially my nephew and nieces.''

"You enjoy other children, even after raising your own and working with kids all day?'' Sarah asked.

"Well, yes,'' Anne admitted. "There are days when it feels like work. But there are so many wonderful times with the children, too. And my nephew and nieces don't live here, so the time I get to spend with them is really special.''

"What about other fun things?'' Szifra prompted Anne.

"Well, I do a lot of needlework, too. And I enjoy yard work and gardening. Okay, before you say anything, Sarah, yes, those both involve work, but I feel good doing them. I need to keep busy, be productive. I know some of it comes from my mother, who believed you should keep yourself busy. She scheduled our time accordingly.''

"Do you ever lie around all day in your robe and watch TV?'' Kathy teased her.

"Well, no,'' Anne replied. "I wouldn't enjoy that. That's not my idea of fun at all.''

"Do any of us ever lie around and watch TV?'' Kathy asked.

"I get into watching sports a lot,'' Mark said. "And movies. I think I can enjoy relaxing okay. Of course, I get so involved in some of the games, and mad when they don't play well, it's probably more agitation than relaxation.''

Szifra was glad Mark had spoken up. He was unusually quiet tonight. Maybe he just feels like listening tonight, she thought.

"I like lying around and listening to music,'' Roger said. "Music has always been a way for me to relax. I put the headset on and crank the music up. I can forget about everything else. I also enjoy reading computer books. I like exploring new things and playing around with my computer at home. It's nothing for me to stay up half the night fiddling with a program idea.''

"Many of you relax by doing some kind of work,'' Szifra commented. "Think about this for a minute. Does your fun have to be productive or useful in order for you to enjoy it? Or can you play just for the sake of playing?"

"I'd say probably not," Roger responded, "except for the music. That is a real let-go time for me. I have so many things I'm interested in, I can't imagine wasting time. Any spare time I do have I like to devote to social issues. You know me, the more controversial and antiestablishment, the more fun it is for me."

"I would never have thought of politics as fun," Anne said, making a face that said it would never be for her.

"Well, fun may not be the right word," Roger responded. "But it feels worthwhile and positive and important. I enjoy talking with others involved in the same issues, too. It's hard sometimes, because I'm not sure what to say and how to act when we aren't involved in something structured. Like the beginning and ending of meetings is awkward for me. I feel real self-conscious. It's easier, though, than some situations, because I know we all have a common goal, a common thread. I can always fall back on some action we've taken or will take. When I know my role, I'm able to relax more in the situation."

"I must be weird," Sarah said. "I don't like doing anything by myself. I like to have people around me, even when I'm reading or something. They don't have to be in the same room, but I like knowing someone's around. I like to sleep in the living room, where activity and people are. I hate to be isolated. I like to cook and go for walks. Both of those are lots of fun for me. I love trying new recipes and sharing them with friends and family. And a brisk walk outside makes me feel like there's something bigger than me out there. I enjoy nature."

"I worked at making a list of what I do for fun," Linda said. "With two daughters, a husband, and working full-time, I don't have a lot of time for fun. I know I take my homemaker duties too seriously. Maybe I could say I enjoy that, because I do. I enjoy making the kind of home I didn't have as a child.

"For pure fun, with no side benefit of getting something

done, I was only able to come up with one thing," she added. "Painting. I like working with both watercolors and oils. And I try to do some painting every now and then so I can feel creative."

"How neat," Kathy said. "I didn't know you were artistic."

"I'd like to be." Linda smiled. "I don't show anything or try to sell it. I do it only for my own pleasure."

"That's wonderful," Szifra said warmly. "You took some time for yourself. Who else would like to share fun activities?"

"I haven't yet, so I will," Susan said. "I'm like the rest of you. I work so intensely at my job that when I get home, I'm tired. So playing for the sake of playing is not something I've done much of. I do play the piano, and I find that immensely relaxing. Especially after a stressful day. I also enjoy reading, but not computer books." She smiled at Roger. "I read popular fiction, just for fun, for escape."

"Playing the piano and reading seem real healthy, Susan," Szifra said. "Fun for you and stress-reducing at the same time. Good combination."

"I agree," Susan said.

"I noticed both of your fun activities are things you do alone, Susan," Michael said. "I've been sitting here thinking of what I do for fun, and everything I think of is something I do alone. My work on ad campaigns is fun. Walking my dog and bathing him is fun. I love working out at the gym. And I like building things, like a train set I'm working on. But now I'm wondering, is this normal fun?"

He looked at Szifra then continued. "It's almost like all these things are work rather than fun, like you keep pointing out, Sarah. My wife says I want too much time alone. It's how I rejuvenate. But it's causing conflict between us. If we go out to dinner with friends or to a movie, I never really relax. To relax, I seem to need to be alone."

"Do you want to change that?" Szifra asked.

He shrugged. "Not especially. Except as far as my marriage is concerned. If my wife needs me to be more available, I'd like to develop some activities we could do together that would be fun.''

"Would you like some ideas?" Sarah asked him.

Michael nodded. "Fine."

"How about walks?" she suggested. "Maybe you, your wife, and the dog could take walks together. I always wanted my husband to take walks with me, but he found them boring. You might try that.''

"I'd be willing to," Michael said. "Of course, with the dog, it usually turns out to be more of a run than a walk, so we might not have as much chance for interaction as my wife is looking for.''

There was a lull after that, so Szifra asked the group to share the fun ideas they'd come up with. "Some of these might give Michael an idea." she said.

"I really got carried away," Sarah said, laughing. "I love being with people, so I listed all kinds of people activities. Things like going to the zoo, that new park, the lake, getting in a volleyball league. The one I'm going to try first is racquetball. I've wanted to know how to play that game for a long time. And right now I still have a lot of anger left, so I thought banging that ball around would be a good way to vent it. To say nothing of getting in better shape now that I've decided to do some dating.''

"Sarah, you didn't seem to have any trouble at all coming up with ideas," Trina said. "I sure did. I guess after so many years of running around to all the bars in town, I'm not much in the mood for social activities. I know I focus on work too much, though, so all I came up with for a new fun activity was to do nothing! Sounds strange, I know, but I think it would be good for me to have a few hours each week where I had nothing planned. Where I'd maybe just sit on the front porch and do absolutely nothing.''

"That sounds like a great idea, Trina," Anne said. "Let me know if that works for you. Maybe I'd try for a half hour.''

"What will you try in the meantime?" Trina asked, looking at Anne with a directness she found unsettling.

"Believe me, I did think about this a lot this week," Anne replied a bit nervously. "Worry about it, would probably be more accurate. I didn't want to come up with something unless I really thought I would do it. So, I only came up with one thing. Since I enjoy summer gardening so much, I decided to expand that to some winter indoor gardening. I have a few houseplants now, but I'm thinking about getting some starts of unusual varieties. Maybe even trying a few bulbs. I know that would be fun. And it's something I'd follow through on."

Trina nodded. "Okay."

"I'm like Michael's wife, I think," Linda said. "I'd like to find some more activities my husband and I could do together. I'd like to go out to dinner with him more often. I think it would be relaxing, and we would have a chance to talk, just the two of us. I'm going to suggest it. Maybe once a month or so." Looking at her list, she added, "I nearly forgot. I also decided I'd like to learn to sew. I think that might be fun. I guess I'll find out if I try."

"Kathy, I see you have a list, too," Szifra commented.

"Not a very long one, though," Kathy said. "My list of what I do now really pointed out how much time I spend alone. Even though I like that, I'd like to learn to have fun with friends. I do a little of that now. Maybe I could learn to relax more socially and enjoy other people."

"My goal is similar," Susan said. "I know I spend too much time alone. I think it would be good to be able to relax with people around. To be able to enjoy myself socially. I'm going to start out slowly. I decided to try asking people out to lunch. That way, if I'm uncomfortable, I know it will only be for an hour. I hope my comfort level will grow. I figure this is a good way to start."

"Seems like a good idea to me," said Kathy. "Maybe we could start out having lunch with each other just to get used to the idea!" She half hoped Susan wouldn't take her up on the offer because she wasn't sure she was ready.

"Roger, how about you?" Szifra asked. "You mentioned some fun activities. Anything new you want to add?"

"I have one thing," Roger said. "I'd like to get out and do some camping. I've never done that. My family is much too shower-every-day-oriented to pitch a tent. It sounds exciting to me. Maybe on a spring break or during the summer I can get away for a couple of days."

"I love the wilderness," Mark said. "I've been on lots of climbs and backpacking trips. One time a friend and I hiked through the Gila wilderness for five days. We never saw another person. It was an incredible experience. You literally forget about all the problems of the world. I get away every chance I can. I guess I should say, every time I can afford it. You should try it, Roger."

"Maybe you can give me a few tips on where to go and what to take," Roger said.

"Oh, yeah," Mark said. "There are wonderful places, some pretty close by, even. I learned to pack light, I'll tell you; when you're hiking up those mountains, you don't want to be carrying any more than you need. And you learn to get by without the extras." He was able to speak comfortably, which was typical whenever he presented cognitive information and shared practical experiences.

"What about you, Mark? Any ideas for new leisure activities?" Szifra asked.

"Well, I talked about playing some basketball again. I haven't found a court yet. I can't afford to join the Y or anything like that. I need to see if there are some open courts at one of the high schools. I'm still planning on that one. One thing I'd love to do for fun is go to some Cubs games." He laughed. "I can't get enough baseball. Having season tickets and the bucks to get to the games would seem like heaven to me. And then short of the Cubs games, I guess I'd settle for some minor league games. But, really, what I need to do is figure out some low-cost fun things. Renting movies gets expensive. It seems like I only like the high-ticket items. Does anyone have any suggestions?"

"Since you like baseball a lot," Roger said, "have you thought about getting in one of the city's slow-pitch leagues? I have a friend who's played for a long time, and he really likes it.''

Mark nodded thoughtfully. ''My schedule makes it kind of rough, but maybe I'll look into that. I played some baseball in high school. I do like it a lot.''

''Can you schedule fun time in?'' Szifra asked.

''Well, I never really tried to do that,'' Mark admitted. ''I guess I could.''

''I think that's what I'm going to have to do,'' Trina said. Anne agreed it was true for her, too.

Everyone realized the easiest course of action was to continue as they were. They also realized it wasn't the healthiest. They agreed that until it became more of a habit, they might have to schedule fun. Szifra encouraged them to do that, telling them they might need to rewrite the ''Don't waste time'' messages.

After discussing this for a while, Sarah said, ''Mark, maybe cooking would be fun for you. I'm going to cook more fun things, things I enjoy. I'd be glad to teach you some of my gourmet tricks.''

''That wouldn't be fun at all for me,'' Mark responded. ''But thanks anyway. You can invite me over to eat any time you want, though! I do like to eat!''

''You know, I was thinking of cooking myself,'' Michael said. ''Maybe Sharon and I would enjoy doing that together. I'd be making the salad while she rolled something fancy in bread crumbs. Does that sound like a fantasy?'' He laughed.

''Not at all,'' Sarah said. ''I think cooking can be a lot of fun. And you'd be spending time together, which you both want.''

''I think I'm going to give that a try,'' Michael said. ''I hope Sharon knows what she's supposed to roll in bread crumbs!''

''Bob, you have a good start with your ability to play, like bringing these balloons tonight,'' Szifra said. ''Are you planning on expanding your repertoire?''

''Absolutely,'' Bob said, laughing. ''I'm adding magic

and a clown suit! . . . Seriously, though, coming in here tonight with the balloons was really fun for me. I'm glad you all responded so enthusiastically. Sometimes my antics are met with weird looks. I would like to be able to have fun with less extravagance, though. Every now and then, balloons and bubble gum are fun. But it feels like I have to go to great lengths to have fun. I'd like to be able to enjoy myself without having such a high need for attention. I'm going to make a real effort to enjoy people contact just for the sake of being with people. Not requiring me or them to do something wild, so it will seem like fun just being with them.''

"I know what you mean," said Trina. "I hope you won't change that other silly, childlike way you have, though. It really helped me have fun tonight."

"I agree," Kathy said. "You are fun to be with."

Bob felt a little strange hearing that. He often thought he was either boring or overbearing. Hearing he was fun felt pretty good, even though it was also a little uncomfortable. "Thanks, guys," he said, looking more self-conscious than usual.

"It's the least we can do in thanks for the balloons," Trina teased.

Szifra realized they'd been meeting for eleven weeks now. Even though some had feared six weeks would be too great a commitment to the group, everyone was still coming. She felt good about that.

My Observations and Reactions to Meeting 11

Anne, 39, child care worker, lost child role in family, father died from alcoholism seven years ago.
Observations/progress noted:

Bob, 50, alcoholism counselor, scapegoat in family, recovering, mother alcoholic, now deceased.
Observations/progress noted:

Kathy, 33, secretary, mascot/responsible role in family, father died from alcoholism this year.
Observations/progress noted:

Linda, 36, nurse, responsible role in family, both parents are alcoholic, living.
Observations/progress noted:

Mark, 30, welder, scapegoat role in family, recovering, father died from alcoholism six years ago.
Observations/progress noted:

Michael, 38, PR/advertising, responsible role in family, father is alcoholic, mother prescription drug–addicted, living.
Observations/progress noted:

Roger, 20, student, lost child/scapegoat in family, recovering, mother also recovering.
Observations/progress noted:

Sarah, 36, high school teacher, responsible role in family, father died from alcoholism five years ago.
Observations/progress noted:

Susan, 32, accountant, lost child/responsible role in family, father died from alcoholism two years ago.
Observations/progress noted:

Trina, 45, shipping clerk, scapegoat role in family, recovering, father quit drinking a few years ago.
Observations/progress noted:

Szifra, therapist
Observations:

Observations about me during this meeting:

My feelings during this meeting:

Issues I'd like to explore further:

My reactions to this meeting:

What I learned about myself during this meeting:

Sharing Feedback with Each Other

"WHAT ARE THE pens and paper for?" Mark asked Szifra as everyone settled in for group. Szifra smiled at his curiosity, noting that he and the rest of the group seemed especially relaxed. Last week's mood seemed to have carried over to this week.

"A different kind of exercise," she responded, explaining that the group would be sharing feedback with each other tonight.

Giving and receiving structured feedback had been useful in other groups. Szifra had waited a while with the ACOA group, to give Anne and Susan time to become more comfortable. In unstructured sessions, she realized, they were able to hide more easily. That was okay; after all, they'd spent their lives being invisible. They would need some time to become comfortable with the high visibility in group.

She had also wanted to give group members time to get to know Mark and Bob before they exchanged feedback— and to give everyone the time they needed to develop more trust and intimacy. "I'd like you to write each group member's name on a separate piece of paper," she instructed them now. "Under each name, I'd like you to list two positive things you can say about that person. Think of what you like or admire. I'd also like you to identify one thing about each person you feel needs work or gets in your way."

Kathy was taken aback by the agenda. She was hesitant about activities that required her participation because she was never sure how vulnerable she'd feel. This one will be a ten for vulnerability, she said to herself as she picked up the paper and a pencil.

Szifra recognized Kathy's apprehension; she'd seen it in other clients. Acknowledging hesitation from Anne and Michael, too, she talked more about how the evening would go.

"I realize it may be difficult for you to do this," she said. "It's very hard to tell others what we really think, and it's hard to hear what they think of us. This is new for most of you, and 'new' isn't usually comfortable.

"Also, this kind of feedback is not something we do much of. We don't generally ask others, 'What do you like about me?' or, 'Is there anything you think I could change?' Most of us don't solicit this kind of input, and that's especially true for Children of Alcoholics."

Szifra sensed that most of the group wanted to hear more about tonight's activity. She decided to expand, hoping they would feel more comfortable proceeding. She spoke gently but with encouragement. "Too often, I know you were subjected to harsh criticism as children. You may have been told, 'You're such a crybaby,' 'You're so naughty,' or, 'You're a stupid, inconsiderate person.' This criticism was not just of your behavior, but of your person as well. After regularly hearing comments like these, I can understand how you wouldn't be enthusiastic about feedback tonight. What we are going to do is different."

"I sure hope so," said Linda. "As you all know, my self-esteem was practically nonexistent after all the criticism I heard growing up. I'm rebuilding it, but slowly."

"What we'll be doing tonight will be constructive feedback," Szifra emphasized. "Some of you may see some humor in that—or believe the two words to be mutually exclusive," she added, picking up on Mark's doubtful look.

"Criticism, contrary to your childhood experiences, can be constructive. We will not be putting each other down.

Our intent is to inform each other, not to communicate blame, to ridicule, or to shame. Although your parents may have unwittingly delivered destructive messages, we will send messages designed to 'save face,' not 'lose face.' If I hear blame, don't worry, I'll interfere!'' She paused briefly to let her words sink in.

"I've often suggested you think of yourselves as a big circle made up of thousands of dots,'' she continued. "Each dot represents one thing about you. There are dots for your behaviors, your looks, your speech patterns, your intellect —dots for everything about you. When someone criticizes one of your dots, you may react by immediately expanding that tiny dot into a huge dot, forgetting about all the other dots in your circle. It's like you are looking through a microscope which is magnifying only that dot.

"For instance,'' she went on, "tonight someone may say, 'I think you could work on better listening skills.' You may enlarge that to mean, 'No one can talk to me. I can't listen. No wonder I have no close friends. Who'd want to be my friend, anyway? I'm self-centered just like Dad was.' In no time you've let a minor criticism destroy your entire sense of yourself. Now, I'm not sure how much we can control that initial feeling. Frankly, I think it's pretty well programmed. Something that sounds like criticism to us will feel bad. We can't be instantly objective. Our task, however, is to turn on our logic. Back to the microscope— your job is to see all the dots again, in perspective. Then remember that only one part of you was being scrutinized, not all of you.''

Szifra spoke quickly, using her hands to emphasize her words. The way she sat forward on her chair and enunciated her speech told the group she attributed a lot of importance to what she was saying. "After you regain your perspective,'' she said, "then you can hear the criticism and evaluate it. You decide if you think it is valid. You can ask yourself if you would respond differently if you had the opportunity to repeat the situation. It's also fine to ask the person how you could behave differently. Sometimes you will decide that you don't agree a change is needed. You consider the feedback, think about the person delivering the criticism, and determine if you have a difference of opinion.''

The group listened intently as Szifra spoke. Michael tried to convince himself that what she was asking them to do made sense. Too bad it doesn't feel like it, though, he said to himself.

"Let's get started writing," Szifra suggested. "Write two positives for each person and one thing that bothers you or that you think needs work. Include yourselves, too. Then we'll share what we've written."

Anne thought how much easier it would be if they could just give the piece of paper to the other person. Speaking to everyone about such personal issues was going to be tough. She looked down at her paper, determined not to get stuck like the time she'd had to write reactions to the meeting. I really like Susan, she thought. I'll start with positives about her.

Szifra glanced around the room as everyone got to work. Feedback sessions were difficult for her, too, yet they were useful. She knew how hard it was for ACOAs to give and receive honest feedback. Years of inappropriate criticism and burying feelings left wounds that took time and work to heal.

After allowing several minutes for everyone to write, she suggested they begin. "I want one of you to share all the feedback you've written," she said. "Share with one person, then another, until you have shared with everyone. Then tell us what you wrote about yourself. Then another person will begin giving feedback."

She asked them to limit their exchange to the feedback and brief acknowledgments, such as thank-yous. "If you want to discuss something in greater depth, save it until all the feedback has been shared. It's fine to write down comments or questions for us to discuss at the end. Who would like to begin? Don't forget," she cautioned playfully, "it gets harder the longer you wait."

They all understood what she meant. She'd told them before that waiting built anxiety.

Linda decided she would go first. She giggled nervously and fidgeted with her clothing, well matched and spotless as usual. Looking at Susan, she began, "I really like your gentleness and I respect your intelligence, Susan." She spoke softly, shifting on her chair and giggling again when all eyes focused on her. "I think you need to work on saying more in group."

Susan blushed when Linda complimented her. It was obvious that compliments were harder to hear than suggestions for change. Szifra knew this would be true for others tonight, too, as it was for many ACOAs.

Linda then turned to Roger. "I can see you've grown a lot in group. You speak up more readily. You've worked hard," she said positively. "What I'd like to see you work on is expressing your real feelings." Roger smiled at Linda, which reassured her. Next she shared her feedback with Mark, then Anne and Kathy.

At last, feeling tense and hesitant, she turned to Bob. "I see you as strong and assertive, Bob. I think those are good qualities. What I think you need to work on is your sensitivity to other people." Her heart beat wildly, her mouth was dry, and she felt dizzy. I'm on the verge of an anxiety attack, she thought, and concentrated on steadying her breathing.

Bob looked surprised. He had no idea what had prompted Linda's comment. Even though he knew that processing was supposed to occur later, he decided to ask anyway: "What do you mean, Linda?"

Linda looked as though someone had struck her. She waited several moments before she replied, her voice trembling, "You mean what I said about you?"

"I thought we weren't going to have discussions until the end," Trina interjected.

"That's what I think we should do," Szifra said. "Otherwise we won't get to hear from everyone." She understood Bob's desire to find out what Linda meant—and told him so—but reaffirmed her decision not to change the group's direction at this point.

Bob backed off, reminding himself that he wanted to be more cooperative in the group, less controlling. Still, he wondered what Linda had meant. Did he bulldoze over people? He remembered his counselor in treatment telling him that alcoholics could be overly egocentric, thinking only of themselves and their needs. And even when they did think of others' needs, too often they quickly denied them so they could drink that night. Bob didn't believe it could be explained away so simply, but he thought about it as Linda continued her feedback with others.

When she had finished, Szifra asked, "Did you write feedback for yourself, Linda?"

"Oh, I was hoping you'd forget," Linda responded shyly, then continued. "What I think is positive about myself is that I work hard and like people a lot. What I think I need to work on is getting more comfortable with saying difficult things to people." She sat back on her chair, with an audible sigh of relief. It was over—except for a further exchange with Bob later. Maybe we'll run out of time, she told herself hopefully.

Although Trina appeared ready to go next, she hesitated. She had usually been willing to speak up in group, but as she'd explained to Szifra in an individual session, that hadn't always been true. Groups used to be very difficult for her; they made her feel uneasy, judged, even stupid.

Suspecting Trina could use some encouragement, Szifra invited her to speak next. When she responded with shy enthusiasm, Szifra knew her perception was on target. Trina started right in, going in order around the circle.

"Bob," she began, "you are outspoken and willing to take risks. Those are my positives. My negative is, you don't always listen to other people like you should."

Bob sat back, frowning. What am I doing wrong in here? he wondered. I'm a counselor, I need to be able to listen and be sensitive to others, but I'm hearing that's not how I come across. His self-doubts grew as he thought about what Trina had said.

Watching him, Trina began to feel a little uncomfortable. Why did I start with him? she asked herself. She glanced at Szifra, who nodded encouragement for her to continue. She spoke to Kathy next. "I think you're funny and you're smart. I think you need to work on being more open with your feelings. You hide how you feel."

She wanted to say more but stopped herself and went on to Michael instead. "I like you, too, Mike. You're so alive. Does that sound weird?"

Michael laughed. "No, it feels pretty good," he said.

Next Trina told Mark, "You are strong. After all, you kicked heroin. And you are able to express yourself well. I think you need to work on denial, because I think you're tricking yourself about drinking."

Mark felt as though he'd been kicked in the stomach. All of these recovering alcoholics are the same, he told himself angrily. They think anyone who drinks is an alcoholic. They don't make any distinctions for individuals. In the next instant, though, he wondered if he was fooling himself.

"This will be one of the hardest things I've had to do in here," Anne began as she, too, took her turn. "You probably all noticed me staring at you as I thought about what I'd write. It helped me think of things to put down. Anyway, I guess I'll start. Kathy, for positives, I wrote 'busy' and 'interesting.' I think your involvement in so many things shows a lot of energy. I'd like to see you realize that you are a neat person."

She was surprised at how easy it was to speak once she got started. She shuffled her papers and moved to Sarah. "You're neat and eager. I'd like to see you relax more." Looking at Susan, she smiled warmly. "Susan, you're kind and intelligent. I'd like to see you be more daring. Once I see you succeed, maybe I'll try it. . . .

"Roger, you're very kind," Anne went on, and blushed suddenly. "You take time to notice all of us, even if we're quiet. And your reaching out to me has helped a lot."

Roger felt good about Anne's feedback. Part of his recovery process was learning to be more aware of others, and he was glad to know he was accomplishing that.

Anne continued sharing feedback with the rest of the group. Then the others took their turns.

Sarah cleverly identified less noticeable qualities, like loyalty and integrity. "Those are the things I look for in people," she explained. Mark had trouble limiting his to single words. He sincerely liked people and found it easy to tell them so.

Most of the comments from others were brief, with the positives more easily stated. Many comments were similar. More than one person told Anne they'd like her to talk more.' Several told Michael how well he spoke, which surprised him, because speaking out didn't come easily for him. Roger received several positive comments about his perceptiveness, which made him feel good.

Linda was amazed when Susan and Kathy both told her they liked how she was able to tell people what she felt. Both commented on her eye contact, even in emotional situations. Susan said that helped her feel more comfortable because she felt Linda was really communicating with her.

"Even though you might be talking about something very personal, you don't back off," Kathy told her. "I admire your ability to do what would be so hard, if not impossible, for me."

Linda responded, "I haven't realized that discussing personal issues is getting easier for me, and that my eye contact helps you feel at ease. I'm glad to know that. Thanks."

When everyone had finished, Szifra asked how they were feeling.

"I was so nervous," Kathy said. "This was the most difficult group session for me. But I will remember these positive comments and try to convince myself I can believe them. And I'm going to work on things like being more open and willing to commit to relationships."

Anne agreed that it had been hard for her, too. Her voice quavered as she spoke, revealing how uncomfortable she had been. "Thanks for helping me realize I'm a person with something to contribute, too," she said.

"I really liked sharing feedback," Trina said. "I never get a chance to hear about what others think of me. Well, not like this, anyway. It helped me a lot. And I'll have plenty to think about, too. I'm glad we did this."

"Is there any specific feedback anyone would like to address?" Szifra asked.

Bob decided not to wait. He'd been phrasing and rephrasing his question to Linda in his mind, and finally he had it worded in a way that sounded good to him. "Linda, what did you mean when you said I needed to work on sensitivity to others?" he asked.

Linda's stomach muscles tightened. She'd expected Bob to ask her to explain herself, but she'd hoped he wouldn't. She'd been rehearsing what to say, just in case. Nervously she responded. "At our meeting a long time ago when we discussed feelings, I said I was nervous. You asked me what I was nervous about, and I said I didn't know. You really pushed me, saying there had to be a reason. Your tone was pushy, and I didn't think you were being sensitive."

"Just because I said you must have a reason, you think I'm insensitive?" Bob asked. "I think you must be oversensitive, then. That doesn't seem like a big deal. Was that really all?"

Linda explained that she'd felt it at other times, too, when he'd spoken in group. She cited a couple of examples. Bob sidestepped each one with, "Yes, I understand what you're saying, but that seems oversensitive to me."

Linda turned to Szifra. Her voice trembled as she began to cry. "I don't know where to go with this."

Szifra asked the others to share their perceptions about interactions with Bob. Trina mentioned he sometimes came off kind of know-it-all. Anne said she was intimidated by him because he seemed so self-assured. Mark disagreed, saying, "I like my interactions with you, Bob."

"It might be helpful to us if you would occasionally say,

'I don't know,' about something," said Kathy. Then she corrected herself by saying, "Well, it would be helpful to me, anyway."

Szifra turned to Linda. "Have you ever felt like this in interactions before? With others?"

Linda thought a minute, then said, "Yes, with my first husband. I always felt like I had to explain my feelings, justify them. Then, no matter what I said, he minimized them. I never had the right feeling or the right reason, it seemed. I used to get so frustrated. I'd try to explain, then I'd finally run off and cry."

"Linda, is how you're feeling now similar to how you felt back then?" Szifra asked gently. When Linda nodded, Szifra pointed out how much she had grown and gave her credit for continuing the interaction with Bob instead of leaving the room. "The option is now open for change, for resolution," she said.

Still crying, Linda said, "Maybe after I stop feeling so much about this, I'll be able to realize I'm doing better. Right now I just feel scared and worn out."

Bob responded, "That helps me understand a little better. I was feeling attacked. My dots are all out of perspective. At first I thought you should have been correcting things, Szifra. Now I'm feeling different, not just attacked. I guess I see what you mean, Linda. My father always demanded reasons. I do it to my children. I think I do it to my clients, too. Maybe I can't handle not having reasons. I don't know why, though."

"You may need to feel in control, Bob," said Szifra, "to be in a position to fix or solve problems. You do have good problem-solving skills. You may not be as strong in your ability to respond with, 'I understand,' 'Yes, I know it really hurts,' or, 'Boy, that's rough.' "

As Szifra spoke, Bob's walls tumbled. He began to cry, releasing his emotions and feelings. Szifra reacted gently.

"I feel like I'm seeing a part of you for the first time, Bob," she said. "You have walled this sensitivity and warmth off from us and the world, and perhaps even yourself."

"It seems strange that we have to be confronted and fall apart before we can show others what we're like underneath," Roger said. "We think the facade we show the world is what everyone will like, but it turns out everyone wants the stuff inside."

"It's hard to take those walls down, though," Susan confirmed. She told Bob, "You deserve a lot of credit for being so brave."

Bob's mood lightened as he said, "Szifra, maybe your 'take credit' statements are paying off. Now we're doing it to each other!"

"Going back to walls, like the old nursery tale," Michael said, "if the walls were brick, we could huff and puff and never blow them down. When it's a wolf huffing and puffing, we need brick walls. But if it's a friend huffing and puffing, straw walls would be better."

"It sounds kind of corny," Bob admitted, laughing, "but it makes sense. I guess we needed bricks as kids with our families, and we probably still do sometimes. But it would be good if we could decide when to substitute wood or straw."

"Bob, I'd like to add another thought, for you and for everyone here," Szifra said. "For each of us, our coping strategies have served us well in some areas and not so well in others. If you did not have your particular qualities, you would not necessarily be confident, get things done, or be an individual willing to take risks. Recognize those strengths. They are assets. Sure, you may want to increase or decrease the intensity of some of your traits. I just don't want you, Bob, or any of you to think that's a bad quality. Better get rid of it. You may want to modify your behavior or its intensity, but don't get rid of anything that may be an asset in its proper place or proportion."

"It's the all-or-nothing virus," Linda said. "We have a special ward at the hospital for people with that disease," she said, laughing.

"Are they all ACOAs?" asked Kathy.

"Is it curable?" Trina asked.

Everyone laughed, glad for a lighter moment.

"Is that next door to the trust-everyone-or-trust-no-one ward?" Szifra asked.

"What do you mean?" asked Mark.

"Well, I was just thinking abut ACOAs and trust, all or nothing. But, as you know, trust is not that way. It's not an all-or-nothing phenomenon. It's as you said, Bob, we need to be able to choose among straw, wood, or brick walls, depending on the person and situation."

"Is it okay to comment on tonight's group?" Bob asked.

"Sure," Szifra encouraged him.

"Well, it was a night!" Bob said.

Trina nodded, and Michael said, "The positives I heard felt very strange and very good. It was hard tonight, but I feel good, too."

"I wasn't thrilled about the activity, but I'm glad we did it," Kathy said.

"I learned a lot from this," said Anne. "I survived while nine different people told me how they felt about me! And I said nine 'negative' things about other people. It's a cinch saying negatives about myself. I'm an expert at that. But to others, gosh! I still can't believe I did it. I really did try to give constructive criticism, though, not put-downs."

"Before tonight," Linda said, "I was afraid I couldn't handle telling Bob what I thought." She looked at him and said, "Thanks for saying so much tonight and showing your feelings, too. I got to see the sensitivity I didn't know was there."

Bob smiled in response and said, "Thanks."

"Another reaction I had," Linda continued, "was being glad I made that connection about thinking that I had to justify my feelings. Group and individual therapy help me fit the pieces of the past together, which helps me work on the present more effectively. It hurt like crazy, and I felt very self-conscious, but I'm glad you pursued that one, Szifra."

"I'm glad, too," Szifra responded.

After everyone finished with their reactions, Szifra reminded them not to carry around just the "negatives" from the evening's session, missing the positives. "If you're feeling like the negatives you heard are overwhelming you," she said, "take a big piece of paper and write them down in very tiny handwriting in one corner. Then use bright colors and big letters to write in the positives. That may help you keep what you heard in perspective. Or else you can draw two big circles with lots of dots. On one of them, make one dot very big and black. On the other, keep the dots the same. Try to realize how out of proportion your feelings about the criticism are.

"Take out the lists from tonight from time to time and look them over," she suggested. "Write 'agree' or 'disagree' next to each item, evaluating the constructive feedback. Think about the comment. If you agree with it, decide how you'll change, and then be patient with yourself. It takes time to change, lots of time. If you disagree, discard the criticism or ask for more feedback from the person who gave it so you'll better understand what they meant. If there are people outside group you trust, ask them to give you two positives and one thing they'd like to see you change. Share tonight's experience with them, if you trust them to treat the material with respect and care."

That's really developing some trust, Michael thought. Maybe I'll try that.

"You all did great," Szifra said, concluding their session. "I sure enjoy being here with you. Thanks for sharing so much tonight. See you next week!"

My Observations and Reactions
to Meeting 12

Anne, 39, child care worker, lost child role in family,
father died from alcoholism seven years ago.
Observations/progress noted:

Bob, 50, alcoholism counselor, scapegoat in family, recovering, mother alcoholic, now deceased.
Observations/progress noted:

Kathy, 33, secretary, mascot/responsible role in family,
father died from alcoholism this year.
Observations/progress noted:

Linda, 36, nurse, responsible role in family, both parents
are alcoholic, living.
Observations/progress noted:

Mark, 30, welder, scapegoat role in family, recovering, father died from alcoholism six years ago.
Observations/progress noted:

Michael, 38, PR/advertising, responsible role in family, father is alcoholic, mother prescription drug–addicted, living.
Observations/progress noted:

Roger, 20, student, lost child/scapegoat in family, recovering, mother also recovering.
Observations/progress noted:

Sarah, 36, high school teacher, responsible role in family, father died from alcoholism five years ago.
Observations/progress noted:

Susan, 32, accountant, lost child/responsible role in family, father died from alcoholism two years ago.
Observations/progress noted:

Trina, 45, shipping clerk, scapegoat role in family, re-covering, father quit drinking a few years ago.
Observations/progress noted:

Szifra, therapist
Observations:

Observations about me during this meeting:

My feelings during this meeting:

Issues I'd like to explore further:

My reactions to this meeting:

What I learned about myself during this meeting:

Dealing with Our Families Now

"HELP!" BOB EXCLAIMED when Szifra asked if the group was ready to begin. Everyone immediately turned to him, surprised by his outburst. Susan seemed to know instinctively that he was serious. Sarah suspected it was another mascot antic.

"My father is coming for a visit," he blurted out. "I don't want to sound too dramatic, but I'm nervous. Last week you encouraged me to tear down my walls. Well, I've got them down, I'm scared about this visit, and I want your help."

Sarah was amazed. What a change. He seems like a real person tonight, she thought. Too bad it took a crisis for him to become a person to me.

"Family visits," Trina groaned. "I can relate."

"So can I," said Michael. "Good luck."

"I'm glad you're speaking up," Szifra said to Bob. "From the responses, I'd say we have a pertinent topic. How does everyone feel about spending tonight discussing family visits and relations with our families?"

"Well, since the holidays are coming up, I think it would be a great topic," Linda agreed. The others did, too.

"Bob, would you like to say more about how you're feeling about your father's pending visit?" Szifra asked.

"Help!" Bob repeated, then got down to the issue. "I'm feeling very uncertain about spending time with Dad right

278

now. For years I've allegedly had my act together. In the last several months, as I've learned more about ACOA issues, I've realized I'm not as together as I thought. I'm in the midst of trying to figure out my feelings, sorting out my childhood, understanding how I was affected. Right now I'm feeling very vulnerable, very fragile. I'm not the person Dad is expecting to visit.''

''Can you say any more?'' Szifra asked.

''Well, I'm not sure he'll see the same me,'' Bob answered. ''And I don't think I'm ready to deal with him.''

''Do you have any viable options?'' Szifra asked him.

''Like asking him not to come now?'' Bob said.

Szifra nodded. ''That's one. Any others you've thought of?''

''Mostly I've been so worried, I haven't been able to think clearly. I didn't expect him to want to visit now. He usually spends the holidays with my sister, since Mom's gone. Frankly, I've been so focused on myself these last few months, I haven't thought at all about how I would interact with my family the next time I saw them.''

''Would asking him not to visit now be an option?'' Trina asked.

''Not a great one,'' Bob responded. ''The explaining I'd have to do would be worse than going through with the visit. It would hurt his feelings. He'd never understand. Neither would my sister, who'd be mad that I was being so selfish. Again, I can't imagine asking him not to come now. Or dealing with my sister because I didn't want him to come.''

''So, do you want to figure out what you can do to make the visit go okay?'' Trina asked, thinking how good she was getting at focusing on the issue at hand.

''I think so,'' Bob said. ''At least that's what I was thinking when I brought it up. At first I thought about just slipping back into my old strong-and-in-control mode. I hate to do that, though. It took me so long to crack that shell. But I don't feel strong enough with what's under that shell to survive a visit from my father.''

"What do you expect during his visit?" Michael asked. "As I recall, your mother was an alcoholic, but you didn't mention anything about your father."

"No, Dad's not a drinker," Bob replied. "Oh, he used to be socially. Maybe he still is. But he's not chemically dependent. I've disappointed him so much in my life. Since I've been recovering, I've tried hard to please him. If he comes now and sees I'm struggling again, he'll be disappointed. That's one issue. The other is, he's a tough guy to get along with. I let him dominate me for years. Then I struck back by drinking and running around. Great method, huh?" he said in a self-deprecating voice. "I really showed him.

"Anyway, once I got sober," he continued, "I didn't see him that much. And when I did see him, we were back into the old pattern. Dad dominates, I submit. Now I'm resisting it, and, as you guys know, it makes waves. What do the rest of you do about family visits?"

Szifra was pleased to see Bob reach out for input from others. He was taking some significant steps away from his former "I've got to know everything and never ask for help" coping style.

"It's a little different for me," Linda said, "because my family all lives here and because my parents are still drinking. But in some sense, my issues are the same. I struggled a long time to become my own person, not to always be at their beck and call. I've had to stand up to my family and let them know I'm making my own decisions and standing by them. Mom didn't like it when I started making my own decisions. Neither did one of my sisters. Maybe that piece is the same for you and me, Bob."

Bob nodded. "Maybe you're right about that. As far as Dad's concerned, I'm still a high school kid who needs some good advice from his old man."

"My mother treats me like that, too," Linda said. "She tells me I get too uppity for myself, whatever that means."

"How do you deal with that?" Bob asked.

"With great difficulty!" Linda replied. "And not always

successfully, to be perfectly honest. I started out by saying, 'Mom, I know you have my best interests at heart. I appreciate your concern. I'll consider your suggestions.' Then when I made my own decision, and it was usually contrary to her suggestion, I'd try to avoid the issue with her. If she asked me about it point-blank, I'd say, 'Mom, I gave my decision serious thought. I think I made the best decision for me. And I'm willing to take responsibility for it.' Then I'd try to change the subject.''

Sarah's jaw dropped as Linda spoke. "You are really strong!" she said. "I'm impressed with how well you handle your mother's interference!"

"Well, I've had years of practice, years of saying the same things over and over to her," Linda said. "For what it's worth, Bob, you might try some of what I did."

"Thanks," Bob said, thinking how important it was to his recovery to hear this constructive feedback. I hate the discomfort, he thought, but I like that I have the chance to change that now.

"I have some of the same issues," Susan said hesitantly. She realized, rather sheepishly, that because Anne wasn't there tonight, she felt shier than she had in a long time. I guess Anne gives me some courage, she thought, then said to the group, "My father is dead, so my relationship struggles are with my mother. They're similar, in that Mom tends to overpower me. I have a history of letting her. I never really liked it, but I didn't realize it could be another way. In other words, that I had choices."

"Even though both of my parents are dead," Kathy said, "I have some of those same experiences. I know I'm changing, becoming a different person in a lot of ways. But my brothers and sisters don't recognize this. It's like they have me stereotyped, and I'll always be silly, fun-loving Kathy who can't add."

"Who can't add?" Trina asked.

"Oh, that's an old one, from childhood days playing cards when I'd count on my fingers. It caught on as another family joke."

"I know what you're saying about your family stereotyping you," Mark said. "I've spent years trying to overcome my earlier behavior. I'm not sure they trust me yet. It's like they're still checking to see if I'm using."

"I sometimes have that, too," Roger added, "from my dad. I think he still looks at me when I come in at night to see if I've been drinking. It's like he's afraid to let his guard down and really believe I'm sober."

"I'm guilty of that," Michael said. "Not with you guys, though. I've only known you as sober, straight people, so it never occurs to me to wonder if you've been drinking or using. But with my dad, it's always the first thing I look for. I think I'm justified, though, because my dad told us for years he had quit when he never had. I think it is a trust issue, like you said, Mark. I have that with one sister, too. You know, we haven't talked much about alcoholism and other problems with sisters and brothers, but I worry about mine a lot. My sister calls drunk sometimes. I worry she'll die young."

Trina echoed those concerns, adding, "Besides worrying a lot, it's also a real pain at times. Although I know not to take their inventory, it sure is hard not to want them to get their acts together."

"I worry about my family, too," Linda said. "Both drug use and other dysfunctional coping strategies I see. . . . A while back, Michael, you talked about your dad." She laughed, noting that they'd strayed from his point.

"No problem," Michael resumed. "Anyway, I just don't trust my dad. He's never done anything to earn my trust. There were too many broken promises."

"I've been straight eight years, though," Mark said. "How long does it have to be before my brother and sisters trust me?"

"I'm not trying to defend their lack of trust," Michael told him. "I understand, though, once that trust is broken, it's awfully hard to earn it back. It's hard for me to trust again."

Szifra noted to herself that Michael had been making

progress, which was especially evident tonight in how able he was to tell Mark his feelings, despite the risk of conflict. It had taken one year of individual therapy plus this group and his Al-Anon ACOA group to bring him to the point where he could "rock the boat" without intense panic and the desire to flee.

"Whether it's changing addictive drinking patterns, becoming more talkative, or giving up the clowning around role," she interjected, "getting your family to recognize change in you is difficult. You can tell them you've changed. Your behavior can reflect the change. But if your family members, and that includes your parents as well as your brothers and sisters, have not been involved in learning about alcoholism and changing themselves, they may not recognize your growth and change. You can, however, hold firm and reinforce the changes you've made. I don't pretend it's easy to do, though. Frankly, I'm the most 'old me' around my family. The encouraging part is I can be more and more myself with them, and others, too. That can happen for you, also."

"Being surrounded by the whole family, though, outnumbers me," Trina said. "I know I'm sober. I know I've grown. If they wanted to see it, they could. But they're all so sick themselves, they can't. I've had to tell myself that what they think is not important."

"That's the most important point," Szifra agreed. "You no longer have to define yourself using their definition. They have really not provided you with a good recipe for living."

"Exactly," said Trina. "For some reason, God only knows why, I still want to maintain some contact with them. I talk to myself before I visit any of them. I plan my visits carefully. And if I feel myself getting sabotaged or undermined, I leave. It only took a year of therapy before I realized leaving was an option." She laughed. "Anyway, I refuse to let myself get caught up in the merry-go-round," she concluded.

"It's not that easy for me, Trina," Kathy said. "I've

found that when I'm with my family I can slip into old habits without realizing it for a while. It's so automatic."

Susan nodded. "I do the same thing. I jump back into old roles of being shy and quiet. I'm still afraid of being rejected in new situations. I don't talk about my feelings often, and yet I'm still afraid others will come to know the real me. I want to give love to small children, for example. I'd love to be more spontaneous with children, but I hold back. I'm ready to go on with my life."

"That's where I'm coming from," Bob said. "I can't try these new things out on my dad. I have to be more strong in them before I'm ready to expose myself to him. Hearing the rest of you say you've been through this helps. Thanks for telling me how you've dealt with it."

"I'm trying to figure out if holidays are worse, or if I'm thinking that because that's about the only time my family gets together, anyway," Sarah said.

"I think holidays can be worse," Linda remarked. "One book on Adult Children I read has a chapter called 'Merry Christmas and Other Disasters.' When I read that, I laughed, but it was a sad laugh. That phrase rang true for me."

"Holidays can compound the problems," Szifra agreed. "Drinking often escalates, which can cause new conflicts and bring back old, bad memories. Many of us have expectations of how the holidays should be. When our expectations aren't met, we feel disappointed, sad, maybe angry. Sometimes it accentuates the 'I don't belong' feeling. Holidays can be very stressful."

She paused briefly, thinking over the turn their discussion had taken. "Maybe we should spend some time talking about how you might handle the holidays differently this year, so they won't become new scenarios in the 'Merry Christmas and Other Disasters' chapter," she suggested.

"I'd like to," Sarah said quietly. "I'm usually very sad around the holidays. I do all the traditional things to make it seem like I'm part of the fun. I make and buy gifts. I wrap everything up nice. I bake. I smile. And I cry. I'm always so glad when they're over."

Sarah went on to explain why holidays were sad for her. There had been so many sad holidays in the past, she told the group, like the time her father had been arrested on Christmas Eve. It had been hard that year to pretend everything was fine.

"My mother went out of her way to make holidays very special for us," Kathy recalled. "Even though we never had much money, she made gifts. She sewed, baked, and made the simplest traditions seem like special activities. I have a mixture of happy and sad memories of holidays. And a lot of appreciation for how much Mom gave. When I was older, though, there were lots of hold-your-breath times when I worried Dad wouldn't be okay."

"Sort of like walking on eggshells," Michael said, and Kathy nodded. "I wish I could say I had as many nice memories as you had, Kathy," he continued. "Holidays were the worst for Dad. That's when he drank the most, started the most arguments, and turned our lives upside down. One of my strongest childhood memories was the year Dad surprised us all, even Mom, with these extravagant presents. I got this huge semi. The cab and trailer detached. It was the ultimate toy that year, and I got it. Even though Dad had been smashed when he came home on Christmas Eve, we kids didn't pay much attention, we were so thrilled with all our wonderful gifts. The day after Christmas, the toys were all returned to the store. Never an explanation. Just gone."

Szifra said, "Michael, I remember you said in an early group that you were angry with your dad because even though he did his best, his best just wasn't good enough."

"I said tonight that if my family wanted to see my changes, they could," Trina interjected. "I saw your expression when I said that, Szifra. I know that maybe they don't deliberately choose to ignore the growth I've made, but I think I feel like Mike did when his dad returned the presents. What an awful thing to do. It's so inconsistent. How the hell are we supposed to trust? So what if that was his best? I agree—it's just not good enough. I have plenty to feel angry and disappointed about. Mike, too. Holidays sometimes reinforce all that.''

The group continued sharing holiday experiences. As the conversation continued, Linda sat back, realizing that what she'd thought had been an experience unique to her was, in fact, common to many others, too. It's just one more example of how much we share, she thought.

"Hearing your memories of past holidays explains why so many of you feel anxious today as the holiday season approaches,'' Szifra said. "This is a good time to remind yourselves you are no longer helpless children who are unable to effect change. Today, you are adults. You can take some control over your holiday experiences. You can create new histories to replace the sad and anxious times. Today, you have power; you have options. How about focusing now on ways to make the holidays more positive?'' she asked the group.

"That would help me,'' Bob agreed.

"Me too,'' said Linda. "I need to switch the focus to something more positive.''

"Good,'' Szifra said. "You can't erase your earlier times. You can dim the impact, though, and you can set the tone for future holidays. Who has some ideas?''

"I do,'' Mark said. "In the last several years, my family has become really important to me. I was the one who used to show up late for holiday dinners. Even though I loved holidays, because of my addiction, my family took second place. Now I try to be with my family at Thanksgiving or Christmas. Christmas is more important to me, so that's usually the one I try for. It means traveling for me, so I have to try to get the bucks together every year. It's important to me, though.''

"I always get together with the family, too,'' Trina said. "But only for a few hours. I go early in the day, when my brothers and sisters are more likely to be sober. I stay only a short while. Then I leave. Mom hates that. She doesn't understand why I won't stay for dinner. But I know what dinner will bring, and I can't take that risk. I go in the morning, enjoy the kids and their presents, hug everyone, then leave.''

''You've found a way to take care of yourself, and still get in on some family contact,'' Szifra confirmed.

''I haven't been able to do that,'' Michael admitted. ''It's been several years since I was with my family for the holidays. Since we don't live in the same town, I don't have the option of going for a few hours. It's just too hard to be around all that drinking and weird behavior, so I stay away. My wife and I have established our own little rituals. It's only the two of us, but we're creating our own traditions.''

''I like that idea,'' said Kathy. ''Since I don't have my own family, the last several years I've usually spent Christmas with my sister and her family. Now that Dad's gone, too, I'm going to have to keep borrowing a family for the holidays. I like your idea, Michael, of establishing my own traditions. I've been reading about surrogate family relationships and learning that I don't have to be related to people to share that family-tie feeling. I think coming up with my own idea of something special to do for the holidays would help me get through this year.''

'' 'Get through,' you said, Kathy,'' Sarah commented. ''That's how I feel. I keep up the front for my kids. I'd never want them to know how hard it was for me. I usually just try to get through it.''

''What could make it easier for you?'' Szifra asked.

Sarah considered the question. ''Not having the interruption in my routine,'' she said. ''It's when the day-to-day routine changes that I feel off balance. Like now is when we're supposed to have wonderful times. The world is celebrating this great holiday together. And once again, I'm not part of the celebration.''

''Since school is out during that time, and you can't teach that day, you don't have a choice about your usual routine being interrupted,'' Szifra reminded her. ''What are some of the things you do have a choice about?''

''I know,'' Sarah said, grinning. ''You're reminding me I have alternatives. Funny, I never thought about that as far as holidays went. What could I do? I figure every house around the world has a mom, a dad, and two and a half children happily eating turkey dinner together. Maybe Grandma's there. There are lots of presents. Smiles. I never realized how much fantasy I was believing!'' She smiled at her newfound awareness. ''Here's nine of us sitting here, and none of us will fit that picture! I guess I better get off the pity pot and work on this. I feel sort of silly now.''

''Don't be too hard on yourself, Sarah,'' Mark said. ''Sometimes I have the same sort of fantasy. I just add Uncle Mark sitting at the table when I paint the picture!''

''My ex-wife and I alternate Christmas Eve and Christmas Day with our kids,'' Bob said, ''so I've always stayed here for Christmas. Since I've had children, I haven't dealt with my parents at the Christmas holidays anyway. I have gone for Thanksgiving, though, and experienced many of the same kinds of things the rest of you have. I guess Christmas has been easier for me since I have kids. They're my tradition.''

''Since I still live at home,'' Roger said, ''I spend it with my parents and grandparents. There have been years when the holidays were too long, but never really bad. My dad likes watching sports on TV. I feel guilty because of you guys having bad times, but I have no fears about the holidays coming up. I always get good presents and enjoy myself pretty well.''

''You're really lucky,'' Linda said. ''Don't feel guilty. It's good. Great, in fact, that you have good memories of holidays and a good time now. I wish ours were like that. Part of why the holidays are difficult, I think, is that here's this group of people who generally don't spend much time together, thrown together for a whole day. No one knows what to do with themselves!''

''I agree,'' said Michael. ''Especially as we got older and developed different interests. We just didn't have that much in common, that much to talk about, not to mention all the weird interactions.''

''Our family usually gets into huge arguments,'' Trina

said. "About anything or nothing. It doesn't matter. There are always people willing to take up both sides of the issue. One year most of the day was spent trying to determine how fast a fly was moving if it was buzzing around in a car going fifty miles per hour. You wouldn't believe the hours of conversation on that. Not conversation, really, loud yelling, shouting, belligerent opinions. That was the year I knew I'd been around for the last full-day holiday."

Several of the others told Trina that their families argued a lot, too, when together. "Well, glad to know, once again, that we all come from similarly nutty situations," she said.

"We always played games," Kathy said. "That made it fun. Mom always wanted Dad to play, but he didn't enjoy them. He always called Monopoly 'Monotony.' I have to admit, now, I agree with him! But then, I wanted him to play. I wanted Dad to join in and do family things. Spend time doing what we liked. Dad usually fell asleep, then we'd all play.

"Your mentioning games gives me an idea for my own traditions," Sarah said. "I've been sitting here trying to figure out what I could do with my boys. They're at that age where just spending time with Mom isn't too cool. Maybe I'll get a neat new game for all of us for Christmas, something challenging enough so they wouldn't get bored with it."

"Church has become a big part of my personal tradition for Christmas," Linda commented. "Well, every holiday, actually. It's a happy time; I connect with very caring people. My husband, daughters, and I have coffee and doughnuts after church and spend a few minutes visiting. I leave feeling very positive. Then, if the rest of my holiday doesn't turn out spectacular, I don't feel like I've missed out on anything. I had a good morning, and I try to hold on to that memory. It means a lot to me that we're our own family unit.

"Oh, speaking of my daughters reminded me I never let you know that my daughter, Lynn, decided not to live with her dad," she added. "She never told me how she made her decision, but I'm glad. I guess you can tell how important she is to me."

"I'd been meaning to ask you about Lynn," Trina said. "I'm glad it's working out."

Linda smiled. "Thanks."

Bob talked about cooking breakfast with his wife, spending their day off together. "I guess we've formed our own family unit, too. I didn't realize we were creating our own traditions, but I guess we are. We make something special for breakfast and linger over coffee. It's something we don't usually make time for. So whenever we have a holiday, we 'do breakfast' as we say."

Several others shared little things they did or might like to try doing with friends or family. "All this input has given me a few ideas for Dad's visit," Bob said. "Even though it won't be for a holiday, maybe we could plan some things so our time together won't be so strained. The more I've heard people talk tonight, the more convinced I am I will not slip back into my old role just to get through this visit. I won't blast Dad, either, which I might have done if we hadn't talked about this tonight. After years of recommending support groups to my clients, I can say I've experienced their real value firsthand. Thanks, everyone," he said warmly.

After everyone left, Szifra thought about the evening's session. I'm so glad everyone's in this group, so they can hear each other and share their ideas and support. Everyone's holidays might be better because of tonight's sharing. What a great thing! If each member positively influences one or two people as a result of this group, so many families can feel better. It can make a dent in the negative generational effects of alcoholism.

My Observations and Reactions to Meeting 13

Bob, 50, alcoholism counselor, scapegoat in family, recovering, mother alcoholic, now deceased.
Observations/progress noted:

Kathy, 33, secretary, mascot/responsible role in family, father died from alcoholism this year.
Observations/progress noted:

Linda, 36, nurse, responsible role in family, both parents are alcoholic, living.
Observations/progress noted:

Mark, 30, welder, scapegoat role in family, recovering, father died from alcoholism six years ago.
Observations/progress noted:

Michael, 38, PR/advertising, responsible role in family, father is alcoholic, mother prescription drug–addicted, living.
Observations/progress noted:

Roger, 20, student, lost child/scapegoat in family, recovering, mother also recovering.
Observations/progress noted:

Sarah, 36, high school teacher, responsible role in family, father died from alcoholism five years ago.
Observations/progress noted:

Susan, 32, accountant, lost child/responsible role in family, father died from alcoholism two years ago.
Observations/progress noted:

Trina, 45, shipping clerk, scapegoat role in family, recovering, father quit drinking a few years ago.
Observations/progress noted:

Szifra, therapist
Observations:

Observations about me during this meeting:

My feelings during this meeting:

Issues I'd like to explore further:

My reactions to this meeting:

What I learned about myself during this meeting:

Living Today

REALIZING THE GROUP hadn't spent much time on reactions the last several meetings, Szifra made a point of checking to see if reaction time was needed.

"Do we get an update?" Sarah asked Bob. "How did your visit go with your dad?"

Bob told her it had gone okay, even slightly better than past visits, but he admitted it was still a long way from being good. "Maybe Dad and I will never really click," he concluded.

The group spent a few minutes responding to his comments. Many empathized, wishing they could figure out how to have a close relationship with their own parents and families yet realizing that may never happen.

Then Trina asked, "Can we talk about relationships with other people? People outside our family?"

"Sounds like a good idea," Roger said.

"I said a long time ago that half my family is alcoholic and the other half crazy," she reminded them. "I wasn't kidding. My only prayer for a good relationship is with someone outside my family!"

"How are your relationships with people outside your family now?" Michael asked.

"Getting better," she said thoughtfully. "With a hell of a long way to go yet. At least I can talk to people at work and not want to drink before, during, and after. I used to avoid educated people, because I assumed they'd think I was too drunk to associate with or talk to. Or, if I was sober, they'd find out I wasn't smart enough."

"It's amazing to hear you say that," Michael said. "I would never guess you have trouble talking to people. You seem so comfortable saying what's on your mind in here."

"Sure, in here," Trina said with a wave of her hand. "And don't forget, I've been working on this a long time."

"It helps me to know we do make changes," Sarah said. "That gives me hope, even if the changes come slowly."

"We need a way to stand back and take a good, clear look at how we're changing and have changed," Bob said. "Like pretending we hadn't seen ourselves for a year. We could note 'what's different today.' "

"I'm pretty hard on myself," Linda admitted. "I probably don't notice changes I've made. I haven't thought too much about how hard it is for me to get close to people, but I'm realizing trust is a big problem for me. Sometimes I don't know if it's me or the other person I don't trust. I often think people are judging me. After I've spent time with someone, I replay the scenes over and over, remembering every stupid or inappropriate thing I said. 'Why did I say that?' I'll ask myself, or, 'She must think I'm really weird. I always mess up.' The tape keeps running." She glanced at Szifra and grinned sheepishly. "Yes, I guess I get the whip out."

"Verbal put-downs or 'whips,' were overused when you were children," Szifra reminded them. "Now you have the power to stop beating yourselves up."

Linda went on, "I can chat with people pretty easily, but when they start to get close, I back off."

"Boy, I understand that," Kathy said. "I do okay with chitchat, too. I run when someone tries to get too close, though. In the past few months I've realized I don't want to be that way forever, always running from relationships. I do enjoy people and would like to be more comfortable."

"It sounds odd to hear you say that, Kathy," Trina commented. "You're so much fun to be with, you could have lots of friends."

"She's right," Roger said. "You're a person people like. Remember all that feedback you got a couple of weeks ago?"

"It's like I told Trina earlier," Michael said. "I'm surprised you're uncomfortable, Kathy. You seem comfortable, and you say such good things. I really enjoy you. You can get close to people. They'll like you."

Kathy's eyes filled with tears. She found the focus uncomfortable and felt they were wrong. She most identified with the sad and dependent parts of herself. This likable part seemed so foreign to her, as if it didn't fit. I'm fun on the outside, she thought. Inside, I'm often sad, lonely, and emotionally dependent. "Emotionally weak," she remembered being called in a past relationship.

Kathy's thoughts wandered as she remembered Szifra working with her to understand what qualities she, Kathy, liked in a person. Much to her surprise, she had learned that she liked strong people who were also down to earth, willing to show their feelings. She smiled to herself as she realized the trait she called "down to earth" in others was the one she termed "emotionally dependent" in herself. Suddenly she realized that she was giving in to black-or-white thinking. If I admit I sometimes feel sad, she thought, then I'm saying I can't ever be fun. Maybe I'm not one or the other, I just have different feelings.

As Kathy detached from the group, Mark, too, became lost in thought. He wanted to ask Michael about his relationships but felt some reservations about speaking up. He reminded himself that he didn't have to wait until he felt totally comfortable before proceeding. Sometimes it was best to take risks and make changes. I'll ask, he decided, even if I feel nervous.

Checking back into the conversation, he waited for an appropriate opening, then asked Michael, "What are relationships like for you?"

Michael was surprised by the question. "Relationships

are pretty hard for me," he began slowly. "I'm okay at work, speaking superficially. I like people a lot, but it's like when we discussed fun. I tend to be a loner. The past year or so has been amazing because I realize for the first time in my life how much better I feel after I've opened up. The other day I discovered it was easier for me to open up in groups than one to one with people. Well, in this group and the other ACOA group I'm in, I mean."

"Yeah," Bob confirmed, "it's not too close, not so intimate. It's easier for me, too."

"Hmm," said Mark, "maybe that's the case for me, too. It's not too intimate. It's easier for me in a group than individually. I wonder if that's a male trait. Is that true for you, Roger?"

Roger shook his head. "It doesn't fit for me. Sharing personal things is very difficult in here. It's much easier for me when it's one to one. I don't believe in male or female generalizations anyway. In one of my groups during treatment, I was the only male, and people were always trying to attribute my feelings to being a man. I got sick of it. It just didn't seem fair."

Szifra smiled to herself, thinking how far Roger had come. He's so much more spontaneous, better able to articulate his feelings and be assertive. He's a far less "lost child," she thought. He's more like a "found child," a visible adult, instead of an invisible child.

Trina asked Michael to continue where he'd left off. "I want to hear more about your relationships," she said.

"I don't exactly remember where I was," Michael said. Szifra mentioned that he'd said he was more comfortable in groups than in individual relationships.

"Oh, right." He nodded. "I never thought I'd be sitting with a group of people talking about personal things, things I've tried to bury and hide my whole life. And then to think I like it," he said, shaking his head. "Well, 'like it' is a bit strong, because it's also uncomfortable as hell a lot. But I'm glad I do it."

He continued, "I know our focus was on relationships

outside our family, but I wanted to mention my sister again. She called and we had a good, long talk. She wasn't drunk. We even talked about some ACOA issues. I surprised myself and told her about my involvement in this group. It felt pretty good sharing what I was learning. I was nervous, but I did it.''

"I was nervous, but I did it," Mark repeated. "That should be a bumper sticker ACOAs could earn. Like the gold stars we used to get in school. Or some kids used to get, anyway." He laughed, remembering how his acting-out behavior often excluded him from the gold-star ranks.

Susan had been hanging back quite a bit during the session. She smiled, though, when Mark suggested the bumper sticker. That must be my cue, she thought, as a recipient of many gold stars, good little girl that I was.

"Too afraid to do anything else!" she spoke up.

Mark looked at her. "You mean you got those gold stars because you were too afraid to do anything else?" They both laughed as Susan confirmed that was the case.

"What about today?" Mark asked her.

"I was nervous, but I did it," Susan said, smiling. "I think it's starting to be true for me. I'm doing more and more all the time, despite my nervousness. I'm better about relationships than I used to be. I go out to lunch sometimes with my coworkers. I say more about my feelings and ideas I sure have a long way to go, though."

"What gets in your way?" Trina asked.

Susan's voice trembled a bit as she responded. "*I* get in my way. I'm so sure I'll say the wrong thing. Sound stupid."

Uncharacteristically, Anne spoke up. "That's what happens to me. I'm convinced I'll say the dumbest thing, so I'm better off just being still."

"Neither one of you ever sounds stupid to me," Roger said. "I always wish you'd talk more. I like what you have to say," he said, looking alternately at Anne and Susan.

"How do you feel, Anne, hearing what Roger said?" Szifra asked.

"Very uncomfortable," she responded in almost a whisper. "I know compliments are supposed to make you feel good, but they do something else to me. I get very nervous."

"And you, Susan?" Szifra asked.

"Basically, I feel like Anne," Susan answered. "I don't know how to respond. I guess I don't know what a normal response is. I suppose it's 'thank you.' It's not so easy for me."

"Is it any easier than it was six months or a year ago?" Szifra asked.

"I guess it is, a little," Susan responded.

"It's back to the idea of not noting progress unless it's enormous," Szifra reminded the group. "Claudia Black says it so well in her book *Repeat After Me*—that for ACOAs to note accomplishment, strict criteria must be met. First, it must be nothing less than moving a mountain; and, second, it must be acknowledged by all."

Everyone chuckled. "What's so funny about that?" Kathy teased.

After the group settled down again, Roger looked at Susan and said, "You do seem more comfortable about things. I think you've changed a lot."

Although she knew Susan was uncomfortable at center stage, Szifra encouraged the exchange. She knew experiencing the feedback from another group member was valuable, a way to expedite progress. She asked Roger to tell Susan more about changes he'd observed.

"For one thing," Roger began, "I can't remember the last time you cried, Susan. I'm not saying it's bad to cry, but it seemed like you were more uncomfortable then. Now you say more personal things and you don't cry every time, so that's good. It's like you have less fear of speaking. You initiate now, too. Early in group, you were more quiet, nervous, and clinging to the wall. Now you're a more active part of the group."

"Thank you," Susan responded, laughing a little at her discomfort and response.

"It doesn't seem fair to comment about Susan's progress without mentioning Anne's," Roger said. He waited a minute, noticing Anne was visibly shaken. She clutched emotionally as the focus shifted to her.

"You're uncomfortable?" Szifra asked Anne.

"Yes," Anne said, pausing a long time. "It's always real hard when the spotlight shines on me. It's a shock. I get so nervous, I want to leave."

"I know," Szifra reassured her. "It is hard. I also know you can handle the uncomfortable feelings."

"I try," Anne said. "And I know it's good for me. I know the discomfort won't last. On some level I want to hear what Roger has to say, even though I know it's going to be hard. . . . Okay, Roger," she said with less trepidation.

"I feel like I'm about to begin some horrible torture," Roger said. "You know I'm a pacifist!" His remark lightened the mood.

"Really, it's okay," Anne said. "I need to hear what people think. Isn't it amazing there's all this fuss to avoid hearing compliments?" She seemed shaken.

"It's not amazing to me," Kathy said, laughing. "That's what I do, too."

Michael nodded. "Me too." He recalled having cried in an individual session when Szifra had told him he was very likable. He wasn't ready to share that with the group, though.

"Would others share how you feel about receiving compliments?" Szifra asked, deliberately giving Anne a short break from the spotlight.

"I like compliments," Linda said, "but I tend to discount them."

"I do that some, too," said Sarah. "I'm getting better. I used to never believe anything positive that people said about me. I pretended I did. Growing up, I didn't get many positives. Maybe that's why I don't know how to handle compliments well now. Since participating in a 'surviving divorce' group this summer, I'm getting more feedback from others and am able to believe compliments more. Maybe I like myself better."

"It shows, Sarah," Trina confirmed. "It's great. I feel like you like yourself better. I'm lots better. I think I'm an okay person, and I guess some other people think so, too." She spoke offhandedly but ended with a hearty laugh.

Szifra asked Mark to respond next.

"I think I'm bad at accepting compliments," Mark said. "I act real cool on the outside, giving the impression, 'Sure, I know, I'm great!' On the inside, I'm full of self-doubt. I think it's left over from the guilt I carry about my addiction."

Roger said he was getting better at accepting compliments but knew he could improve more. "Some part of me shuts compliments out. It's related to my relationship with my father. He compliments me, but his actions don't fit with his words. So I find myself thinking others' compliments are phony, too."

He turned to Anne. "Well, should I tell you how I see you've changed?"

"Sure," Anne said. "I guess it won't kill me." She laughed nervously.

"Even that last remark shows you've changed," Roger said. "You couldn't joke much when we first began meeting. Anything involving a one-on-one interaction would send you running. But now, you teased me, and you looked right at me. You are saying more in here, and more that is personal, too. I think you're doing great."

With a sheepish grin, Anne thanked Roger. Mark and Trina added their agreement that Anne had changed a great deal, and she thanked each of them, then sat back.

"I liked tonight's group," said Michael. "I think we should talk about relationships again sometime. It helps to hear you all talk about it. When Anne and Susan said they sometimes felt stupid, I realized maybe I'm being too hard on myself, too."

"I have to announce something," Linda said, realizing group was about over. Her voice let them all know it was something important to her. "After a lot of deliberation, I've decided I want to take a leave of absence from group. I feel like I need a break. I might decide while I'm taking a break that I really am done, or I might come crawling back, asking if I can rejoin!" She glanced at Szifra, who nodded encouragingly.

"I know we agreed to announce at least one week ahead of time if we intended to leave group," she continued. "Next week will be my last week. I want to have time to say good-bye." Her eyes filled with tears as she finished speaking.

"Will you get any support?" Anne asked, suddenly aware how much she herself would miss the connections she'd made if she stopped coming to group.

"I know there's an ACOA support group I can attend. I'll probably try that," Linda told her. "I also asked Szifra if I could see her individually if I needed to. And I've made a couple of friends who are very supportive."

"Boy, I'll be sorry to see you go," Roger said.

"Me too," said Susan.

"You do seem ready, though," Kathy commented. "You seem to feel comfortable with where you are now and the work you've done so far. I feel bad that I'm not ready, to tell you the truth."

Bob was feeling very uncomfortable. He did not think Linda was at all ready to leave, but he couldn't decide whether to say anything about his reservations. I wonder if it's because I'm a counselor, he thought. Maybe I just can't drop that role.

Trina wanted to blurt out, "The hell you're ready. You're no more ready than the rest of us." But she reminded herself not to take anyone else's inventory. In the past, she had interpreted that to mean "mind my own business—never interfere." Now she decided it meant that she could say anything she wanted if it was out of concern for the person.

"I'll miss you, too, Linda," she said assertively. "I don't feel the way Kathy does, though. I think you still have plenty you could do here."

Linda stiffened. She did not want to doubt her decision. Before she could think of a response, however, Bob said, "I was feeling the same way but was afraid to bring it up for fear I'd look like 'Mr. Counselor.' "

Anne felt her stomach muscles tighten. She tried to remind herself that even if conflict emerged here, it would not be like the conflict in her family. I sure wish I could convince my stomach of that, she thought. This is awfully uncomfortable.

Linda said, "I really have thought this out and feel it's the right decision for me." It was clear she did not want to discuss the matter further.

Szifra knew Linda's shut-off signals. She also felt there were group "rights" as well as individual "rights." Group had the right to ask Linda to explain. Linda had the right to refuse, recognizing she might not be acting responsively to the group.

Bob and Trina backed off, and Szifra asked them why. "Because Linda seems decided," Bob said.

Szifra agreed, then told him that Linda's decision didn't preclude his asking her to explain if he wanted more information.

Bob faltered, unsure how to ask. Finally he said, "Well, Linda, I'd like to know why you think you're done. Have you finished everything you came here for?"

"I feel done enough for now," Linda responded. "I joined this group to help me feel better about myself. And I feel like I've come a long way with that. I also wanted to learn how to keep my parents' alcoholism from dominating my life. Although I still haven't entirely resolved that, I am able to focus more on my life. I know I could do more. I plan to. I will even try a group again. Right now I need time away from therapy."

The group processed more of Linda's motivation and needs. Susan's final comment summed up most of their feelings: "We hope you're making a good choice for yourself, Linda. We know you'll be okay. We wonder if you could still benefit from staying, though. And we feel guilty and selfish because we also know we'll miss what you give us.''

Linda cried as Susan spoke. Trina and Sarah hugged her. Szifra added, ''We'll take time next week to talk more about Linda's leaving.'' The collective sigh of relief was audible.

Szifra closed by praising the group for opening up, and she encouraged them to continue. ''You have so much to offer yourselves and others. Some of you have old tapes running that keep you safe, and lonely. It can be scary to reach out to new people, and scary to open up more to people we know. You may have had bad experiences in the past that taught you to play it safe. I don't want to minimize the emotional risk of reaching out and opening up. Nor do I want you to minimize the costs of being lonely and staying stuck in old patterns.''

Szifra paused a moment before continuing, ''What we work hardest at hiding is often exactly what makes us all most alike. We hide our fears and insecurities. We show our most secure parts, never wanting others to discover we are confused or afraid. We want to seem normal, not realizing 'normal' is a person with strengths and weaknesses, a whole person. Normal does not mean 'all together.' Normal does not mean no self-doubt. Normal does not mean perfect.

''It's a paradox. We're taught to hide imperfections. We learn to cover them up. To have healthy, fulfilling relationships, we need to open up all these areas. We need to unlearn the old messages. When we are strong enough to share our tears and fears, we can make close friends. We can then be more intimate with our partners. We can stop hiding, and feel free.

''That's what's so wonderful about our ACOA group,'' Szifra concluded. ''You open up here. You share your insides, and discover that we all feel similarly. We all experience hurt, fear, confusion, insecurity. You feel connected when you open up and share. It's exciting. You can do it with others, too. You have so much to offer, people will line up to share with you! Let them in!''

Realizing she'd spoken a long time, Szifra laughed and said, "Okay, Lecture 303, 'You Are Great; Start Believing It,' is now over!" The group laughed with her as they stood up.

Bob said he was glad they'd talked about relationships; it had helped him see things differently. Others echoed his feelings.

"One quick note about next week," Szifra said. "I'd like you to spend some time reflecting on where you are now in dealing with various ACOA issues, what your current goals are, and what you think you can do to achieve these goals. Try to keep this in mind this week. See you next Tuesday."

My Observations and Reactions to Meeting 14

Anne, 39, child care worker, lost child role in family, father died from alcoholism seven years ago.
Observations/progress noted:

Bob, 50, alcoholism counselor, scapegoat in family, recovering, mother alcoholic, now deceased.
Observations/progress noted:

Kathy, 33, secretary, mascot/responsible role in family, father died from alcoholism this year.
Observations/progress noted:

Linda, 36, nurse, responsible role in family, both parents are alcoholic, living.
Observations/progress noted:

Mark, 30, welder, scapegoat role in family, recovering, father died from alcoholism six years ago.
Observations/progress noted:

Michael, 38, PR/advertising, responsible role in family, father is alcoholic, mother prescription drug–addicted, living.
Observations/progress noted:

Roger, 20, student, lost child/scapegoat in family, recovering, mother also recovering.
Observations/progress noted:

Sarah, 36, high school teacher, responsible role in family, father died from alcoholism five years ago.
Observations/progress noted:

Susan, 32, accountant, lost child/responsible role in family, father died from alcoholism two years ago.
Observations/progress noted:

Trina, 45, shipping clerk, scapegoat role in family, recovering, father quit drinking a few years ago.
Observations/progress noted:

Szifra, therapist
Observations:

Observations about me during this meeting:

My feelings during this meeting:

Issues I'd like to explore further:

My reactions to this meeting:

What I learned about myself during this meeting:

Where We've Been; Where We Want to Go

WALKING INTO GROUP Tuesday night, Bob waved hello to Mark as he pulled in the parking lot. He waited while Mark parked, then asked him how he was doing after their outing the night before.

For quite a while, Bob had wanted to ask Mark if he'd like to go to an AA meeting. Finally he'd called, and to his surprise, Mark had eagerly agreed to attend. He's said he was curious about AA; and although he hadn't made the decision to abstain from drinking, he wanted more information. "At the least," Mark had said, "I'll understand my dad's disease better."

Mark had seemed relatively comfortable during the AA meeting, so on the way home Bob had suggested coffee. In the restaurant, he and Mark had had a heart-to-heart talk, and their conversation had progressed naturally to sharing their backgrounds.

"Being addicted was such a full-time job," Mark told Bob, "it left no room for anything else in my life. And the longer I was addicted, the more it took. Before long I had used up all my resources, all my friends, and all my self-respect. And to escape that reality, I continued." He glanced at Bob, smiling wryly. "Being a counselor, you've probably heard all this before."

More gently than usual, Bob answered, "Mostly I've dealt with alcohol addiction. It's interesting for me to hear about other drugs. If you want to keep going, I'm interested.''

"Thanks," Mark said, sitting back in the booth as he relaxed into his "storyteller" mood. "I remember so clearly the withdrawal from opiates. The symptoms began with sniffles and aches, and a craving that would cause you to sell your own mother to the devil for five minutes of relief because you know what's coming.

"But as it progresses, I can only equate it with being plugged into a light socket, causing all your nerve endings to light on fire. And the feeling in your head is ten times worse, until you wonder if the top of your skull is going to blow off. And then you wish it would.''

He paused to take a sip of his coffee, then continued. "And the craving that would cause you to sell your mother to the devil? Well, you can't do that because you already did that the day before yesterday. And your intentions of kicking, a very real and true desire, are lost in the countless attempts to do so.''

Mark sat quietly a minute, smoking a cigarette, inhaling deeply. He stared at the glowing tip. "This is a bit of what the physical effects were. And, yet, they don't hold a candle to the remorse and guilt and hate you hold toward yourself.'' He spoke softly, regretfully. "Unfortunately, it manifests itself on those around you, as well.

"You see," he continued, "the pain and guilt you have stuffed inside you never escape. They can haunt you for a lifetime.'' He shook his head. "I'm no longer addicted to heroin, and my legal problems are history, but I'm still on a tethered chain. That's the nature of the beast of addiction, as you probably know.''

Bob tried hard not to respond as a counselor. Practicing AA's Twelfth Step, reaching out to others in need, was important to him, though. He didn't want to ignore the opportunity to reach out to Mark. "I think you have a reason to be aware of that 'tethered chain,' '' he said. "Frankly, I'm relieved to hear you say you recognize that. Whether it's one drug or another, you know the risk.''

Mark nodded. "On a lighter note," he said, "I do feel real hopeful. I like learning about ACOA issues. It's hard, but I feel I am getting better."

"Me too," Bob said. "Recognizing that recovery is a lifelong process helps me. The more I learn about myself and others, the more freedom I add to that chain. One link at a time. I grieve the loss of childhood, I take responsibility for today, and I go on." They chatted a while longer before calling it a night.

Seeing Mark's enthusiastic greeting now, Bob knew their interaction the night before had created a bond. "Do you remember what the topic for tonight is?" he asked Mark.

"Something about stopping for an intersection," Mark responded.

"Oh, yeah, we're going to take a look at where we've been in group and decide where we want to go from here." Walking into Szifra's office, Bob joked with Mark, asking if he'd remembered his road map.

As group began, Szifra reminded everyone that tonight was "assessment night." "Tonight, you'll review your accomplishments thus far in group, then address your goals. We'll also leave time to process Linda's leaving. How about getting started with our assessments first?

"To help you evaluate, you might ask yourself some questions. 'What else do I want for myself?' is a good one. Or 'How am I going about getting what I want?' 'What possible roadblocks will I encounter?' "

Trina jumped in first. "I thought a lot about this in the past week. I want better relationships. I'm hopeful I can have them now that I understand my past better. In fact, I know I can. I've already begun to, at work. I'm thankful I'm dealing with these issues and taking care of the little girl inside."

Michael picked up the conversation. "I'm determined to change. I'm trying to feel in the present, instead of thinking, One day everything will come together, or, Someday I'll be happy or relaxed. I'm practicing living every day, trying to stop always waiting for tomorrow. I'm also trying to find a way to settle back and just live, rather than always having to figure it out.''

"You'd like to spend some time free of monitoring and evaluating," Szifra said.

Michael nodded. "That's what I mean."

"I'm feeling like that a lot myself," Linda admitted. "Like a plateau would be okay for a while."

"I'm feeling just the opposite," Mark said. "I've spent so much of my life coasting, not thinking enough about the time going by, I want to get busy now. I hope to get to know myself better and sort out more of what's going on for me."

"I've done a bit of that sorting out," Roger said. "I'm changing the things I can to feel better about me little by little. I'm learning to notice the small changes I make. And that motivates me to keep on. I've started giving myself credit for these changes, too." He laughed. "Obviously Szifra's indoctrination is working."

"Motivation to keep on is a big part of this whole process," Anne said, feeling pleased that she had joined the conversation on her own. "At times I am overwhelmed when I think of how much needs to be done. Sometimes I wonder if it would be easier to go back and pretend I didn't know what I've learned so far. But then when I think about going back to the way I was before, I say, 'No way!' That's not what I want. I want to keep moving forward. I wish my husband and children could understand a little more about what goes on inside me, but I have to learn how to deal with that. Anyway, I'm relieved to know why I am the way I am and glad I can do something about it. It's going to take time. I need patience, but I know I'm not alone."

Anne stopped abruptly, as she sometimes did in conversations. It was hard for her to begin talking and sometimes difficult for her to end smoothly. She'd start feeling self-conscious and stop talking. She was aware of it but no longer let it slow her progress in initiating conversations.

"I like what you said about being glad you can do something about it, Anne," Sarah said. "I think that's a very bright part of all this—we can do something about it."

"I liked what you said about realizing it would take time," Susan added. "That's one area I need to work on. I want to be easier on and nicer to myself. I've decided I'm not going to look in a mirror and only notice flaws. I'm going to see positives and progress, too."

"And that's progress," Szifra said.

"So many of us are hard on ourselves," Roger said. "It's so ridiculous, too. We are okay people! When we evaluate ourselves, we're too critical, probably much like our parents were. It's hard to turn these ideas around, I know. I'm glad we're here, though, because I think we are all better than we used to be."

"I'm better at being more forgiving when I make mistakes," Bob said. "I'm not great at it yet, but I'm working on it. I have a difficult time relaxing, having fun, too. And I have difficulty with intimacy, in trying to relate to others. I'm learning to listen and to express my feelings to the important people in my life. And that includes all of you. I know I have a long way to go, of course. I want to keep growing and feeling good. I don't want to be sucked into sickness anymore."

"Sucked into sickness," Trina repeated. "That's pretty graphic. No wonder you want to avoid it!"

"I think a lot of my growth has to do with resolving my relationship with my dad," Bob continued, "at least emotionally working some things out, and then, if I can, having a good relationship with him."

Szifra noticed Bob was more serious than usual. It made him seem more authentic, she thought. She knew his clients would benefit from the positive, healthy changes he was making.

Kathy spoke up. "I know I still carry a lot of alcoholism's effects with me. Sometimes I'm thankful for what I've learned. Other times I wish I could have my childhood back and it would be different.

"Sometimes I'm sad," she continued. "I'm happy, too. I do slip into old, automatic roles, so I have to work to keep my perspective. Slipping into old patterns is often easier than pushing myself. But the reward after the push is a real positive rush, and worth the effort. I'm much less mascot than I used to be. I'm glad, too, because I got tired of wearing that smile, always feeling like I had to entertain. Sometimes it's fun to just sit back.''

"I understand what you're saying," Michael said. "I hope you'll still keep a good part of your humor, though. We've enjoyed it.''

Sarah nodded. "That's true, Kathy.''

"Well, I'm trying to save the humor for more appropriate times," Kathy said. "I'm focusing on being more open with people. And taking more risks at work, trying more challenging assignments. I'm realizing that learning is a process, and that's how I'll learn. I used to avoid risks, for fear I'd make a mistake.''

"It's hard for us to really accept that everyone makes mistakes," Szifra said. "Successful people all have failures. No one gets by without mistakes and failures.''

"That's a hard lesson for me, too," Michael admitted. "I'm using the message, 'It's okay,' to get over it. It says everything to me. My feelings are okay. I'm okay. It's okay. When I tell myself that, I feel better. It helps me keep my perspective.''

"I use self-talk a lot, too," Linda said. "It's how I get the nurturing I didn't get as a child. This progress we're all making feels so good to me. I know there's hope for each of us.

"For me, not resenting my parents so much is a big change," she went on. "My resentment was eating me up. I never knew how to deal with it. I didn't really even know what it was. Without realizing it, I kept avoiding the issue. Group has helped me resolve a lot of this. And individual time with Szifra, too. In a way, I feel sorry for my parents. They can't take charge of their lives. They've never had the strength to stop drinking. They're like young teenagers who never grew up.''

Uncharacteristically, Roger was very somber and almost tearful as he shared with the group. "I feel sad sometimes because I tried to be different from Mom with my alcohol use. I thought I'd show her I could master alcohol like she couldn't. I didn't recognize how futile and destructive that was. I want all those years back, and I can't have them.''

Trina told him she understood how he felt, reminding him he had years he wouldn't have had if he hadn't stopped drinking.

"You're right, of course." Roger smiled his thanks to Trina for her support.

"I'm learning about myself, too," Susan said. "I'm not the quiet, inadequate, and terrified shy person I used to see myself as. I enjoy talking about my feelings and experiences, at least more often than I used to, and I like hearing others share. This new feeling of connecting with others is wonderful. Still a little scary, but wonderful!''

"Great!" said Szifra. "You've updated your self-image, Susan. The new one fits you very well."

"Thanks," Susan said.

"What a positive thing to say, Susan," Kathy said. "You are so articulate. You communicate so well." Even as she spoke, she realized how much Susan had changed. If I met her today, I would never think she was once quiet or shy. I wonder if I've changed a lot, too, and can't see my own progress, she thought. I hope so!

"A new self-understanding has been really important to me, too," Sarah said. "Learning about alcoholism really opened my eyes. I can see why I was the way I was. I've been able to forgive myself, too, and to accept my children the way they are. It's been a great freedom, but I know it doesn't undo the damage they've felt from growing up with an alcoholic father and codependent mother. I feel real bad that they have problems to overcome.

"I also recognize that I did the best I could, given the circumstances," she went on. "Sure, I wish someone had intervened. But they didn't. Now I'm open with my children and tell them what I'm telling you. I've made amends to each of them. And we're closer because of it."

"Attaching the label *alcoholism* to all that craziness

helped me, too,'' said Trina. ''Now I understand there was a reason for it. It makes it easier for me to work through some things. I can't say it always makes it easier for me to accept, though. The thinking part of me seems to accept the cause, but the child part says, 'Why me?' I know I'm one of the lucky ones, though, because I'm sober and I can have these debates with myself.'' She smiled broadly, pleased with herself.

''One of the things I'll have as a 'forever' to work on is the acceptance that it's okay to be me, weak or strong,'' Susan said.

''For me, it's worrying,'' Anne said. ''I'm trying to worry less. If my son is out with the car, I worry. Now, I've learned to give myself some positive messages, such as 'He's a good driver' and 'He's responsible,' to help me counter the worrying.''

''You can't always control those automatic thoughts,'' Szifra reminded them. ''It's what you do with them that counts. That's what will make the difference in how you'll feel.''

''I used to really worry, too, Anne,'' Michael said. ''About my family, about me, about anything. I'm working on that same issue. We'll have to check each other's progress from time to time!''

''I've learned my ACOA issues can get in my way as a therapist,'' Bob said. ''My personal life, too. Group has been a great place to work on this, because then it's safer 'out there.' '' He pointed to the window, indicating the rest of the world with a wave of his hand.

''You have come a long way, Bob,'' Szifra told him warmly. ''It amazes me how open you're able to be. I'm glad for you, and for your clients.''

''I've also become aware of how difficult new situations are for me,'' Bob continued. ''Although I appear outgoing, my control issues rear their ugly heads when I don't know what to expect in a situation. 'Gotta be perfect,' you know! ACOA motto!''

Kathy laughed with him and said, ''Until recently, and

sometimes still, I pretended I knew something rather than admit I didn't. Now I'm trying to ask for more explanation. I've found it also improves my relationship with that person, who's generally pleased to help me. Also, I used to spend a lot of time reliving conversations or evenings, wishing I'd said certain things differently or not at all. Now I try to think a little more before I speak. My behavior used to be so dictated by my emotions. Now I'm letting my head take over more often!''

"You all have been exceptionally perceptive tonight, seeing your own progress and identifying where you want to go," Szifra said. "It's great that so many of you are feeling really good. You've worked hard! We could go on longer, and I'm guessing some of you wish we would."

Uncharacteristically Roger said, "I just want to hear what Trina's dealing with still."

Everyone seemed surprised. Trina said, "You're just getting too well, Roger, being assertive, even interrupting the therapist!" She laughed, then admitted, "I still have a real hard time showing sadness and other soft-type emotions. I'm working on it, though."

Roger said, "Okay, back to you, Szifra."

After a few moments, Szifra said, "Let's move on to Linda's decision to leave group. After four months of being together, she has become an integral part of our group. Her leaving will affect us all."

"This is so hard," Linda responded. "I do want to try it on my own for a while. I think I'm ready. I know I have many things to work on, but I think I'll keep working, making progress, and growing."

Bob leaned forward, then forced himself to sit back again. He felt strongly that Linda wasn't ready to leave, but he was facing the "counselor versus group member" dilemma. Leaning forward again, he finally spoke up. "Linda, I'm not convinced you're making a good decision. Maybe it's none of my business. Maybe I'm playing counselor. But here goes. You mentioned so many problems at last week's meeting. I can't remember them all, but I remember you saying that trust is a big problem for you, that you back off when people get close. You said you discount compliments and feel like people are judging you. Why leave when those are issues we deal with so much in group? Linda, look, I'm worried about you. I haven't known you all that long, being a newcomer in here. But you were really making good changes. I wonder if you're sabotaging yourself by leaving."

Linda felt herself alternately on the verge of tears and ready to scream, "Stop!" Before she had a chance to say anything, however, Trina spoke up. "I'm worried, too, Linda. I wonder if you're copping out. Maybe we're getting too close."

"I don't think that's it," Linda replied. She was convinced she was being honest, but the intensity of her response made others wonder if Trina had hit home. "I really just need a break from therapy," she reiterated.

Roger surprised everyone by his almost angry response. "We all want a break, Linda. We don't like working on this stuff all the time, either! But it makes us well. We are all so much better, and so much happier more often. I think maybe Trina's right, that you're copping out."

The confrontation from Roger shocked Linda, who burst into tears. Watching this exchange, Anne shifted nervously on her seat. Why doesn't Szifra do something? she wondered.

Kathy felt terrible for Linda. Why does she have to go through all this? she thought. Good-byes are so hard.

After a few moments Szifra asked Linda to tell the group how she was feeling.

"It's very hard," Linda responded. "I want to trust my judgment and not have everyone doubt me. I think I'm doing what's right for me now."

"You know, you might be right," Susan said. "How can any of us really know?"

"Whatever you choose, we're still behind you, Linda," Kathy said gently.

The discussion continued, which seemed to bolster Linda's resolve and dispel the doubts expressed by Trina, Bob, and Roger. "I'm still going to take a break," Linda said. "I realize I may not be as ready as I thought, but I still want to go. I'll work a while with what I've learned here. Practice in the real world. Try to grow more all the time. Believe me, I'm not walking away from this issue! I've learned a lot here, and I won't forget it."

"If you find yourself wanting to return, could you?" Szifra asked.

"If you mean, will I stay away because of pride, no, I don't think so. At least I hope not," Linda said.

"I'm open if you change your mind," Bob told her. Others assured her that she was a success whether she made changes outside of group or sought group support again to make changes more rapidly.

"Whatever you do, you're doing great," Sarah said warmly.

As group wound down, Susan spoke up. "Before everyone leaves, I have a poem I wrote this week when I was thinking about Linda leaving. I want to give it to you as a going-away present, Linda. Although my poem is especially for Linda, it's to all of the group, too," she explained as she handed copies to everyone.

"There is enough time to read it, if you'd like, Susan," Szifra said. Susan decided to, feeling a little uncomfortable but pleased she was asked.

COAs

The days pass by like years, the minutes like days.
Reminders of the past enter into almost every facet
of our lives, directly or indirectly.

Happiness is here, then fleeting. Yet at times
seems mountainous.

Life forges on and we do not control it.
And there are stages for every season of our growing up.

We cry at pain. We laugh at ourselves. We have to.
All for a better tomorrow and a time when we
finally accept ourselves.

Susan's heart was racing. She was nervous, but she didn't let that stop her from saying what she had planned to tell Linda. "Linda, you have felt through so much, and now you can accept yourself more. We're aiming there, too," she said. "Good luck, and please keep in touch. I'm not very good at initiating, but as a good adjuster, I'm good at responding."

"Thank you, Susan, and everyone," Linda responded warmly. She had tears in her eyes as she said, "I promise to keep in touch."

"You better!" Trina said, hugging her.

Szifra spent a half hour after group finishing up some business before leaving for the night. When she walked out to the parking lot, she noticed an after-group group going on. It had become a common Tuesday occurrence. Tonight, Trina, Linda, Susan, and Roger were talking. Nearby, Mark, Bob, and Kathy were laughing over a funny story Bob had told.

My Observations and Reactions to Meeting 15

Anne, 39, child care worker, lost child role in family, father died from alcoholism seven years ago.
Observations/progress noted:

Bob, 50, alcoholism counselor, scapegoat in family, recovering, mother alcoholic, now deceased.
Observations/progress noted:

Kathy, 33, secretary, mascot/responsible role in family, father died from alcoholism this year.
Observations/progress noted:

Linda, 36, nurse, responsible role in family, both parents are alcoholic, living.
Observations/progress noted:

Mark, 30, welder, scapegoat role in family, recovering, father died from alcoholism six years ago.
Observations/progress noted:

Michael, 38, PR/advertising, responsible role in family, father is alcoholic, mother prescription drug–addicted, living.
Observations/progress noted:

Roger, 20, student, lost child/scapegoat in family, recovering, mother also recovering.
Observations/progress noted:

Sarah, 36, high school teacher, responsible role in family, father died from alcoholism five years ago.
Observations/progress noted:

Susan, 32, accountant, lost child/responsible role in family, father died from alcoholism two years ago.
Observations/progress noted:

Trina, 45, shipping clerk, scapegoat role in family, recovering, father quit drinking a few years ago.
Observations/progress noted:

Szifra, therapist
Observations:

Observations about me during this meeting:

My feelings during this meeting:

Issues I'd like to explore further:

My reactions to this meeting:

What I learned about myself during this meeting:

FINAL MEETING

Using Our Tools for Recovery

SO MUCH HAS changed in the past six months, Szifra thought as she prepared for that evening's group, and now more is changing. She reminisced about the group's collective experiences, as well as individual milestones. Two seasons had gone by since Trina's father had died. Roger had been arrested at a rally. Sarah was dating a photographer she'd met several weeks before.

Michael and his wife had realized they were undecided about having children, instead of resolute that they would not. They'd agreed to keep their options open.

Anne had been able to talk to her sister about her father's sexual advances. Her sister had been able to accept Anne's inaction at the time. They'd had a good talk about her pain and had gotten closer.

Although Linda had left group almost three months ago, she'd kept in touch with Sarah and sent hellos frequently.

During the last several weeks the group had discussed spirituality, crying, sex, trust, relationships, anger, control, conditional love, and fear of abandonment. As with earlier topics, they'd discovered many common feelings and worked together for resolution.

Tonight, Michael and Susan would leave. John and Nancy were to start group in two weeks, and Szifra had decided to bring in another therapist to co-facilitate group with her.

It will be hard, a kind of grieving, Szifra realized, thinking about all the changes. True, it's a smaller grief than death. Are there small deaths? she asked herself. Maybe life losses. She wondered if group members realized how much she enjoyed working with them. She loved being intricately involved in their growth and had told group members she felt privileged to accompany them on their journey.

Each group is so different, Szifra thought. The way the group flows, the focus, the interactions, and the feelings are greatly determined by the individuals participating. I've really enjoyed this particular group and each person in it.

Bringing her mind back to matters at hand, she focused on the evening's agenda. Good-byes to Michael and Susan would be part of it. That usually brought a mixture of tears and backing off. After that, she might have to play it by ear—do whatever feels right, she told herself, grateful for the freedom from the worry and self-consciousness she'd felt early in her practice. I'm glad I can cry now if that feels right or hug someone good-bye, she thought. I'm glad I trust myself more. It's taken years of working on my own issues and self-doubts. I've finally learned to worry less about what others think. What a relief!

She thought of ACOAs who came into treatment expecting instant changes—perfection, with no more problems—after a year of therapy. It was difficult for them to hear that none of us is problem-free.

But then, who wants to have the same unresolved issues at fifty you had at twenty? she thought. I'd rather chip away, even if it is slow sometimes. She smiled to herself. I'd prefer new problems at fifty!

Just before seven P.M., Szifra heard the waiting room door open. She left her office for a fresh mug of decaf.

Michael had arrived. He greeted Szifra and said, "Well, it's going to be hard saying good-bye tonight. I'm feeling worse than I anticipated."

Szifra told him that was understandable, acknowledging it might be harder yet once the evening's session began. They talked until Bob arrived, then Michael and Bob began chatting. After that, group members arrived one or two at a time. Szifra noticed Susan and Trina were standing outside, talking away. How different from when the group first began meeting, she thought.

Group began promptly at seven P.M. Three weeks ago Michael and Susan had announced that tonight's group would be their last. Michael was moving to take a new job with a bigger ad agency. Susan felt she was ready to take what she'd learned and practice on her own. Last week she'd alluded to group being like tennis lessons. She'd laughed and said she might be back for more lessons later.

Some group members talked about how they felt. Roger said he wished they could stay: "I just don't like your leaving." Kathy told them that saying good-bye was hard.

"I've been thinking about your leaving," said Mark. "I thought I'd gotten used to people coming in and leaving groups from when I was in treatment, but I realize this group is different. This is probably the closest I've come to experiencing what a healthy family might be like. We talk. We listen. We reassure and support. We don't ignore each other or put each other down for our feelings. And it's the same people, week after week. We open up more, get to know each other. It feels bad you two are leaving," he said sincerely. "Michael, you always say things that are helpful to me. And, Susan, your changes are an inspiration to me."

"Really? Like what?" Susan asked.

"Being able to speak up, and ask for input, like you just did," Mark responded. "When I first joined group, which was a while after you did, you were still pretty quiet and nonassertive."

Susan blushed. "It embarrasses me, but I really like hearing how I've changed. I don't know why, but I still don't easily notice the changes."

"Does that mean you do see some?" Mark asked.

"Yes, I guess. I better say that if I'm saying I'm ready to leave!" Susan said. Her humor had really emerged in the past several months. "I'm a lot less afraid in here, and outside, too. I'm not so hard on myself, I guess. I've put the big whip away, although I think I have too large a supply of small and medium-size whips I still use! I have the skills now to put them away. I hope someday I don't even look for them. And''—she looked at Mark—"thanks for the compliment.''

There was a pause, during which Szifra asked that others let Susan know what changes they'd seen. Since Susan and Michael were leaving, she wanted this to be a time for feedback, when group members could look at how far they'd come and what still remained to be done. By now the group was comfortable with spontaneous feedback. Interactions that used to be threatening had become almost routine. They talked about the "real issues" quite easily.

Michael spoke up. "You let your sense of humor show more often, Susan. You're really funny, you know."

"I'm just learning that," Susan said. "Thanks for saying so.''

"You seem relaxed, like you're more comfortable overall," Sarah said. "I remember earlier meetings when you'd grip the arms of the chair so tightly. Now you're sitting there like it never was a habit you had." Others agreed that Susan seemed more open and more talkative.

"And generally I can talk without crying!" Susan said.

"The crying was not an issue for me," Trina said. Someone else reminded Susan that she was more assertive now, and she gave and received feedback more easily.

"You share more personal issues," Kathy added.

Szifra reminded Susan of her family's implicit rule of keeping thoughts and feelings to yourself. "It's great that you've learned a new rule: 'It's okay to talk about what really matters and to feel good about it, too.' "

"I hadn't thought of it that way," Susan said slowly. "I am able to do that more and more."

"Let's continue sharing changes we've observed," Szifra suggested. "Michael, why don't you start by telling the group the changes you've noticed in yourself and others?"

Michael decided to share how different he felt about being likable. He told the group his experience in an individual session when he'd burst into tears after Szifra had told him he was likable.

"Although I still feel very strange saying this, I do mostly like myself and think I'm a pretty likable guy," he said. "I couldn't handle hoping for things before, because I felt too afraid I didn't deserve them, or I wouldn't get what I most wanted, which was for people to like me and think I was okay. I also couldn't figure out a way to fit in with the self-image I'd had for so long."

"I guess you trust yourself more now," Anne said.

Michael nodded. "And others, too. I've realized even more how messed up I got because of the way my family functioned. I realize I have alternatives. I can change. I used to say, 'It's okay,' to myself a hundred times a day, and believe it about ten times. Now, I really believe it a lot. My feelings are okay, and I can even experience more than one feeling about the same situation, even if feelings seem to be opposites. I can be angry with my wife, and also understanding and sympathetic with her about the same issue."

"I see other changes in you, too," Bob said. "You talk about more personal issues."

"Yeah," Sarah agreed. "A good example is your sharing the time you cried in an individual session. You wouldn't have been so open before."

"You seem more relaxed and confident," Kathy said.

"You do seem a lot more comfortable with yourself," Roger said. "I'm kind of jealous. And you seem to have such an easy time talking to people."

"Thanks," Michael said.

"And you can take a compliment now," Szifra told him. "They were nearly impossible for you when we first met! I also remember you telling us you used to deal with feelings by keeping busy, running from them. Then you'd get physically ill and end up in bed. Changes I'm excited about seeing include less running, less frantic and forced 'busyness.' And being stuck in bed less often and for fewer hours when you do get sick."

Michael laughed. "How could I have forgotten that? I hated that, and still do when it happens. But it really is much better. My anger is better, too. I think I've finally experienced constructive anger, and I can talk with my wife about anger now, too." He smiled broadly, pleased with how far he'd come.

Mark mentioned that Sarah exhibited a lot more independence and self-acceptance, and Susan was better at receiving compliments, too.

Susan laughed. "I actually like them now!" she said. "At least on some level."

"What do you mean, at least on some level?" Kathy teased.

"Well, Kathy, I'm not perfect yet!" Susan responded.

"When will we ever give that one up?" Anne asked.

"That will be the last to go, I suppose," Trina joined in. "How about, ACOAs who can let themselves be imperfect earn an A plus!"

As the group laughed together, Szifra remarked how much freer their laughter was. "You are so much more spontaneous," she told them.

The focus shifted then back to Michael. Several of the group members congratulated him on his changes and asked him to keep in touch. Michael's demeanor during the exchange reflected his increased comfort.

"My only regret is that I can't finish here. Frankly, I'm kind of scared," he said. "I depend on this group for support and perspective. I'm worried about backsliding when I leave." His voice trembled as he told them, "I'll really miss you."

Kathy wished she could leave the room, she so disliked saying good-bye. Sarah hugged Michael, then told him teasingly that she'd wanted to hug him for months, and this gave her a good excuse. Trina got up and hugged him, too.

"That's one way you've changed," Michael told Trina. "You're more demonstrative about your feelings."

Trina laughed. "Pretty fancy word, Mike!"

"And I'll miss people teasing me, too," Michael said.

Trina decided to go next by sharing some ways she felt she'd changed. "Breaking the pattern, first of all. Coming here for counseling was a huge first step. I've discovered a lot of good things about myself during therapy. My ability to talk about my family has improved," she said. "Even when I talk about the incest and battering, I feel much less guilt. I don't feel like I'm bad if I share what happened in my childhood. I'm more comfortable with all of you, too." She smiled as she looked around the room. "My trust and intimacy are improving, I suppose, and I'm a little more assertive."

"A little?" Bob said, teasing her. "I'd say a hell of a lot more than a little. You're much more assertive."

"Really?" Trina asked.

"Yes." Bob recounted two different situations in group—one where Trina had represented herself very assertively, and another when she'd told Susan she ought to speak up more because she said good things.

"We always talk about this," Trina said, "but, once more, it really helps me to hear what changes you see. I guess I'm too close and don't see the changes."

"At the beginning of group, Trina," Bob said, "you might have said something, but you would have been very careful and more apologetic."

"I guess you're right," Trina admitted. "Well, good for me. I'm getting even more well than I thought!"

"I'd like to back up a little bit, Trina," Bob said, "to when you said you feel less guilt. Guilt about what?"

"Everything," Trina replied. "I used to feel guilty because I'd been molested, like it was my fault. Now I know it's never a two-year-old's fault. And when they start that young, you're bound for trouble. Actually, no matter what the age of the child or adolescent, sexual abuse is never the kid's fault. I'm finally believing that. Before, I knew it in my brain, but not in my emotions.

"I don't feel so much guilt about talking about my family and how screwy they are, like I used to," she continued.

''Now I feel I'm reporting the facts so I can be free and more healthy. I really don't love or like them any less because I see them more clearly. I don't hate them anymore, either. I do get more angry about what happened to me, but, ironically, getting angry about the real stuff has also allowed me to realize they did what they could. Sure, I got ripped off, lost my childhood. I'm real mad about that. So now I don't have to walk around being resentful in general. I'm not so tied up in my family, going to them almost exclusively to get my needs met, all the while knowing they can't meet them. I think I had to get real angry at all I lost, all they did to me, to get free.''

''You have changed, Trina,'' Bob added. ''There's a kind of forgiveness, which doesn't mean you let them off the hook for screwing up, but which frees you from being eaten up inside. I'll bet your recovery is much more complete and healthy because of it.''

''I'd never thought of that, but I agree,'' Trina said. ''I must admit some of my AA pals are Adult Children who never dealt with their Adult Child issues. Many are sober, but not healthy emotionally. They survive, not thrive. Or their relationships are still real bad. Intimacy, trust, and control are unresolved. Many of the women in AA were molested, I know. Unless the person molesting had intercourse with them, they think they're overreacting. They say, 'It really wasn't much.' Then they feel guilty about feeling upset about it.''

She spoke softly, somberly. ''I know how long I covered my feelings up. With booze for a long time, with any defenses I could find. After I was sober awhile, I realized through therapy that the incest did mess me up.

''And some women I know who had two or three incidents of being fondled got messed up, too,'' she added. ''They feel threatened by men, or feel men want something from them. Or they see men as pigs. Many are still so fearful or angry with men in general. Some are real uptight about sex, and can't enjoy it. I guess I could help by letting them know how much help I got once I worked through this in therapy. I think I'll bring it up in my women's AA group. I'm ready for that now."

She gazed around the circle, smiling warmly. "I'm so glad I'm in this group. I've still got things to work on, of course. I want to feel more secure in my recovery. I want to become more patient and tolerant of others, and figure out some goals for my life. In the next few weeks I'd like to figure out what some of those are."

"Me too," Anne said.

Szifra acknowledged Trina's sharing. "You deserve lots of credit, Trina, for working so hard, and for your commitment to keep on working."

Trina smiled. "Thanks, Szifra. Now it's someone else's turn. Move the spotlight, please!"

"Who's ready?" Szifra asked.

"I'll go next," Anne volunteered. "I think what's changed for me is I say more in group, and I'm more comfortable here." She looked mostly at Szifra as she spoke but made eye contact with some others in the group.

Roger noticed and said, "You used to look only at Szifra, especially when you were saying anything even slightly positive about yourself."

"That's true," Anne admitted. "I still really want to look at Szifra only, but sometimes I force myself when I realize I'm doing that. I'm a little better at showing my feelings. For example, a woman at work really frustrated me. She asked me a direct question about her behavior, and instead of being a wimp, I told her how I felt."

"That's great," Trina said. "I knew you had it in you."

"I want to say a little more about that situation with the lady at work," Anne said, and went on to elaborate some for the group.

When she'd finished, Trina said, "I noticed you said 'I want to say more about it,' and you did. That was great. Gold star for you. I remember you telling us your style was to do what others wanted, or what you thought they wanted. I see how far you've come. You speak up and say, 'I want. . . .' You must be pleased."

Anne nodded. "Sometimes I'm glad about it. Usually I am. It's hard, though, because I never know how much is okay for me to want for myself. What's selfish? I know Szifra says there's 'okay selfish' and 'not okay selfish,' but I can't always tell the difference."

"And, of course, we have broken gauges when it comes to that," Kathy reminded her. "I've noticed your changes, too, Anne. They seem so positive to me."

"Thanks," Anne said, smiling a bit self-consciously.

Trina spoke up. "Actually, I think the biggest change is that you carry your diet pop cans in here, right into our group. You didn't do that at first. You probably thought it wouldn't look right!" Everyone laughed, enjoying the light-hearted moment.

"You've got me pegged," Anne said. "I'd never have done that at first. I probably still wouldn't if Linda hadn't always come in with one."

"You also initiate more conversations, in and out of group," Susan mentioned. "You seem much more assertive in here and with your family, from what you've shared with us."

"I'd say more relaxed, too," Roger added. "You sit differently, and you laugh more."

"You really are funny," Sarah said. "I'm so glad you opened up. You make great wisecracks, and they're especially great because none of us expect them from you. Initially your 'Be quiet and stay out of the way' family rule was strictly enforced in group."

"I like that you share more of your opinions and feelings," Michael offered. "I notice a new positiveness that I'm not sure you're aware of."

"You're right, Michael," Anne said. "It's hard to see all the changes."

"Something I notice and am glad about is that you bring issues up before eight-twenty," Szifra said. "Early on, it seemed you held back, sharing only when there was a short time remaining. Now you can risk more. You're okay with being more vulnerable. You seem to need less control. It is nice to see the additional freedom, Anne. It becomes you.''

"Thanks, everyone," Anne said.

"You seem to be hiding, Kathy," Szifra commented. "I know this is one of your least favorite pieces of group, getting feedback. Maybe if you cover everything about yourself that's changed, there won't be anything for anyone to add!''

Kathy laughed, then began. "I'm more able to share personal things.'' She let some of her mascot role come through as she continued, "You may not think what I say is real personal. For me, it's my deepest, darkest stuff. I'm more comfortable with myself and with all of you. I'm not as intense. I'm a little more laid back.'' Then she held up her organizer and added, "Well, not too laid back! I'm trying to learn to play, not to have to be productive all the time. It's slow, but I'm a little better. Okay, now nobody needs to add anything, right?!''

"You wish!" Roger said. "I think you're more friendly. I like that. I also think you're more serious, not always ready to do the mascot routine, and I like that, too.''

"And you cry sometimes, too," said Sarah. "Instead of hiding behind walls. I'm glad you're able to do that.''

"I can't believe you have to try to be laid back," Mark said. "I know you're real organized, but your smile and fantastic sense of humor in group make it hard to believe you're 'all work and no play.' ''

"Thanks," Kathy responded. "It is hard for me to play. I'm getting better, although just a trace so far.''

"I'm still working on that, too," Anne admitted. "I still judge a lot of my self-worth on how productive I've been that day.''

"I just think you're great, Kathy," Michael said warmly. "I guess the change is that you let us in more; maybe that's why I think you're great. I get to see you're not perfect, either.''

"I like you being the mascot," Trina said, "even though I know you're supposed to be giving that up. Your humor kills me. Another thing, I used to feel cheated because you didn't share more. I don't anymore.''

''I used to feel that if people knew the real me,'' Kathy answered, ''they'd think I was boring. I still have some of that, but much less.

''And I've realized another change,'' she went on. ''I handled all this feedback better than I thought I would. I guess it is easier than it used to be to hear others comment about me and for me to tell them my opinions. A few months ago I would have been much more tense. Then I would have gone home and cried. I'm okay now. That's really good news.''

Szifra realized how far Kathy had come since her first visit. ''I remember you telling me you wished you could be more aware of others' feelings and be able to acknowledge them more,'' she said. ''You felt selfish, being so self-focused, self-absorbed. You've come a long way since you started group, Kathy. Are you aware of that change?''

''You know,'' said Kathy, ''I hadn't thought of it, but I really am. I guess there is hope for me after all.'' She smiled and sat back. ''There's hope for me, and for all ACOAs!''

Roger was next to speak. Dressed in faded overalls, he sat with his feet up on the footstool, crossed at the ankles, and appeared quite relaxed. ''Well, my goals for group were to get in touch with my feelings,'' he began. ''I'm a little better at that. And to communicate better. I'm somewhat better, with plenty of room to gets lots better. I also wanted to learn about anger. I think I'm only one percent better with that. And I wanted to learn to be more assertive. I think I'm much better with that. I think I'm doing okay in here.''

''I think you are, too,'' Susan agreed.

''Me too,'' Anne said, chuckling.

''You're really amazing tonight, Anne,'' Trina commented. ''I hope you keep letting this part of yourself out.''

''Roger, you are so much more relaxed,'' Bob observed. ''Look at the way you're sitting. You used to shift around uncomfortably in your chair, crossing and uncrossing your legs.''

"And you'd fold your arms across your chest like you were hiding something," Sarah added. "Like you were keeping us out. Now you're more open."

"Now we have to focus on what our body is doing," Roger said, grinning. "Even our body language gets processed!"

"And you smile much more," Sarah said. "And say more personal things. I used to think you were real quiet. I don't anymore. You talk and contribute good things, too."

Szifra noticed Roger seemed comfortable. This was true with others, too. Early in therapy, ACOAs tended to discount positives about themselves. At some point they began to believe pieces were true. Later they noted positive changes, were able to affirm themselves and accept compliments from others.

The group gave Roger lots of positive comments about his group participation and changes. Roger's eyes filled with tears, and Szifra asked if he could tell them how he was feeling.

"I'm not sure, really," he responded, his voice trembling. "I know I feel awfully conspicuous, and part of me wants out of here. I'm really sorry."

"Sorry?" Szifra asked.

"For crying," he said.

"Please don't be sorry for that," Susan said softly. "It makes me feel so much better to realize that others cry, too."

"But I have no good reason." He sounded bewildered.

"You must, or you wouldn't be crying," Susan said.

"But, you were all saying nice things," Roger said. "Then I cried. Like I couldn't handle all the nice."

"I hate that, too," said Kathy. "I can hear the negative better, in a way, and unless I've earned the positive, I can't handle it. It's like it's not okay to be liked just for being ourselves."

Roger nodded. "That's how I feel, I think. I didn't realize it before, but I think, 'I don't deserve all this good stuff. If they only knew . . .' "

"It seems like that thought could make you cry," Szifra suggested.

"But it's not very rational," Roger said.

"How about we allow ourselves to have irrational reasons?" Szifra asked.

"Irrational reasons. I like that," Roger answered.

"You really have changed, Roger," Sarah said. "I can't tell you how many times I've seen you run from your feelings. You didn't do that at all tonight. Even with tears. You stayed with the feelings. What a change."

"I don't know," Roger replied. "I feel pretty shaky inside."

"Sure," said Sarah, "but you didn't run. You're not going to feel real comfortable. Why should you? It's hard enough to cry and feel okay about it when you're by yourself, let alone in front of people."

"I want to go back to what Sarah said to you, Roger," Szifra interjected. "She mentioned you continued with your feelings as opposed to closing off. I've noticed you stay with and share feelings more, too. Both sad and happy feelings. When we rewrote our family rules, wasn't your rule something like 'It's okay for me to have feelings and share them'? I think another was 'It's okay to cry.' "

"I wish I felt more comfortable about it," Roger said.

"I don't blame you," Szifra replied. "I wish that for me, too! But it would be pretty weird to feel real up while you're feeling down. I've gotten to the point where I feel okay about being sad. I call it an 'okay sad,' as I mentioned before, which is the kind I know won't devastate me. There's okay crying, okay sad, okay lots of feelings."

"I guess," Roger said. "It still feels uncomfortable, though."

Nevertheless, he seemed generally pleased. He knew he had changed and had surprised himself tonight by getting choked up in the first place. Imagine, crying because people like you, he thought. He'd also surprised himself by letting

people in while he was "out of control." He'd been trying
to believe that crying was a courageous act, which meant
fighting the "You're weak" tape. It wasn't easy.

"I think I know how you're feeling, Roger," Michael
said. "When I told people about crying in that session with
Szifra, it was really hard to admit. I admire you for being
gutsy enough to cry in front of everyone. I've always been
scared I'd break down during one of these sessions, but you
know, in another way, I wish I'd been able to. I probably
would have thought I was weak somehow, probably all
those stupid 'Boys don't cry' messages I got. But I think in
another way, I'd have felt good.

"As a child," he continued, "I never got to express my
feelings and be understood. Now I want to be nurturing to
myself. Crying when I feel like it is one way. Just like
buying something for myself. I deserve some things, just
because. . . . Roger, I hope this makes sense, and helps,"
he concluded.

Roger was amazed. It was as if Michael had read his
mind. "Thanks, Michael," he said, then realized he wanted
out of the spotlight. "Hey, we haven't heard about your
changes, Mark."

"Well, I started playing basketball. I knew my body
was in bad shape, and I was right," Mark said. "But it's
getting better. I can play for a while now without getting
exhausted. And I'm a little better with anger. I read some
books on anger recently and talked with Szifra. That
helped. I'm also actively seeking other releases, so I don't
become verbally abusive when I let out my anger and
frustration.

"I've also decided to take a good look at my drinking,"
he continued. "I'm not convinced I'm an alcoholic, but I
realized I don't have to be in order to quit. I think there are
too many strikes against me. Maybe the risks are great for
me becoming physically or psychologically addicted or dependent. It's clear I have an addictive personality. Whatever I do, I do to extremes. I have a family history of
alcoholism. My father, and so many of my mom's relatives.

The genes may be against me. My body is already damaged from chemicals.''

"I am really glad you've decided to look at your drinking, Mark,'' Roger said. "Congratulations. I know it's hard to decide, to break out of the denial that lets you 'drink sometimes,' even when you know underneath you really would be better off not drinking at all. It's so easy to keep procrastinating, buy yourself another week, another month.''

"Thanks, Roger,'' Mark said. "I guess I'm glad, too. To be perfectly honest, I'm also scared to look at it real honestly, because it probably means I'll have to quit.''

"I don't blame you for being scared,'' Bob said. "But, you know, I really think you'll make it, especially if you keep opening up like you have been.''

Szifra suggested Mark feel free to bring up his drinking issues in group. Many had quit social drinking as a result of learning about alcoholism and ACOA issues, she said. Mark agreed to use the resources available in group.

"Does anyone have any observations to share with Mark?'' Szifra asked.

"I do,'' said Anne. "You don't seem so nervous. And you talk about and show your feelings more. Like even how you told us about your decision. It was told differently. You didn't seem so distant.''

"That's what I've noticed most,'' Kathy said, nodding. "You're closer, not so distant.''

"And you don't pace so much,'' Sarah added. "You're more relaxed.''

Trina told Mark she was glad, too, that he was thinking about not drinking anymore. She urged him to bring it up in group—the troubles, the rough spots, knowing there could be some tough times.

After she'd finished, Szifra asked someone else to share the changes made.

"I'll go,'' Sarah said. "What I'm thinking of most is that meeting where I said, 'Don't label me.' I sure was rigid then—so rigid I projected it to everyone else. When we talked about roles we played in our childhoods, I wanted no part of that. Now it seems like a different person who was so defensive. I'm sure I could get like that again, if the issue touched off one of those vulnerable spots.''

"I remember that meeting," said Anne. "I was so nervous. The tension was too much for me. I was so upset that I didn't even think about how rigid you were being."

"I remember it, too," Trina said. "You couldn't believe a high achiever could feel inadequate.''

Sarah suddenly laughed and said, "Now I can't believe how a superachiever could feel anything but inadequate if the motivation was to compensate for family dysfunction, to prove oneself, or to feel okay the only way you knew how. I don't have to be successful to be an okay person—what a flip in my thinking!''

"It's really good to hear you say all this, Sarah," Kathy said. "I was worried about how you used to see these things. You do seem so much better now. Generally more 'together.' ''

"You say more, too," Michael observed, "about yourself, your family.''

"You're more assertive, not aggressive, either,'' Bob said.

"And more open,'' Mark said.

"Several months ago,'' Szifra said, "I remember we talked about feelings. At the time you said you mostly felt angry. And you said anger covered up many other feelings, like fear and loneliness. You used anger to keep from feeling vulnerable. I worried it also diminished your power, not seeing what was behind the anger. You are much better at looking at, identifying, and dealing with the real feelings. You are more open and seem much more confident.''

"Thanks, Szifra," Sarah said. "I really do feel better, too.'' She sat back on her chair, relaxed and amazed at how comfortable she was feeling. It no longer felt awful to be the focus, she realized, even when she was discussing personal changes.

Szifra asked Bob to share next.

"The major changes I see in myself are that I play counselor less and person more," he began. "I don't use 'smart language' as much. I talk less when I am tempted to preach, teach, and lecture, and I talk more when I am feeling inadequate or insecure. I'm less wordy and less pompous, I think, and I'm trying hard to realize that my way isn't necessarily the right way. Even in therapy I used to think there was one way to treat addictions. Now I'm trying to realize that people are different, and may require different treatment."

"You know, I like the way you put that," Trina said. "You're right, too. At first, I did feel you were acting one-up, like a know-it-all who was here because you wanted to help your clients. I thought you thought you were 'all together.' I really haven't felt that for quite a while. In fact, I'd forgotten I used to think that about you."

"You *are* more real, Bob," Michael said.

"Yeah, much warmer," Roger agreed. "And you do things from feelings now. Before, it seemed like you were all head, no body. Like a computer, I guess. Now you seem more balanced, like feelings count."

"I agree," said Mark. "You're more open, more relaxed. I like it better. I think group has helped you be a better counselor, probably. Not because of 'I'm here to learn about ACOAs,' but because you learned about you and your ACOA issues."

Szifra asked Bob how he was hearing this, knowing he might filter out the positives, shrink them down, and hold on to and enlarge the negatives.

"Well, I must admit, I didn't realize how others saw me before," Bob said. "I'm glad I'm different now, but it does kind of sting to hear all these negatives, too."

"I'd be wiped out if people told me this stuff," Anne said.

"I wouldn't like it," Susan said. "In fact, I'd probably crumble. I think it makes sense for you to feel uncomfortable, Bob. Hopefully it won't last too long, so you can focus on how far you've come. I'm giving myself the same pep talk, because I can get focused on what's bad about me, what I used to do wrong. Then I ignore the positives.''

"Bob, can you address this?" Szifra asked. "Guess for us how long you'll be thinking about this.''

"Oh, I really think it's okay, even good for me,'' Bob responded. "I need to hear it. And I realize it. I think I'm better about not whipping myself excessively. And, if I start to do that, I know I can reach out. I can call you for an individual session, or even a five-minute perspective change by telephone. I can go to an AA meeting and talk. I can call my sponsor or a friend. I used to keep it in, because I'd never want anyone to know I felt anything but secure and happy with myself. Now I'm better at being 'untogether.' ''

The group laughed. "What a gang!'' said Trina. "We come here and pay to cry, to feel okay about being less 'together'!''

Michael added that he liked Bob's ability to be more open, even to the extent of crying and feeling that it was okay to cry.

"And you've been very attentive to others' feelings and needs,'' Susan told him.

Bob thanked her and then said he was finished.

Group felt long tonight. Szifra asked everyone to take a few minutes over the week to write reactions so they could be shared at the next meeting. Then, everyone said their good-byes to Michael and Susan. There were lots of hugs and some tears. Addresses were exchanged and promises to write made. Teary-eyed, Szifra told Michael and Susan that she'd miss them. It was an okay cry, an okay sadness.

Szifra knew next week's group would begin with a discussion of how different it felt without Michael and Susan. The loss would be felt acutely at first, then the group would take on a new flavor. They'd work on current issues. Soon there'd be new members, with fresh perspectives.

She remembered something a former client had said upon leaving an earlier group: "What I learned in this group is that I am not forever cursed by my ACOA legacy. I know now that none of us, ACOA or not, is born perfect, free from fault or pain. But once we are aware, the possibilities are endless."

The possibilities for growth are endless, Szifra thought. The ACOA group provides the necessary ingredients— support, honest feedback, nurturing, motivation to help and be helped, blamelessness, and empowerment.

As always, she looked forward to next week's group, another piece of the journey. She thought again how lucky she was to have found a job so rewarding, so challenging, where she was able to share in the lives of the group members.

Locking up the office, she glanced at a framed calligraphy piece hanging by the front door. It was a gift from a client, a poem he'd written during an earlier group.

> We came
> Sad, hurt, and confused
> We talked
> We cried
> "That's okay," you said.
>
> We came
> Hopeful, yet cautious
> We talked
> We cried
> "That's okay," you said.
>
> We came
> Happy and excited
> We laughed
> We cried
> "We're okay," we said.
>   Ed

My Observations and Reactions to Final Meeting

Anne, 39, child care worker, lost child role in family, father died from alcoholism seven years ago.
Observations/progress noted:

Bob, 50, alcoholism counselor, scapegoat in family, recovering, mother alcoholic, now deceased.
Observations/progress noted:

Kathy, 33, secretary, mascot/responsible role in family, father died from alcoholism this year.
Observations/progress noted:

Mark, 30, welder, scapegoat role in family, recovering, father died from alcoholism six years ago.
Observations/progress noted:

Michael, 38, PR/advertising, responsible role in family, father is alcoholic, mother prescription drug–addicted, living.
Observations/progress noted:

Roger, 20, student, lost child/scapegoat in family, recovering, mother also recovering.
Observations/progress noted:

Sarah, 36, high school teacher, responsible role in family, father died from alcoholism five years ago.
Observations/progress noted:

Susan, 32, accountant, lost child/responsible role in family, father died from alcoholism two years ago.
Observations/progress noted:

Trina, 45, shipping clerk, scapegoat role in family, recovering, father quit drinking a few years ago.
Observations/progress noted:

Szifra, therapist
Observations:

Observations about me during this meeting:

My feelings during this meeting:

Issues I'd like to explore further:

My reactions to this meeting:

What I learned about myself during this meeting:

WHAT'S YOUR NEXT STEP?

IN *TOGETHER WE HEAL,* group members' dialogues and interactions are primary to my role as facilitator. During the weekly group sessions, we hoped you would learn by your own form of participation in the group. Experiencing the group process offers more than simply reading about it.

Now that you have participated in our group, you likely have questions, reactions, and new feelings. You may even decide to seek a group of your own. Or you may have gotten what you needed from reading. In this closing chapter, we'd like to suggest ways you might further use *Together We Heal.*

IF YOU WANT TO JOIN A GROUP

You may already be attending Twelve-Step–based AA or Al-Anon groups or an ACOA group affiliated with the National Association of Children of Alcoholics. If so, you may want to incorporate some of the topics from *Together We Heal* in your meetings or bring up issues that came to mind as you read. The topics in our book can be introduced easily and effectively at Twelve-Step or other ACOA support group meetings. Perhaps Susan's statement in meeting 4, "Sometimes it seems Mom's protectiveness affected me more than Dad's drinking," triggered something for you. Issues of an overprotective parent may be relevant for you, too, and something you'd like to suggest as a support group topic. In the same meeting, Michael mentioned that he felt guilty because he didn't see his parents. Many ACOAs relate to this and would like to know about others' experiences, too.

We hope you'll feel free to take topics and issues from *Together We Heal* for further discussion in your own sessions. Maybe it would be helpful to find out how other ACOAs are dealing with family members who are still using chemicals, how others feel about their nonalcoholic parent, how to move from acquaintanceship to friendship, or how to deal with perfectionism. The experiences, strengths, and hope shared by others can be a source of growth and recovery for you.

IF YOU WANT TO JOIN A THERAPY GROUP

After reading *Together We Heal*, you may want to explore the possibility of joining a therapy group similar to this one. Several factors can contribute to your decision. If your issues are interpersonal, such as problems with assertiveness, listening, or making and keeping friends, a group may help you gain interpersonal skills. If you frequently wonder what normal is or generally feel as if you don't belong, you may find answers in group therapy. If you want to hear more from others who grew up with alcoholism and codependency, group therapy may be the ideal treatment choice.

Many individual reasons contribute to your decision about group therapy. If you're wondering whether a group is the appropriate next step, you might find it useful to review the following list of feelings and characteristics. Use them as a preliminary screening guide, realizing that individual needs vary greatly.

Reasons for Joining a Group

You frequently feel like a fraud or imposter.

You often feel like you're on the outside looking in.

You think everyone else is fine except you.

You believe everyone else has the "rulebook" for how to act.

You feel that no matter what you do, it's never good enough.

You think no one would like you if they really knew you.

You try to be what others want you to be in relationships and friendships.

You feel you have to be needed in order to be liked.

You're nervous about meeting new people.

You seldom speak in group situations.

You are afraid to trust others.

You would rather have your feelings hurt than risk hurting someone else's.

You want to talk about yourself more, but the words won't come out.

You have trouble representing yourself if someone expresses a point of view different from yours.

You wonder what normal is.

You hesitate to let yourself be vulnerable.

You have difficulty listening well.

You have trouble dealing with conflict.

You find it difficult to ask for what you want or need.

You are troubled by someone else's drinking.

You want to express your feelings but can't.

You don't feel anything or don't know what it is you feel.

You want to be able to express yourself better emotionally and to increase your emotional vocabulary.

You see few, if any, options for yourself.

You isolate yourself from other people.

You are still living a rigid family role and don't know how to get out of it.

You have trouble getting along with people at work, in your family, or in your personal life.

You suffer from the "I'm always right" syndrome.

You want to know how others handle problems.

You want to talk about how being an Adult Child continues to impact your life today.

You have been working a good AA or Al-Anon program but haven't talked much about your own childhood.

You want to know about patterns you learned in your family that you might be passing on to your children.

You want to learn how to deal more effectively with family members who are still using.

If you identified with some of these feelings and behaviors, it's likely you could benefit from group therapy designed to address such issues. I suggest you meet with a therapist to discuss the type and style of group available and the suggested treatment for you. Although your issues may be appropriate for group, the timing may not be right. For instance, I sometimes suggest that a client first participate in a divorce group to resolve more immediate issues. For others, individual counseling may be recommended before joining a group. Group therapy may be too big a step from where you are right now. If you're reluctant to trust and you've not seen a counselor individually, some individual sessions may help build the trust you'll need to share in a group. Making a decision about readiness for group therapy is more complicated than having the "right issues." It's important that you don't immediately assume a group is the only answer. You and an experienced ACOA therapist can make these important determinations together.

Whether and when you decide to join a group may depend on the group's style and format. They vary widely, depending on the therapist and participants. Some groups are time-limited, lasting a designated number of weeks or months. Other groups are ongoing, with participants spending months or years working at their own rate. Rarely does anyone know how long they will stay in a group when they first join. Most stay in my groups six to eighteen months, though several have chosen to stay two years or more to accomplish their goals.

It's often best to participate in a group in conjunction with individual therapy. During the first several weeks of group, I generally see my clients weekly or every other week, tapering off as group continues. Once group has been under way a few months, I see most clients as needed. Many group therapists I know operate similarly, though a wide range of options exists. If a group member is in individual therapy with another therapist, I keep contact with that therapist to ensure the group is meeting the client's needs and that we are all working together.

CHOOSING A THERAPIST

If you decide individual or group counseling will be your next step, but you don't know whom to see, here are some suggestions. Some ACOAs find therapists by asking for a recommendation from people they know. If you feel comfortable asking, this is a good way to proceed. If you don't find a therapist through an individual referral, you might start with the Alcoholism listings in the telephone book. See if any ads list "Adult Children of Alcoholics" as an area of expertise. Also check the listings under Counseling, Marriage and Family, Psychologist, and Social Worker. List therapists or agencies with ACOA expertise, then call to ask a few questions. It is perfectly acceptable to inquire before scheduling an appointment. Ask what services they provide, how long they've been working with ACOAs, and if they lead groups. You'll also need to know their fees. If the price is out of your reach, ask if they offer any fee adjustments or will let you work out a payment arrangement. Your insurance may cover part of the cost, so you may want to check with your insurance company first to determine its coverage.

Sometimes, calling can feel intimidating. Using the following format might make it easier:

"Hello. I'm   (your name). I'm looking for a therapist who works with Adult Children of Alcoholics. I just finished reading a book about groups for Adult Children and may be interested in trying one. Do you offer any?"

"Yes, I do."

"Could you tell me the cost, when they are, something about the way your groups operate, and how I go about joining?"

Feel free to ask how long the therapist has been facilitating ACOA groups and whether the group is time-limited or ongoing. If it's time-limited, are there options for continuing in another group when this one ends? If the therapist does not offer groups, ask who in the area does.

This call will give you an initial introduction to the therapist. Did you feel comfortable? Did you get good feelings about the person? Does the person seem informed? Are you inclined to make an appointment to meet, or do you find yourself thinking of checking with someone else first? Use your feelings as information, although many people, therapists included, are not at their best over the telephone.

If, after your telephone call, you decide that you'd like to meet with the therapist, you can schedule an appointment to see if that therapist is someone you feel comfortable with. You'll want to find someone solid, predictable, and consistent, someone with whom you feel safe.

I suggest you also look for flexibility and openness to

new ideas; ability to admit limitations and learn more about ACOA issues and a counseling style that allows the therapist to respond to your questions rather than turning the question back to you. For ACOAs, it's especially important early in recovery that therapists answer questions. These may be as simple as "What is normal in this situation?" or "Why do I feel this way?" Together you can establish a rapport where you will feel you are being treated as a capable person who simply needs more information. A therapist who responds directly to questions functions more as a consultant than a manager of your life. Of course, therapists working with ACOAs are more effective if they are informed about alcoholism, codependency, and their effects on Adult Children.

Some other characteristics are also important. You might want to look for a therapist who

- understands you
- learns your strengths and deficiencies
- helps you identify how you are thinking, feeling, and behaving
- can question, confront, and dispute illogical reasoning without attacking your character
- encourages you
- uses creative approaches in therapy
- adds humor when appropriate
- seems healthy

A therapist's ability to laugh, smile, and be joyful in group deserves special mention. Group members are often working through difficult and painful situations, feeling hurt and deeply sad. It is easy for the therapist and group members to slip into a somber, grim state. Sometimes, of course, we need to be serious, very serious, to get the necessary work accomplished. It is appropriate to be sad when the situation is sad. When the tone and style of the group are consistently grim, it can too closely resemble the grim, tense, depressed, and serious homes of alcoholics and codependents. One of the challenges facing ACOAs is learning to have fun and to take themselves and life less seriously. In my groups it's essential to smile and laugh, to see the humor in some of the predicaments we're in. Sometimes we need to be able to laugh at ourselves without putting ourselves down.

When you meet with the therapist, you'll also want to ask if you'll be joining a group that is just forming or one that has already been established but accepts new members from time to time. If the group is already meeting, ask how the therapist plans to introduce you and help you fit in. The other members will already know each other and may have developed bonds from sharing their personal experiences. Unless the therapist takes special care to welcome and integrate you, you could feel an unnecessarily intensified sense of "I don't belong here." In groups that adhere to a strict psychoanalytic therapy model, therapists leave it up to group members to decide when, how, and if a new member is welcomed and integrated. I don't think this style works well for most Adult Children. Too many ACOAs already feel left out, rejected, or unwanted. To combat the sense of isolation, I try to add two new members at the same time. Having someone else who is brand new, who doesn't know other people or the rules in the group, decreases the discomfort of being the only stranger. In my groups, the goal is to create an environment safe enough for clients to feel comfortable and begin to take risks.

I also help current group members prepare for new members before they join. When one member leaves, I frequently wait two or three weeks before adding someone new. During this time the ACOAs still in group talk about what it's like now, changes they anticipate when a new member joins, how they felt and what helped them get comfortable when they first started, and what they need to do to get ready for the addition of new members. This helps current members regain stability before encountering new changes. Because of the condensed format of *Together We Heal*, new members joined the meetings in this book more quickly than in my typical therapy groups.

In your pregroup interview, you'll also want to discuss experiences common to many group participants. At first, for example, many members will have the urge to ''run''— to leave prematurely. This can even happen after you've been in the group for a while. Preparing yourself ahead of time won't keep the feelings from emerging, but it might help you stay in the group and work through them.

In general, when you're deciding on a therapist and/or a group, it's important, understandable, and okay for you to take the time you need to know if this is the therapist or group you'll feel comfortable with and where you'll be able effectively to make progress.

WHAT TO EXPECT WHEN YOU JOIN A THERAPY GROUP

As you prepare for a group, it's also important to think about your expectations and to understand clearly a group's purpose. Therapy groups are largely a place to learn and practice the skills you'll need to create a full life on the outside. They are generally not a good source of social friends. (In fact, some therapists strongly discourage contact with members outside the group). Even though you will likely develop a very close bond with fellow group members, this connection isn't intended to replace the need for outside social relationships.

If you decide to participate in a therapy group, you'll encounter many new feelings and experiences. I'd like to share what a number of ACOAs have experienced in groups and how they've handled new feelings and perceptions.

Earlier I mentioned that you might sometimes feel an urge to run. When that happens, try to talk about how you feel rather than act on those feelings. Often the feelings are a clue that you are dealing with something vital. Maybe as a child you ran or fantasized about being able to run from the trouble at home. The urge to leave now may be an attempt to remedy some past trauma. Running almost never works, however. Your need or urge to leave may have been the result of a no-win situation you were trapped in. But your situation is different now. Your group members are not your family of origin. They will listen to you, validate your feelings, and encourage you. Talking about your feelings in your family may have brought beatings or verbal humiliation and abuse. Talking about your feelings in group, on the other hand, can result in greater freedom and closeness. Recognize these differences and try to work through the discomfort. Remember, too, that the urge to leave prematurely is normal and expected.

You may also experience rapid changes initially. You may think you have resolved your ACOA issues and that you are, in fact, "done." I encourage you to be patient. It takes a long time for changes to be integrated in the many parts of your life. Unless you continue working, old patterns and behaviors can easily take over again, covering up your new learning. Be sure that the new learning is well enough integrated in your behavior and life to be a part of you. You will recognize this evolution when the new behavior seems to be the automatic response, replacing the old, instinctive behavior. For example, Trina's old automatic response was, "How do I cope with this situation?" She looked for ways to adapt and adjust no matter how bad the situation. In group therapy she learned to ask, "What can I do to make this situation better for myself? What are my options?" Her changes are so well integrated that it is now automatic for her to ask herself and others, "What are some other options?" Be patient with the process; you cannot rush it effectively.

At times you may hear a voice inside suggesting, "Things aren't so bad" or, "Why are you working so hard at this? Don't make such a big deal about life." A part of you may desperately prefer to leave things alone. This part is afraid to venture out and take risks. Although you need to hear this voice, you do not need to heed or give in to it. You can listen, instead, to the braver voice that tells you how important you are and how important your life is, and that you have what it takes to stop the generational dysfunction and unhappiness. Give yourself affirming messages, such as "I can do it; I want to be happier and more free."

Sometimes during group therapy you may be confused or upset by another person's style or personality. After learning that children in high-stress families develop survival strategies to help them cope, it is often easier to understand their behavior. For example, if your role was primarily that of a lost child, it may be difficult for you to understand how ACOAs who took on the scapegoat characteristics could act or talk the way they do. If Trina were in your group and talked about her childhood experiences, you would get a different view of scapegoat behavior. You might even feel empathy toward her. On the other hand, if you grew up with scapegoat tendencies, you might have little tolerance for "goody-goody" heroes. It might never have occurred to you that this was as much a survival strategy for them as yours was for you. Underneath the mask, they hurt, worry, and feel inadequate, too. In our group, for example, Mark understood responsible hero behavior in a brand-new way. He learned that Susan had been too afraid to be anything else, that Kathy found peace in structure and accomplishment. Understanding this will help you understand others— not only in your meetings, but also at work and at home. You may also understand your siblings better after learning more about the various survival roles. Invariably there will be others who remind you of your siblings. At the beginning you may not feel much empathy for the "sibling's" coping style. Within a short time, however, a more empathetic relationship usually emerges, which often results in changed relationships with biological siblings. Of course, not everyone becomes best friends with a sibling as a result of group, but generally the distance between you decreases and understanding increases.

A side benefit of this transition is learning that others' behavior is not necessarily reflective of or directed at you. Instead, you realize that each of us adapted strategies in childhood that may be continued as coping strategies today.

As you read *Together We Heal,* you most likely noticed that ACOAs freely engaged in dialogue, often commenting on what others said or did. If you've participated in a support group, you know that cross talk is carefully monitored.

In a support group, for example, you may want to know more about how to make friends. You may present your topic by saying, "I'd like to talk about making friends. In my family, things were pretty closed. My parents didn't have friends in, and we avoided bringing friends home. I am good at meeting people and chatting because that's what I did at school, but I don't know what to do once someone is an acquaintance. I think I want to be closer, but I really don't know how. Am I supposed to call them? Would I be pushing if I did? What should I do with friends, and how often? I realized this was a problem for me recently when I was talking with someone I really like. I thought about asking her if she'd like to meet for lunch, but I got too nervous. I'd like to hear how others feel, if you have experienced similar feelings, and what you do now to make and keep friendships going."

The support group format lets the group know exactly what you want from them without inviting cross talk that suggests what you should do. Those who speak will be sharing their own experiences and what is true for them. They may relate an anecdote of success or share similar feelings of frustration. They may say, "What I tried that worked for me was . . ." What they won't say, though, is "What you should do is . . ."

That same technique can also be used effectively in therapy groups. I encourage groups to avoid "you should" cross talk, which can be destructive to the recovery of both the sender and the receiver.

WHAT WILL RECOVERY LOOK LIKE?

At some point you'll begin to wonder, "What does recovery look like?" You may also wonder how much farther you have to go! After a while, however, you'll realize that feelings and behaviors are lifelong. You won't be in therapy forever. You may or may not attend support group meetings, but you will continue to develop new coping strategies and insights for years to come.

Although the following list is by no means all-inclusive, many ACOAs add these tools to their toolbox, creating a happier, healthier self:

- Greater ability to identify feelings and a more extensive feeling/emotional vocabulary
- Wider range of feelings expressed more openly and more assertively
- Enhanced listening skills
- Ability to give and receive compliments more comfortably and freely
- Comfort socializing with peers
- Growth in self-confidence and decrease in self-consciousness
- Ability to accept alcoholic and codependent behavior for what it is

You'll see changes as you are able to

- Be more open
- Ask for help when you need to
- Trust more when the situation warrants it
- Avoid self-defeating situations and relationships
- Take responsibility for yourself
- Set more reasonable expectations for yourself and others
- Nurture yourself
- Discuss feelings and attitudes more easily
- Take risks

- Feel more comfortable both when you're with people and when you're alone
- Like and accept yourself more
- Forgive yourself
- Forgive others
- Enjoy life
- Have fun
- Feel relaxed

Please don't think you'll be able to check off all the items on this list. Remember, recovery is a process. It takes time. You will feel increasingly better; however, you'll never be perfect.

Recovery is a journey, not a destination. Take time to recognize this fully. Will you take a minute right now? Glance over the list of recovery behaviors and feelings. Draw a line under those that applied to you a year ago. Now circle ones that are truer for you today than a year ago. (You may circle ones you've already underlined.) Now draw a star next to those that are true for you today but were not a year ago today. Assess your progress, then give yourself a big pat on the back for your accomplishments. Write a few sentences about how pleased you are with your progress and how proud you are of yourself. It's okay to tell yourself nice things, affirming things. And it's a useful tool to a speedier and happier recovery. Please don't shortchange yourself even though it's hard to remember and to feel comfortable giving yourself credit.

Where do you want to be a year from now? How will you help yourself achieve those goals? It may be useful to do some planning. Remember balance, though. Sometimes ACOAs are so busy working their recovery that there's no time to smell the roses, hug the kids, or slow down enough to be self-nurturing.

CLOSING REMARKS

You have taken a brave step. Reading *Together We Heal* meant breaking many old family rules. It takes courage to look at yourselves and your families, especially when you've known all your lives that it wasn't okay with your families. Now you know that others share some of your feelings, thoughts, and experiences. You have had the opportunity to see other ACOAs healing. My hope is that participating in our group has helped you heal, too. I hope that reading *Together We Heal* has given you an increased sense of your own worth, competence, and belonging, greater freedom from old hurts and from feeling alone, or hope for healthier relationships with yourself and others.

You are on the recovery journey. It's an exciting place to be. Kathy said it best in her introduction: "You don't have to hurt alone anymore. Together we can help each other. We can recover from our families' alcoholism." You can go to meetings, join a support or therapy group, talk to other ACOAs, or read more books. Remember that you are no longer powerless, nor do you have to be alone in your quest for greater freedom and health. Today you have choices.

I feel honored to have been a part of your recovery process. Thank you.

A NOTE TO THERAPISTS

ADAPTING *TOGETHER WE HEAL* TO THERAPY GROUPS

If you are a therapist considering starting a group or adapting some of *Together We Heal* to a current group, I'd like to share a few thoughts and suggestions.

I believe the meeting topics in our book make a good model for other groups. Besides the issues in *Together We Heal*, you'll likely identify others particular to your group. And *Together We Heal* may even trigger new subjects you hadn't thought of.

Please remember, though, that the individual ACOA progress in *Together We Heal* was escalated for the reader's benefit. In reality it takes more time for ACOAs to feel comfortable, to be willing to open up as much, and to achieve their individual goals.

Unless you are working with ACOAs who are far along in recovery, I recommend that several early meetings focus on learning about alcoholism, codependency, and what I call "ACOA-ism" and that your ACOAs be given more time than we have in *Together We Heal* to receive, process, and understand what may be new information. It is common for ACOAs in my groups to spend three to four weeks on topics such as family roles and family rules, instead of the one meeting we devoted to each of these issues in our book.

You could give *Together We Heal* to clients who are uncertain about whether or not to join a group; reading it may help them decide if group therapy is what they are looking for. Reading our book could also be useful as an introduction to clients who are just beginning a therapy group. Prospective group members can get an idea of the kinds of issues that are appropriate for group, some of the ground rules of group therapy, constructive ways to give and receive feedback, and commonly addressed themes. This advance information makes the job easier for both client and therapist. Your clients will know how to be group members and how best to use the group process.

Over the years I've started and led many groups. Much of what I've learned is reflected in *Together We Heal*. Some specifics that may help you:

• **Ground Rules.** In meeting 1, you'll notice I cover the expectations I have for group members. Members are expected to attend weekly and to call if they'll be absent. When a member decides to leave, it's announced at least two weeks in advance. I make sure to talk about confidentiality in group, even though I've discussed it with each person individually. Trust is so important that I bring up confidentiality from time to time as a gentle reminder.

At the first meeting I review my guidelines, then solicit feedback from members about their expectations and needs. Recently, for example, an ACOA in a first meeting asked about sharing phone numbers. My client wanted to know how the group was handling this and was ambivalent about whether or not she wanted to exchange numbers. Since I do not have a black-and-white policy on interactions outside of group, I asked the members what they thought. After they finished, I brought up the pros and cons I saw for each position. They decided to put the decision on hold for a while. As we had to be selective, I elected not to include that process in *Together We Heal*. (It really was difficult to decide what was most salient and readable.)

• **Commitment.** I now ask for an eight-week minimum commitment from group members when they join. In this way I ensure stability for current group members and help ACOAs fight the urge to flee.

• **Education/Skills Building/World of Feelings.** These are essential components of treatment for ACOAs. The three areas overlap, of course, but generally I think early group treatment needs to be focused educationally. During this phase ACOAs learn about alcoholism, codependency, and ACOA-ism. Next they learn some skills, as we've outlined in the introduction and throughout *Together We Heal*. After some foundation is built, ACOAs can more effectively handle the strong feelings that emerge when we focus on emotions.

Use your judgment, assess the person, then decide how best to do treatment. Go back to the toolbox. If the person is in early ACOA recovery, has good interpersonal tools—strong intimacy skills, close friends, and supports—but is unable to free herself from thinking she's a bad person, dealing with childhood issues may be most appropriate. No hard and fast rules apply here, but my rule of thumb is that the earlier the stage of recovery, the more likely I'll recommend a treatment group that begins with education. The progress of the client determines how quickly I move. Eventually I try to have all clients adept at identification, expression, understanding, and comfort with a wide range of feelings. In group this is done in the context of the interpersonal group process.

Most of what we do in *Together We Heal* is in the areas of education and feelings. As many excellent books are available to teach skills building, I decided not to focus on this issue. Negative self-talk and distorted thinking, a common problem for ACOAs, is dealt with very well in David Burns's book *Feeling Good*. Learning to change distorted thinking has been useful to many of my clients.

Two books I have recently found helpful in my own work are *Let Go and Grow*, by Robert Ackerman, and Marsha Vannicelli's *Group Psychotherapy with Adult Children of Alcoholics*. Ackerman's book does a good job of describing how ACOAs are different from each other. I believe understanding this is essential to good ACOA treatment. He also covers ways to make peace with spouses, children, members of family of origin, and self. Vannicelli's book, a text for therapists, covers an array of issues, from the ACOA as ACOA therapist to themes that frequently emerge in ACOA groups. Though my therapy style and orientation are different from Ms. Vannicelli's, I found her book valuable.

To be honest, I believe that this particular topic—addressing ACOA issues and group therapy adaptation for the benefit of the therapist—requires a separate manual to accompany *Together We Heal*. However, until such a manual exists, you can read the book itself for topic ideas, ACOA themes and experiences, group progress information, and therapist/leadership style. No matter how you use it, I do hope you find it helpful in your work. Working with ACOAs is challenging and wonderful; ACOAs can and do make changes. I wish you and your clients a strong, healthy, and joyous recovery.

BIBLIOGRAPHY

NONFICTION BOOKS SPECIFICALLY ABOUT ALCOHOLISM, CODEPENDENCY AND THEIR EFFECTS ON THE FAMILY

Ackerman, Robert. *Children of Alcoholics*. Holmes Beach, Florida: Learning Publications, 1983.

———— *Let Go and Grow*. Pompano Beach, Florida: Health Communications, 1987.

Beattie, Melody. *Codependent No More*. New York: Harper/Hazelden, 1987.

Black, Claudia. *It Will Never Happen To Me!* Denver, Colorado: M.A.C. Publishing, 1981.

———— *Repeat After Me*. Denver, Colorado: M.A.C. Publishing, 1985.

———— *My Dad Loves Me, My Dad Has a Disease*. Denver, Colorado: M.A.C. Publishing, 1982.

Brooks, Cathleen. *The Secret Everyone Knows*. San Diego, California: Joan B. Kroc Foundation, Operation Cork, 1981.

Deutsch, Charles. *Broken Bottles, Broken Dreams*. New York, New York: Teachers College Press, Columbia University, 1982.

Drews, Toby Rice. *Getting Them Sober*. South Plainfield, New Jersey: Bridge Publishing, 1980.

Gravitz, Herbert and Julie Bowden. *Guide to Recovery—A Book for ACOAs*. Holmes Beach, Florida: Learning Publications, 1985.

Greenleaf, Jael. *Co-Alcoholism, Para-Alcoholism*. Denver, Colorado: M.A.C. Publishing, 1988.

Hastings, Jill M. and Marion H. Typpo. *An Elephant in the Living Room*. Minneapolis: Comp Care Publications, 1986.

Johnson, Vernon. *I'll Quit Tomorrow: A Practical Guide to Alcoholism Treatment*. New York: Harper & Row, 1980.

———— *Intervention: How to Help Someone Who Doesn't Want Help*. Minneapolis, Minnesota: Johnson Institute, 1986.

LeBoutillier, Megan. *Little Miss Perfect*. Denver, Colorado: M.A.C. Publishing, 1987.

Lerner, Rockelle. *Affirmations: Daily Inspirations for Adult Children of Alcoholics*. Pompano Beach, Florida: Health Communications, 1985.

Maxwell, Ruth. *The Booze Battle*. New York: Ballantine, 1976.

Malloy, Paul. *Where Did Everybody Go?* New York: Warner Books, 1981.

Marlin, Emily. *Hope: New Choices and Recovery Strategies for Adult Children of Alcoholics*. New York: Harper & Row, 1987.

Seixas, Judith S. and Geraldine Youcha. *Children of Alcoholism: A Survivor's Manual*. New York: Harper & Row, 1985.

Seixas, Judith. *Living with a Parent Who Drinks Too Much*. New York: Greenwillow Books, 1979.

Somers, Suzanne. *Keeping Secrets*. New York: Warner Books, 1988.

Wegscheider-Cruse, Sharon. *Another Chance, Hope and Health for the Alcoholic Family*. Palo Alto, California: Science & Behavior Books, 1981.

—— *Choicemaking*. Pompano Beach, Florida: Health Communications, 1985.

Wholey, Dennis. *The Courage to Change: Personal Conversations About Alcoholism with Dennis Wholey*. Boston: Houghton Mifflin Company, 1984.

Woititz, Janet. *Adult Children of Alcoholics*. Pompano Beach, Florida: Health Communications, 1983.

—— *Struggle for Intimacy*. Pompano Beach, Florida: Health Communications, 1985.

—— *Marriage on the Rocks*. New York: Delacorte Press, 1979.

BOOKS WE RECOMMEND FOR HEALING AND SKILLS-BUILDING

Bass, Ellen and Laura Davis. *The Courage to Heal: A Guide for Women Survivors of Child Sexual Abuse*. New York: Harper & Row, 1988.

Bloomfield, Harold. *Making Peace with Your Parents*. New York: Bantam, 1982.

Boston Women's Health Collective. *The New Our Bodies, Ourselves*. New York: Simon and Schuster, 1984.

———— *Ourselves and Our Children*. New York: Random House, 1978.

Briggs, Dorothy. *Your Child's Self-Esteem*. New York: Doubleday, 1970.

Burns, David. *Feeling Good*. New York: Morrow, 1980.

Colgrove, Melba, Harold Bloomfield and Peter McWilliams. *How to Survive the Loss of a Love*. New York: Bantam, 1976.

Gordon, Thomas. *Parent Effectiveness Training*. New York: New American Library, 1975.

James, Jennifer. *Success is the Quality of the Journey*. Seattle: Bronwen Press (3903 East James, Seattle, Washington 98122), 1986.

Jasinek, Doris and Pamela Ryan. *How to Build a House of Hearts*. Minneapolis: Comp Care Publishers, 1988.

Jourard, Sidney. *The Transparent Self*. New York: Van Nostrand, 1964.

Lerner, Harriet Goldhor. *The Dance of Anger*. New York: Harper & Row, 1985.

———— *The Dance of Intimacy*. New York: Harper & Row, 1989.

Lew, Mike. *Victims No Longer: Men Recovering from Incest and Other Sexual Child Abuse*. New York: Harper Collins, 1990.

McKay, Matthew, M. Davis and P. Fanning. *Thoughts and Feelings*. Oakland, California: New Harbinger Publications, 1981.

———— *Relaxation and Stress Reduction Workbook*. Oakland, California: New Harbinger Publications, 1983.

———— *Messages: The Communication Book*. Oakland, California: New Harbinger Publications, 1983.

Newman, Mildred and Bernard Berkevitz. *How to Be Your Own Best Friend*. New York: Ballantine, 1971.

Sandbek, Terence J. *The Deadly Diet*. Oakland, California: New Harbinger Publications, 1986.

Satir, Virginia. *Peoplemaking*. Palo Alto, California: Science and Behavior Books, 1972.

Weekes, Claire. *More Help for Your Nerves*. New York: Bantam, 1987.

SOURCES OF INFORMATION AND LITERATURE

Al-Anon, Family Group World Service Headquarters
P.O. Box 862
Midtown Station
New York, NY 10018

Alcoholics Anonymous-General Service Office (A.A.)
468 Park Avenue South
New York, NY 10016

Children of Alcoholics Foundation, Inc.
200 Park Avenue, 31st Floor
New York, NY 10010

CompCare Publications
2415 Annapolis Lane
Minneapolis, MN 55441

Hazelden Literature
P.O. Box 176
Center City, MN 55012

Health Communications
2119 A Hollywood Blvd.
Hollywood, FL 33020

M.A.C. Publishing
5005 East 39th Ave.
Denver, CO 80207

National Association of Children of Alcoholics
31706 Coast Highway, Suite 201
South Laguna, CA 02677

National Clearinghouse for Alcohol Information
P.O. Box 2345
Rockville, MD 20850

National Council on Alcoholism
12 West 21st Street
New York, NY 10010

National Institute of Alcohol Abuse & Alcoholism
5600 Fishers Lane
Rockville, MD 20852

Parkside Publishing
205 West Touhey
Parkridge, IL 60068

Perrin & Treggett, Booksellers
P.O. Box 190
5 Glen Road
Rutherford, NJ 07070

RESOURCE ORGANIZATIONS

Adults Molested as Children United
P.O. Box 952
San Jose, CA 95108

American Anorexia/Bulimia Association Inc.
133 Cedar Lane
Teaneck, NJ 07666

American Atheist Addiction Recovery Groups
2344 South Broadway
Denver, CO 80210

Incest Resources
Women's Center
46 Pleasant Street
Cambridge, MA 02139

Incest Survivors Anonymous (ISA)
P.O. Box 5613
Long Beach, CA 90805

Incest Survivor Information Exchange
P.O. Box 3399
New Haven, CT 06515

New York State Coalition of Children of Alcoholic Families
P.O. Box 9
Hempstead, NY 11550

Rutgers Center for Alcohol Studies
Rutgers University
P.O. Box 969
Piscataway, NJ 08854

Sex and Love Addicts Anonymous
Augustine Fellowship
P.O. Box 119
New Town Branch
Boston, MA 02258

SOS (Save Our Selves) National Newsletter
Codesh, Box 5
Buffalo, NY 14215

Utah Alcoholism Foundation
2880 South Main Street, Suite 210
Salt Lake City, UT 84115

Women for Sobriety, Inc.
P.O. Box 618
Quakertown, PA 18951

RECOVERY MUSIC

My Way of Saying Thanks, Laurel Lewis (available through Hazelden Literature, P.O. Box 176, Center City, MN 50012)
Survivor, By Request Only, Daylight, c/o Nancy Day, P.O. Box 8317, Pittsburgh, PA 15218
Wes, I Need to Believe, Tidal Waves, c/o Night Vision Productions, P.O. Box 249, Kittery, ME 03904

GAMES

Choose for Yourself. Apalachee Drug Education Program, P.O. Box 1782, Tallahassee, FL 32302

Family Happenings. Kids in Progress, 2749 Third Street, Eau Claire, WI 54703

Social Security. Ungame Co., P.O. Box 6282, Anaheim, CA 92806

The Stamp Game. Claudia Black, M.A.C. Publishing, 1850 High Street, Denver CO 80218

Talking, Feeling and Doing Game. Creative Therapeutics, 155 County Road, Creskill, NJ 17626

Ungame. Ungame Co., P.O. Box 6282, Anaheim, CA 92806

RECOVERY ART PRINTS

Daylily in Bloom, Raggedy Ann & Andy—Recovery Takes Time, c/o Claudia Wearstler Paeth, 7226 S 625 W, West Point, IN 47992

Abuse
emotional neglect, 220, 222
physical abuse, 218–219
resolution of, 223–24
sexual abuse, 214–225
verbal criticism, 220, 221–222, 224
Achievement, overachievement, 157, 160
Ackerman, Robert, 19
Acting-out child
as adult, 25
characteristics of, 17–18, 25
group members experience of, 153
needs of, 25
Addictive behavior, discussion of, 229–239
Adjuster
as adult, 26
characteristic of, 18, 26
group members experience of, 155, 156
needs of, 25
Adult Children of Alcoholics
beginning of movement, 2–3
reasons for joining group, 353–355
sensitivity of, 19
therapist, choosing, 356–360
Adult Children of Alcoholics meetings, 12–14
Al-Anon, 74

Al-Anon Adult Child meetings, 11–12
Alcohol, group members discussion of drinking, 229–239
Alcoholic family
becoming aware of problem, 69–80
denial in, 70
Alcoholic-like behavior, 75
Alcoholism
as family disease, 29, 95
modeling after alcoholic parents, 114–115
All-or-nothing phenomenon, 271–272
Anger, 177–178
fear of, 112–113
physical release and, 183
Another Chance: Hope and Help for the Alcoholic Family (Wegschneider-Cruse), 19

Betrayal, feelings of, 78–79
Black-and-white thinking, 91, 106, 184, 297
Black, Claudia, 16–17, 19, 33, 124, 152, 155, 300
Blame, 184–185
Burns, David, 177

Chemically dependent person
characteristics of, 20
needs of, 20

Chief enabler. *See* Codependent

Closed groups, 10

Codependent, 7, 98
  characteristics of, 21
  needs of, 22

Compliments
  difficulty related to, 301–302
  difficulty with, 265

Comprehensive Alcohol Abuse and Alcoholism Prevention, Treatment, and Rehabilitation Act, 2

Control, need for, 166, 270

Criticism
  constructive criticism, 262–263
  See also Verbal criticism.

Crying, 135, 270–271

Denial, 29, 70

Depression, 176
  recalling past and, 88–89

Drug addiction, prescription drugs, 236–237

Drug withdrawal, 312

Egocentrism, of alcoholics, 266

Empowerment, 5

Family Freedom (Wegschneider-Cruse), 18

Family hero
  as adult, 24
  characteristics of, 17, 23
  group members experience of, 155, 156–157, 158, 160
  needs of, 24

Family relationships (present), 278–290
  family recognition of change, 283
  holidays, 284–290
  old roles/habits and, 283–284

Family roles, 16–19
  carried into adulthood, 153
  chemically dependent person, 20
  codependent, 21–22
  family hero, 17, 23–24
  group therapy session on, 152–162
  lost child, 18, 26–27
  mascot, 18, 28
  scapegoat, 17–18, 25

Family rules
  effects in adult life, 202–203
  examples of, 198–201
  new rules, 203–205, 212–213
  rewriting of, 197–206

Fantasy life, 135

Fear
  in childhood, 114, 115–121
  as persistent feeling, 179–180

Feedback, 300–301, 302
  structured feedback, sharing of, 261–273

Feeling Good (Burns), 177

Feelings
  about parents, 77, 119, 184
  altering with drugs, 182
  blocking of, 175
  feelings list, 171–175
  group members experience of, 177–187

lack of recognition, 175, 176–177
learning to recognize, 175–176
mixed feelings, experience of, 183–184, 185–186
numbing of, 169, 182
shut-down of, 78, 89–90, 113, 140
See also individual feelings.
Flexible thinking, 91
Fun
being alone and, 251
therapy group discussion, 244–256
work related fun, 247–250

Giving versus taking, 72
Goal setting, by group members, 313–318
Guilt, 79, 107, 123

Higher Power, 159
Holidays, 284–290
new ways to celebrate, 286–290
old experiences, 284–286

Intervention, with alcoholic, 109–110, 233
Isolation, in childhood, 134–143
It Will Never Happen to Me (Black), 19, 124

Let Go and Grow (Ackerman), 19
Lost child
as adult, 26
characteristics of, 18, 26

group members experience of, 153, 154, 159
needs of, 25

Mascot
as adult, 28
characteristics of, 18, 28
group members experience of, 155, 160
needs of, 28
Memories, 151
blocking of, 141
Mental problems, alcoholism disguised as, 72, 74

National Institute on Alcohol Abuse and Alcoholism, 2
Needs, taking care of self, 105–106
Neglect, emotional, 220, 222
Normal, perception of, 184–185

Open groups, 10
Overachievement, 157, 160
Overexposure, group member's feeling, 230
Over-protective parent, 117–118

Parenthood, of Adult Children, 73, 143
Parents
betrayal feelings about, 78–79
death of, 152, 168, 195–197
love/hate feelings toward, 77, 184
Perfectionism, 184, 318–319

Physical abuse, 218–219
Physical illness, 182
Placater
    as adult, 28
    characteristics of, 18, 28
    needs of, 28
Powerlessness, of children,
    223

Rage, societal, 112
Rageaholic parent, 29
Recovery, as lifelong process,
    313
Relationships, 295–306
    discomfort related to, 296,
        297–298
    sharing past with mate,
        130–131
Relief, in therapy process,
    107–109
Repeat After Me (Black),
    300
Responsible one
    as adult, 24
    characteristics of, 17, 23
    needs of, 24
Role changes, 192–193

Sadness, denial of, 90–91
Scapegoat
    as adult, 25
    characteristics of, 17–18,
        25
    group members experience
        of, 158
    needs of, 25
Secrets, about sexual abuse,
    216, 218, 223
Self-criticism, 86, 123, 179,
    296, 315
Self-pity, 94

Self-talk, 177, 316, 318
Sense of self, reformation of,
    193–194
Serenity Prayer, 142
Sexual abuse, 214–225, 333
    covert type, 222
    group members experiences
        with, 215–218
    secret-keeping and, 216,
        218, 223
Sleepiness, anxiety and, 169
Social discomfort, 65, 76, 92,
    136
Speaking-up, difficulty of, 76,
    92–93
Support groups
    Adult Children of Alcohol-
        ics meetings, 12–14
    Al-Anon Adult Child meet-
        ings, 11–12
    style of meetings, 12–13
    versus therapy groups, 13–
        14
Survival tactics, in childhood,
    116–117

Therapy group
    addictive behavior, discus-
        sion of, 229–239
    assessment session, 313–
        318
    awareness of alcoholism
        effects, 67–80
    changes in members, dis-
        cussion of, 330
    closed groups, 10
    dealing with sexual abuse,
        214–225
    development of, 6–7
    family relationships, dealing
        with, 278–290

family roles discussion, 152–162
fun, group discussion of, 244–256
getting acquainted meeting, 46–60
goal setting in, 10
group information sheet, 45
introduction of new group members to, 166–171
issue of early ignorance about alcoholism, 93–100
issue of isolation in childhood, 135–143
learning aspects of, 3–5, 7–9
member leaves group, 303–305, 319–322, 328–333
member's feeling of overexposure, 230
open groups, 10
outside interaction of group members, 11
recognition of feelings, 171–187

relationships issue, 295–306
rewriting family rules, group session, 197–206
role of therapist, 14
rules of, 10–11
sharing childhood experiences, 105–124, 132–144
size of, 9
structured feedback, sharing of, 261–273
versus support groups, 13–14
Twelve Steps, 12

Verbal criticism, 140, 220, 221–222, 262
adult self-criticism and, 296
Violence, in home, 118–119, 138
Vulnerability, 262

Wegscheider-Cruse, Sharon, 17, 18, 19, 33, 152
Workaholism, 247
Worrying, overcoming, 318

ABOUT THE AUTHORS

Kathy Mayer has been a partner at Mayer & Samuelson Writing/Editing Services since 1987 and regularly writes nonfiction articles for business and consumer publications.

She is actively involved in organizations working to help recovering alcoholics and helping survivors of domestic violence and their families.

Szifra Birke is a certified mental health and alcoholism counselor. She has facilitated on-going therapy groups for Adult Children of Alcoholics for the past six years in addition to her work with adults and children in high stress families.

Ms. Birke conducts both professional training seminars and educational workshops for ACOA's nationwide.

If you are interested in receiving additional information, please write to: Szifra Birke, Alternatives Counseling and Consulting, P.O. Box 285, North Chelmsford, MA 01863.

SOBERING INSIGHT FOR THE ALCOHOLIC . . . AND THE LOVED ONES WHO WANT TO HELP THEM